Surviving
James Dean

Surviving James Dean

WILLIAM BAST

BARRICADE
BOOKS

Fort Lee, New Jersey

For Paul Huson

Published by Barricade Books Inc.
185 Bridge Plaza North
Suite 308-A
Fort Lee, NJ 07024

www.barricadebooks.com

Copyright © 2006 by William Bast

Library of Congress Cataloging-in-Publication Data

Bast, William.
Surviving James Dean / William Bast.
    p. cm.
  Includes index.
  ISBN 1-56980-298-X
    1. Bast, William. 2. Television writers—United States—Biography. 3. Dean,
James, 1931–1955. I. Title.

PN1992.4.B38A3 2006
791.4302'8092—dc22   2006040729

First Printing
Manufactured in the United States of America

Contents

Acknowledgments

MY SINCERE THANKS ARE DUE TO A NUMBER OF PEOPLE WHO have rendered me invaluable assistance during the course of this project. To Seita Ohnishi for his extraordinary generosity in allowing me to draw from his collection of Sanford Roth's photographs (inquiries about which may be addressed to him at oscarforjimmy@earthlink.net), to Elaine Schatt for finding a print of her husband's 1953 photograph of me, to Ron Martinetti for the use of photographs from his American Legends collection, to Martha Millard for her unwavering faith in this project, to Max Gershunoff and Leon van Dyke for their invaluable tips and guidance. And for their generous advice and encouragement, I must also express my gratitude and love to Penny Fuller, Niki Marvin, Clive Hirschhorn, Celia Brayfield, Marion Rosenberg, Ron Lyon and Jenny Paschall, Mark Shelmerdine and Susan Jeffers, Martin Jarvis and Ros Ayers.

Also, thanks go to Harcourt Inc. for permission to reprint the book cover from *The Little Prince* by Antoine de Saint-Exupéry, copyright 1943 by Harcourt Inc. and renewed 1971 by Consuelo de Saint-Exupéry, English translation copyright © 2000 by Richard Howard, reprinted by permission of Harcourt Inc.

But most of all, for his unflagging moral support and his expertise as an editor and collaborator in this enterprise, I owe my greatest debt of gratitude to Paul Huson, my longtime friend, critic, partner, and coconspirator in life.

Introduction

BASED SOLELY ON HIS PERFORMANCE IN HIS FIRST FILM, *EAST OF Eden*, James Dean had become Hollywood's most promising new young star of 1955, when at the early age of twenty-four, his life was suddenly cut short in a tragic car accident. The public outpouring of grief started with his funeral and gained momentum with the subsequent release of his last two pictures, *Rebel Without a Cause* and *Giant*. Fanned by generous help from Warner Brothers' publicity machine, the press coverage of the Dean-worship that followed catapulted him to near sainthood. Based on the public's reaction to Valentino's death decades earlier, one might reasonably have expected its obsession with James Dean to persist for a year or so. Not only has it persisted for more than two generations, it has now endured for more than half a century. In that time, he has come to be considered an American icon, right up there alongside JFK, Marilyn, and Elvis.

For a handful of years, the last five years of his short life, in fact, I considered Jimmy my closest friend. I've now survived him long enough to have witnessed his transformation into a commodity marketed all over the world. His life has been the subject of a never-ending series of books, some well researched, too many grossly speculative, some pure invention, his image stamped on T-shirts, mugs, dish towels, postage stamps, you name it, anything and everything that can be sold from Los Angeles to London to Tokyo.

His death was a devastating blow to me personally for reasons that will become apparent shortly. Psychologically, my recovery was facilitated by setting down a simple chronicle of our years of friendship, which was published within a year of his death. Ironically, as a result of that book, I found myself cast in a role I had naively neither anticipated nor sought. Overnight I became in the eyes of many of his fans his chief apostle, someone who could provide a sense of being in contact with their lost idol. Mail flooded in from the moment my book hit the stands in 1956; since its publication, hardly a week has gone by without some incident involving James Dean affecting my life. He has remained a constant backdrop to everything I do and has often, at times too often, taken center stage. In fact, there came a time that, whenever I shook a hand, I no longer knew if the one extending it was greeting me or seeking James Dean. Still, for what it's worth, it has allowed me to experience the depth, if not the perversity, of the Dean phenomenon.

Stephen Sondheim once noted, ". . . the best reason for all biographies of recent lives: to record the facts correctly, before the peripheral figures forget and distort too much." My first youthful biographic portrait was just that: an attempt to record the facts correctly before I forgot and risked distorting too much. Of course, despite my intentions, the publication of my book did nothing to stem the subsequent tide of what I came to see, in all too many cases, as profoundly distorted accounts of Jimmy.

A cavalcade of Sondheim's "peripheral figures," journalists and biographers, each with his or her own ax to grind, has since stepped forward to lay claim to "the real James Dean." If you try to glue all the frequently contradictory bits together, you come up with a schizoid colossus. People seem to forget, Jimmy was only a kid of twenty-four when he died.

In fairness though, I will admit that Jimmy himself may have contributed to the problem. Having been witness to the way he lived and functioned over his last five years, I was able to observe how mercilessly he played with people's heads and hearts, mine included. Some of the other "peripherals" who got to know him may, therefore, be forgiven for having painted such disparate portraits of him. Worse still was the problem confronting the would-be biographer who had only these conflicting stories from which to fashion a portrait. Jimmy was a chameleon, protean by nature and by profession, with the power to assume different characters, become different creatures, in order to avoid capture. Only if caught and held would the Greek god Proteus confide the truth. Few ever caught and none ever held Jimmy.

So, over the progression of half a century, now I have seen happen what I worried about at the time of Jimmy's death: the gradual reinvention of James Dean. Thanks to the foresight of a friend and advisor who persuaded me to write my first book, I did set down the details while they were still fresh in mind—the superficial ones at least. My failing, if you can call it that, lies in what I omitted. Feeling obliged to conform to the proprieties of the time, I shied away from dealing with what would have then been considered unacceptable truths about Jimmy and about myself. Unfortunately, that lapse seems to have been an open invitation to a certain amount of biographical speculation, wishful thinking, and, in some cases, salacious invention.

My problem at the time is simply stated. I had just turned twenty-five. Of course, Gore Vidal was only nineteen when he started publishing his first novels dealing with homosexuality, but then, they were fiction. I had never written a book, much less a chronicle of an intimate relationship. There was also the not-so-negligible matter of my respect for the memory of that friend, his image, and my concern for his reputation. And, indeed, I was concerned for the reputations of others involved in the tale, not to mention fear of reprisals. "There are harpies on the shore," Jimmy often warned me, cryptically quoting André Maurois. There was certainly fear for my own image, my reputation, my safety, for the year was 1956 and the era was puritanical and punitive. My family would have had to face the embarrassment of my coming out in print at a time in history when I would have been considered both deviant and criminal. But more to the point, I took seriously what some sage once cautioned: Tarnish an idol in the eyes of the crowd, and they will stone you in the streets.

And then, of course, there was my publisher. Could I blame their legal department for my omissions? Not really, as I had censored myself. Had I told the entire story, they would never have published my book. They had already pressed me to delete certain "unpublishable" passages. Furthermore, the Teenage Book Club of America only agreed to order the paperback edition of the book in substantial numbers—a major coup at the time, I was assured—with the proviso that certain other "objectionable" passages be excised from the hardcover edition, rendering the paperback edition even less forthright. What all these objectionable passages could have been I have no idea—obviously very innocuous and piffling by today's standards.

So in an effort to make up for my youthful shortcomings and omissions, I think now after more than fifty years it's time to fill in the gaps in Jimmy's tale and provide the missing links. I chose the title *Surviving James Dean* because I felt it encompasses the two themes of this book: how I survived the influence of an intimate, but thoroughly unpredictable friend while he was alive; and how I survived the onrushing juggernaut of the myth that has evolved around him since his death, from my initial sobering realization that death is final to my gradual discovery that, for legends and for those who survive them, it is never final.

1

UCLA, 1950

THE YEAR WAS 1950, AND NO ONE COULD BE TRUSTED WITH MY secret. I was a budding homosexual and quite terrified that I might be found out and considered a pariah. I couldn't afford to face the humiliation of discovery. Even after a semester in the Theater Arts Department at UCLA, I hadn't made any close friends. As a result, I was destined to waste a great deal of precious time, for I couldn't foresee that I would only have him in my life for the next five years.

In the darkness of UCLA's cavernous Royce Hall Auditorium, I slipped deeper into my seat and braced myself for more garbled Shakespeare. It was late, and we were rehearsing *Macbeth*. Joanne, the girl I'd been dating, was playing Lady Macduff, which was my sole reason for hanging around. I'd selected a row far enough behind the director and production staff so I wouldn't be overheard spontaneously muttering critical comments, a bad habit of mine. Seated in the row directly behind me, her chin resting on her crossed arms, which were propped on the back of the empty seat next to me, was one of the girls working wardrobe on the play. Jeanetta Lewis, a spunky, dark-haired Texan, was a friend of Joanne's.

On stage, the final scene was unfolding as Macduff, having vanquished Macbeth, presented what was supposed to look like Macbeth's severed head to young Prince Malcolm, who was now hailed as the new king of Scotland. Our "Malcolm" was a young, sandy-haired kid with nicely chiseled facial features and a pair of knobby knees showing beneath his kilt. Unfortunately, he suffered from bad posture and a pronounced rural Indiana accent and dreadful diction, neither of which, to my ear, had improved throughout rehearsals. As he stepped downstage to direct his curtain speech to the house, this is what I heard:

"We shall not spind a large expinse of tom befer we reckon with yer sevral luvs, and make us evin with you . . ." I cringed as he twanged on relentlessly to the end: ". . . We will pur'form in misure, tom, and place. So thanks tuh all at once and tuh each one, whom we invaht tuh see us crowned at Scone."

"It's pronounced 'Skoon,'" I groused impatiently under my breath, "as in 'spoon.'" It was Shakespeare, for Pete's sake. When was he going to get it right?

Jeanetta shushed me, afraid I'd be heard, and insisted in her own seductive Texas drawl that she thought him "turrifuck," then boasted, "We been datin'."

"Well, they say love is blind. Guess it's deaf, too," I teased.

"You are so mean!" she retorted, bopping me gently on the head. "He's really very sweet. You'll see."

"What's his name again?" I asked casually, more interested than I let on.

"Dean . . . James Dean."

"Where'd you say he was from?"

"Indiana," she replied. "Maybe he's just a plain ole farm boy, but I think he's delicious."

Earnest, maybe, but delicious? Still, her keen interest in this specimen was a challenge. I leaned forward to study young James Dean, now center stage, taking his spotlight and trying to look regal. Hmm, not bad to look at, I granted to myself.

The one commodity at a premium at UCLA was acting talent. Out of the few hundred students enrolled in the department, there was then less than a handful that could be called truly talented. They, fortunate souls, were constantly being cast in the lead roles of one production after another while the rest of us lesser talents were forced to compete desperately for the few choice bit parts left. As a result, competition for us ran heavy at audition time, but the faculty took every opportunity to remind us: "There are no small parts; there are only small actors." Slim solace that to the ambitious young.

Still, tough competition was understandable. Because of the school's proximity to Hollywood, it was a potential source of new talent for actors' agents. As a result, every so often, some lucky student actor or actress was plucked from among us and cast in a feature film. Whenever that occurred, a ripple of excitement ran through the student body as the Chosen One's success was experienced vicariously and, for all, hope rekindled. It mattered little whether that success was achieved in the field of acting, directing, or writing. The affirmation that success was possible in any area of the film or theatrical arenas was all that counted to us in the end.

During the rehearsal break, the dressing rooms that lined both sides of the Green Room just beneath the stage were a muffled buzz of activity. Wardrobe people were helping players with alterations on problem costumes; makeup people were trying to redefine the characters played by some of the actors with the aid of Max Factor's magic; principals and bit players were running lines or lamenting "the sad state of the American theater"; while others were trying to study for tomorrow's exams through bloodshot eyes. Only a fortunate few had found secure niches where they were dozing off in exhaustion.

The stage manager finally appeared and announced that that would be all for the night and dismissed us. As I headed for Lady Macduff's dressing room to collect Joanne and see if she wanted to stop for coffee on the way home, Jeanetta waylaid me. She was determined to introduce me to her friend, Jimmy, and prove how wrong I was about him. I allowed her to drag me into his dressing room although I knew I'd have a hard time finding something complimentary to say about his performance should the subject come up. And how could it not? He was an actor.

As we entered, he was standing before his dressing-table mirror, still in costume, his back to us. I could see him reflected in the mirror, quietly amusing himself by doing what appeared to be pelvic bumps, rhythmically bouncing his sporran, the leather pouch that hung down in front of his kilt, off his crotch.

"Hey, that looks like fun," I commented, rather good-naturedly I thought.

Stopping, he turned to glare at me over the top of his horn-rimmed glasses. Up close, I noticed he had intense blue eyes, set in a finely chiseled boyish face and wore his glasses perched on the bridge of his equally finely chiseled nose. I gathered he was not particularly amused by my remark.

"Jimmy, this is Bill Bast," Jeanetta chirped breezily, unaware of any tension. "He's a friend of Joanne's."

"Hi," I offered, unsure whether to extend my hand or bite my knuckles.

He grunted, turned his back, sat down in front of his mirror, and started to remove his makeup. Finally realizing that he wasn't in the mood to chat, Jeanetta suggested that she and I collect Joanne while he changed, then all of us grab something to eat down in Westwood Village. He grunted approval. Quickly ushering me back into the Green Room, Jeanetta covered our exit with an inane non sequitur: "Jimmy's a Sigma Nu, you know." Then, out of earshot, she reassured me, "Don't mind him. He was just concentratin' on his part."

"I noticed."

She didn't pick up on it.

We corralled Joanne, and the four of us drove down to a favorite late-night eatery, a deli in Westwood Village, where Mr. Dean seemed more relaxed and communicative, in fact, almost gregarious. I was still uneasy after the icing he'd given me in his dressing room. But Joanne seemed to like him, so I made an effort and began to relax.

That was the first of a number of double dates we shared during the play's rehearsal period, and with each, Jeanetta's "plain ole farm boy from Indiana" became more accessible. In fact, I gradually started to see him in a somewhat different light. Over the next week or so, I saw that he was actually pretty lonely and surprisingly insecure. In fact, it seemed to me that, in his way, he was almost begging for acceptance. If I had his looks, I recall marveling to myself, I wouldn't be begging anybody for anything.

When among new people, particularly those he seemed to like or admire, he behaved like a little kid trying to fit in where he felt out of place. He laughed a little too hard, listened a little too intently, and agreed a little too eagerly. At times, he was so attentive that he made me feel uncomfortable. And when he felt out of his depth or at a loss, he'd often smile guilelessly and utter the same meaningless phrase, "Well, then, there, now." Evasive, but I found it at once endearing and oddly sad. I was actually growing fond of this guy.

Over the following weeks, he confided that he hadn't developed any really close friendships since coming to UCLA, not even among his fraternity brothers, with the possible exception of one James Bellah, the son of a successful Hollywood screenwriter. I could sympathize with his problem. Having transferred to UCLA from the University of Wisconsin the previous semester, I'd also found that most of the denizens of the Theater Arts Department were a bit aloof, mainly the Beverly Hills contingent. Cliquish, probably because they had been to high school together and had known one another for years, they seemed to consider the rest of us outsiders.

Shortly after *Macbeth* opened, *The Bruin*, our campus newspaper, came out with its review. Though sometimes considered a bit too tough, theater critic Harve Bennett's reviews were generally respected. However, as far as I was concerned, this one was right on the mark, at least on one count. Although he lit into the production and was only mildly impressed with most of the acting, Harve panned one performance in particular: "Malcolm (James Dean) failed to show any growth, and would have made a hollow king." He didn't even mention Joanne's performance as Lady Macduff, a slight she deeply resented. However, she was more upset for Jimmy than herself. Well, perhaps not so oddly, considering her maternal bent. I'd yet to notice how readily Jimmy's little-boy-lost act tended to bring out the maternal instincts in women.

I couldn't bring myself to ask Jimmy's reaction to the review, if any. Surprisingly however, and despite the panning, he'd managed to snare himself an agent as a result of his performance, which is more than any of the other cast members could say. According to Jimmy, one night during the run, an independent actor's agent, Isabel Draesemer, had appeared backstage after the performance, given him her card, and suggested he give her a call if he were interested in representation. *If* he were interested? You should've seen him shine. Within a few days, he was one of her clients; within a week, she'd snared him a job in a Pepsi-Cola TV commercial. She may not have been one of the biggest agents in town—in fact, she was probably among the smallest—but she was his, and he was flying high. Was I jealous? Not a bit.

Jimmy said that, prior to *Macbeth,* he'd felt a comparative outsider at UCLA. I, of course, could sympathize. In his case, though, I found it hard to understand. Here was this good-looking kid of medium stature, a great build—except for a chronic slouch—with a boyishly killer smile, roaming the campus for months without a friend? Granted, he hardly ever projected himself beyond his horn-rimmed glasses, but when you got to know him, he could be a charmer. Maybe they saw him as just a simple, withdrawn Hoosier shit-kicker not too long off the farm, which in fact he was. But forget the "simple" part. He was far from simple once you got to know him. Light-years. Only, I was yet to learn that.

Hunched over his coffee after lunch in the student union, he told me that he'd elected pre-law as his major and theater arts as his minor during his freshman year at Santa Monica City College, much as I had at the University of Wisconsin, where I'd also switched majors my first year. Realizing that he was devoting less time to the pre-law curriculum at SMCC and more to theater arts studies, he'd transferred to UCLA, which claimed the best theater department in the West. Again, as with me, his family—in his case, his father—didn't approve of the theater, especially acting, as a suitable career. Until then, I'd had no idea we had even that much in common. Maybe he sensed it, but I obviously didn't.

The weekend after *Macbeth*'s run ended, Jimmy, Joanne, Jeanetta, and I drove Joanne's parents down to Tijuana in their car. There, they caught a plane to Mexico City to spend a week. The four of us then continued further down the coast of Baja California to the port town of Enseñada for dinner, intending to return to L.A. that night. However, because of a heavy fog, we found ourselves stranded in Enseñada and obliged to rent motel rooms for the night, one for the girls, one for Jimmy and me. Later in the darkness of our room, sharing the one double bed, Jimmy and I confessed to each other that, aside from "fooling around," we'd never as yet had real sex with a girl.

When Joanne's parents got back from Mexico, we tried to explain our predicament to them, but the mere mention of the word "motel" was enough to stigmatize the whole episode. Even the motel bill indicating that we'd paid for two separate rooms wasn't enough to persuade them of our innocence, possibly because it didn't indicate the exact sleeping arrangements.

A week or so later, Jimmy threw me a curve. I'd told him how miserable I was, stuck in a crummy off-campus dormitory for the term, so he suggested that I consider joining his fraternity, Sigma Nu. I explained my dim view of fraternities, but he insisted that I at least join him for lunch at his frat house the next day and see how I felt about the idea after checking out the scene. Not wanting to offend him, I finally agreed. Anyway, what harm could a little luncheon do? At least it would be free.

As it turned out, there was a price to pay, after all. Because of a revised rehearsal call, Jimmy was unable to join me at the lunch, so I found myself on my own, surrounded by a dozen or so jocks, at the big table in the frat-house dining room. The ritual of interrogating a prospective pledge quickly became boring and not a little intimidating. Almost half an hour was spent reviewing the present and former frat-house members who had attained fame as athletes. As sports weren't my meat, I knew then and there that I could only disappoint. There followed a long account of house history, traditions, rules, and rushing procedures. By the time we got to dessert, I was at a loss for anything to say.

They wanted to know my major. When I told them it was theater arts, the room fell silent. The house president cleared his throat and explained awkwardly that they didn't usually rush theater arts majors, that, in fact, there were only two in the house: Jimmy—who, it was carefully pointed out, was only *minoring* in theater arts—and another pledge who had made the football team and would therefore probably have been acceptable had he been majoring in ballet. They asked if I had a job. I was relieved to report that I'd recently applied for part-time work with the Columbia Broadcasting System in Hollywood, where I was almost assured of being hired. Disappointed, the prez explained that they didn't like their members to work because too many outside interests kept them from participating in house activities and interfered with their house chores. It was pretty much downhill from there.

Later in the campus cafeteria, I apologized to Jimmy for making a mess of it and admitted uneasily that I would have found it hard to endure the smug, condescending attitudes of his frat brothers. I thought I detected a hint of bitter accord as he nodded understandingly. I genuinely thanked him for trying, resigning myself to life at the off-campus dorm, at least until I got the CBS job and could afford a better place. I was surprised to see how disappointed he appeared, though I must admit, I was flattered.

2

There is No Top

UNHAPPILY, DESPITE A SCHOLARSHIP AND SOME HELP FROM MY grandfather, money was proving to be a problem for me. So while waiting for a job at CBS to materialize, I turned to the UCLA Student Employment Bureau. They arranged an interview for a temporary part-time job teaching a woman to drive. Never mind that I'd only been driving for a few months myself. The address I was given turned out to be just off Sunset Boulevard among the posh mansions of Brentwood.

Having just seen the recently released movie *Sunset Boulevard*, I half-expected Eric von Stroheim to answer the door. But Eric turned out to be Magda, a middle-aged woman in a black uniform and little white apron. She did have an accent; however, unlike von Stroheim's heavy German, hers was Hungarian. She also had a Middle European sobriety and monosyllabic terseness that belied a generous nature beneath. During a brief interview, I learned that this was the home of composer Cole Porter, for whom Magda was housekeeper and cook. I was thrilled at the prospect of possibly meeting Mr. Porter in person, but she explained that he was away in Europe and would be for some time. (It would be a decade before we met, Mr. Porter and I.) Magda had purchased a serviceable used car for her errands, but it had been standing idle in the driveway for want of a qualified licensed driver, which as yet she was not.

Over coffee and some of her sublimely rich homemade cakes, we settled on the terms of my employment: I would teach her to drive for one hour every day after my classes in exchange for wages already set by the UCLA Student Employment Bureau. As I couldn't always rely on borrowing Joanne's car, the problem of my getting to and from Brentwood daily was instantly resolved by a dismissive wave of Magda's hand.

"Take da car. I couldn't use it, could I? It just sits dere."

So, each day I drove Magda's car back and forth from Westwood to Brentwood, determined to teach her the skills of driving. Seat belts were a thing of the future, and riding with Magda took considerable nerve. It wasn't that she drove too fast, in fact, quite the opposite. Irate drivers, trapped behind us, leaned on their horns and barked rude epithets in passing. Magda paid them no heed, dismissing them airily with the same comment at every stoplight as she invariably pulled up beside them.

"Americans!" she marveled, shaking her head, "Hurry up and vait! Alvays, it's hurry up and vait!"

Gradually, I was becoming something more than a driving instructor to Magda; I was becoming a friend. As Christmas holidays approached, she started to bake cakes and cookies to give as presents, turning out the richest, most velvety, deep, dark chocolate confections I have ever tasted. Out of kindness, she baked batches for me to give to my friends at Christmastime, as well. Aside from Jimmy, who managed to dispose of more than his share, they were also a huge hit with Joanne's family and helped to improve my standing after the suspicious motel incident.

"You know, you and I would make a good team," Jimmy suggested as we sat in the rear of a bus headed back from Hollywood to Westwood one night a month or so after our first meeting. In the flat glare of the bus lighting, I could see his anxious eyes searching mine for a reaction. In the moment before I responded, I couldn't help thinking how odd it was that this guy, whom I'd never intended to cultivate as a friend, had become a part of my life in such a short time. Yet, despite the fellowship that seemed to be growing out of our shared experiences recently, I still had this continuing resistance to him. I supposed it was because I hadn't picked him as my friend, the girls had. Not that there was anything wrong with him; he was nice enough, though maybe a bit of a hayseed. It was just that I still felt we had too little in common. In truth, I was ashamed to admit to myself, I'd only hung out with him this long because I was in no position to be choosy about friends, having few at UCLA myself. Suddenly, the thought brought me up short: I'd been *indulging* him. Wasn't that exactly what those jerks at Sigma Nu had been doing to me at that ludicrous luncheon? So who was *I* to indulge *him*? Looking into his expectant face, I suddenly felt ashamed.

"How do you mean, we'd make a good team?" I probed.

"Well, we sort of complement each other," he ventured. "I mean, you know a lot of stuff I should know. And there's a lot I could help you with, I guess. Maybe, if we stuck together—you know, combined forces—it might make for easier going. I mean, look at what happened today."

Indeed, a lot had happened. That morning, Magda had called to say she couldn't make her afternoon driving lesson. A friend had offered to take her on an outing, so she would need her car for the day. Having separate business in Hollywood, Jimmy and I managed to bum a ride into town with Art Munch, another student in the theater department, who had to drive in to work. It was Art who had encouraged me to try for the job I was awaiting word about at CBS studios in Hollywood. Ushers were needed to shepherd audiences waiting to attend live broadcasts there. Already on the ushering staff, Art had introduced me to the guy in charge of guest relations (i.e. ushers), who'd said there might be a spot for me in the near future. On Art's advice, I'd been pestering the guy several times a week since. That day, after more than a month of perseverance, I was told that the next opening was mine.

As for Jimmy, he'd gotten a tip from another aspiring actor on campus that the Jerry Fairbanks production company in Hollywood was casting several television movies. His first attempt to get in to see the casting director had been unsuccessful, but, thanks to his new agent, he'd been granted an interview that day and come away with the promise of getting to read for a part in one of the upcoming movies.

After his interview at the Fairbanks Studios, Jimmy had joined me over at CBS, only a few blocks from there. I'd been rehearsing for one of the CBS Radio Workshop productions. It had nothing to do with ushering, but was a series of radio dramas for the United Nations, which we were to record shortly. It didn't pay, but it was excellent experience in front of a microphone, and our tutors were professionals. When Jimmy had shown up after his interview, I'd introduced him to our producer, Elliot Lewis. Upon learning that Jimmy was also an aspiring actor, Elliot had offered to let him read for an open part in that week's production. Jimmy read well, and Elliot promptly cast him in the role.

As our bus jogged along through the darkening streets toward Westwood, Jimmy continued. "I mean, if you hadn't brought me into the workshop today, I never would've got a crack at that part, and that was great experience. See what I mean?"

He then reminded me that I'd been hoping to find an agent myself and, to my surprise, offered to introduce me to Isabel, suggesting that she might take me on as a client, as well. He was sure he could convince her that we wouldn't be competition for one another, as we were totally different types, one being dark, the other fair. I was touched by the way he seemed so pleased to be able to offer me something of value. It was the carrot, and I was inclined to take a bite. Why not?

"You know," he confided, turning serious, "there's something I ought to tell you. The other night at the Sigma Nu beer bust, they started riding me. I didn't like the stuff they wanted me to do for initiation. So, they started on me for being in theater arts and all. Like there's something a little, well, peculiar about a guy who'd go in for that kind of stuff."

Being sensitive to the issue, I got the point. The fraternity jocks had obviously guessed my secret over lunch that day, probably just from the way I talked or held my fork. When I said I was a theater arts major, that must have clinched it.

They probably figured, Dean's in theater arts, too, and Bast is his friend, ergo, guilt by association.

"Guess I just can't take a riding," Jimmy was saying guiltily. "Happened once before in high school. Took a poke at a guy that time, too."

"Too? You mean you slugged one of your fraternity brothers?" I could barely disguise my delight.

"Yeah, guess I did," he admitted, now looking sheepishly pleased with himself. "So, they kicked me out."

"Out of the beer bust?"

"Out of the fraternity," he corrected. "Anyway, now I've got to find someplace to live. I was thinking, maybe we could get a place together. I mean, you're always complaining about that dump you live in."

He's out in the cold, and it's my fault, I was thinking. Well, maybe not entirely my fault, but I certainly felt responsible to some extent. How could I say no? On the other hand, did I feel guilty enough to room with him? I mean, aside from hopes of a future in show business, what did we have in common? Because there seemed little, in some part of my mind, I'd been keeping him at arm's length. He surely must have felt it, yet here he was, proposing that we room together. He wanted to be my friend.

So, why was I hesitating? Maybe it wasn't such a bad idea after all. Everything considered, I wanted to get the hell out of that dorm, didn't I? Okay, so Jimmy was being manipulative, offering to introduce me to his agent like that, but maybe there was something to what he was saying. I knew instinctively there were other ways he could help me. He had qualities I felt I lacked: strength, self-assurance, and drive, among them. Also, he had this sense of urgency, this intense determination, attributes I secretly admired.

Sure, I wanted to succeed, but how hard would I try? I was fairly bright, but how much would I go on developing? Goals are easy to dream up, but much harder to attain. Maybe he could help teach me how to invest in my future. Besides, the truth was, he was growing on me. I was reluctant to admit it, but I was actually beginning to like the guy. Only now, more than that, he'd suddenly touched something that resonated inside me, unlocking something new and exciting. I admired him, and I wanted to be closer to him, though I hadn't yet admitted to myself exactly how close.

"You know," I finally conceded, "maybe you're right. We probably would make a good team. I hear there are lots of cheap little apartments down in Santa Monica."

His face lit up like a kid's. "Yeah, we could start looking tomorrow."

So we shook on it, an innocent handshake that would turn out to be the most binding contract I would ever make and last some fifty years.

With lots to think about suddenly, we each drifted off into our own thoughts for a few blocks. For me at any rate, this was a big deal, and I wondered what I was getting into, where it would lead me, lead us. Then, suddenly it hit—for the first time in my life, there was an "us."

Jimmy stared out the window into the night for a few minutes then turned to me abruptly and blurted, "I never told this to anyone else. Guess I always thought they'd think I was crazy, so I just kept it to myself. But I think I can trust you." He paused, as if to gather courage, then, searching my eyes for reassurance, plunged in.

"Have you ever had the feeling that it's not in your hands?" he started, then paused again, as if grasping for the words, as if looking for a way to express something he'd never given voice to before, but had held, closely guarded, in his heart. "Do you ever just know you've got something to do and you have no control over it? See, all I know is, I've got to do something. I don't know exactly what it is yet, but when the time comes, I'll know. I've got to keep trying until I hit the right button. See what I mean?

"It's like, I know I want to be an actor, but that isn't it. That's not all. Just being an actor or a director, even a good one, isn't enough. There's got to be more than just that.

"I figure there's nothing you can't do if you put everything you've got into it. The only thing that stops people from getting what they want is themselves. They put too many barriers in their paths. It's like they're afraid to succeed. In a way, I guess I know why. There's a terrific amount of responsibility that goes with success, and the greater the success, the greater the responsibility.

"But I think, if you're not afraid, if you take everything you are, everything worthwhile in you, and direct it at one goal, one ultimate mark, you've got to get there. If you start accepting the world, letting things happen to you, around you, things will happen like you never dreamed.

"That's why I'm going to stick to this thing. I don't want to be just a good actor. I don't even want to be just the best. I want to grow and grow, grow so tall nobody can reach me. Not to prove anything, but just to go where you ought to go when you devote your whole self and all you are to one thing.

"Maybe this sounds crazy or egocentric or something, but I think there's only one true form of greatness for a man. If a man can bridge the gap between life and death, I mean, if he can live on after he's died, then maybe he was a great man. When they talk about success, they talk about reaching the top. But there is no top. You've got to go on and on, never stop at any point. To me, the only success, the only true greatness for man lies in immortality. To have your work remembered in history, to leave something in this world that will last for generations, centuries even. That's greatness.

"I want to grow away from all this crap. You know, the pathetic little world we exist in. I want to leave it all behind, all the petty thoughts about the unimportant little things that'll be forgotten a hundred years from now anyway. There's a level somewhere where everything is solid and important. I'm going to try to reach up there and find a place I know is pretty close to perfect, a place where this whole messy world should be, could be, if it'd just take the time to learn."

So much yearning, so many dreams captured inside this strange little man. Where did he come from? What did he want with me? Where were we going?

He paused, smiled sheepishly, a little embarrassed, and said, reverting to the yokel act again, "Well, then, there, now," words I would hear him say a thousand times and still echo in my heart today. "Guess I shot my wad. Anyway, now you know what a nut I am." I thought to myself, if there were some shit handy, he'd surely kick it. But looking at that sheepish smile, it was like seeing him for the first time, and I wanted to reach out and embrace him somehow. I didn't, of course.

As we got off the bus in Westwood and started walking toward the campus, I realized that I was smiling to myself. Want him or not, here he was at long last, a friend, or, more correctly, a "teammate"—and most intriguingly, a teammate with a dream.

Only one thing troubled me: the problem of my secret life.

3

The Closet, 1950

IF THE COMING FIFTIES WERE TO BE RELATIVELY LIBERATING YEARS in terms of sexual enlightenment, the late forties were holding fast to sexual repression in America—that is, until Dr. Kinsey came along. Even then, true liberation was a long way off. Still, I was from the deep Midwest and, despite the sophisticating experience of a brief, but magical adventure in New York the summer of my sixteenth year, I'd remained pretty naïve, especially when it came to matters sexual. Even at eighteen, I was still hopelessly inexperienced and far from wise in the many forms of human sexuality.

Despite my sexual naiveté, I was relatively happy in my first semester at the University of Wisconsin, except with my curriculum. Having enrolled as a pre-med major, motivated by the knowledge that my long-lost real father was a doctor, I soon realized that there are no such things as professional genes and finally admitted to myself that I wanted to study the arts more than the sciences, theater arts in particular. Having been involved in theatrical projects while attending high schools back in Wisconsin, in both Kenosha and Milwaukee, and even semiprofessionally while briefly presiding as moderator on a radio teen talk show in New York at sixteen, I was already hooked. So, at Wisconsin, I started to satisfy my craving through extracurricular involvement in campus theater productions by night and sleeping through my liberal arts courses by day. It didn't help my grades, but it did wonders for my spirit.

By the end of my first semester, fate stepped in and solved my problem. My parents abruptly announced that they, as well as my grandparents, were buying small businesses in Los Angeles and moving to California before the beginning of the next semester. Up until then, as a resident of the state, my tuition at the University of Wisconsin had been comfortably modest. But when my family moved out of state, as a nonresident, my tuition would increase beyond the reach of my scholarship. My parents suggested a simple solution: move to Los Angeles with them and transfer to UCLA.

Because UCLA boasted one of the best theater arts departments in the country, it seemed an ideal chance to realize my secret ambition. So, I agreed to join them in California, but there was to be no more evading the issue: I would enroll at UCLA, but only as a theater arts major. I wasn't to know until I got there that there was one snag. For the first year, until I became a legal resident of California, my scholarship wouldn't cover the cost of out-of-state tuition as well as living on or near campus. For that year, I'd have to forfeit independence and live at home, not the happiest of compromises. Still, transferring to UCLA and moving to exotic Los Angeles seemed worth the price.

I arrived in Los Angeles on a gray February day after a freak snowfall, which I promptly read as a bad omen. In fact, I hated the place on sight. My parents met me at the station and drove me via the "sights" to what would be my new home. First stop: the fabled intersection of Hollywood and Vine, purportedly L.A.'s equivalent to New York's Times Square and for years touted by radio comedians like Jack Benny and Bob Hope to represent the heart of glamorous Movieland USA. Having once lived in New York, albeit only for several months, I could see at once that this was no New York. For one thing, there were no skyscrapers; for another, downtown Hollywood looked suspiciously like downtown Milwaukee. In truth, it was so unglamorous, so tacky, that even the tourists looked perplexed, as if wondering if they'd come to the wrong town.

Adding to my disappointment, my family had settled in North Hollywood near their new business, perhaps as much as twelve or more miles from the UCLA campus and, almost insurmountably, over mountains! (Mountains, it should be understood, were a big thing, as southern Wisconsin was basically flat.) Being carless, due to both economics and the fact that I didn't yet have a driver's license, initially I would have a serious transportation problem getting back and forth to Westwood where UCLA was located.

I was far from alone among the student body at UCLA in having to rely on public transportation or other options to attend classes. In fact, only a fraction of the student body then lived on or near campus. The majority was scattered elsewhere in sprawling Los Angeles, most forced to commute by public transportation. Ergo, UCLA's early reputation as "the Streetcar College."

As any native Angeleno of the day could tell you, public transportation in L.A. was inadequate at best and hopeless at worst. In the late forties, it was so hopeless, in fact, that it was said that the wealthy of Beverly Hills and Bel Air rather insensitively dismissed buses as transportation exclusively reserved for their domestic help. Contrary to that snobbish view, it wasn't the company on the bus, which turned out to be surprisingly convivial, but getting up before dawn to make my first class and getting home after dinner that made me eighty-six the bus as my transportation of choice. Instead, I opted for hitchhiking, not always reliable, but certainly faster and less expensive. In the end, however, it would prove to be much more adventurous than I had bargained for.

Like Los Angeles itself, UCLA was also a disappointment to me. Initially, I felt isolated and friendless. The Theater Arts Department seemed predominantly populated by the offspring of the Hollywood movie colony, many boasting the familiar surnames of famous stars, producers, directors, writers, and composers in the film business. They wore expensive clothes, they drove expensive cars, they went on expensive holidays, and they were cliquish. As a naturally gregarious person, I felt left out for the first time in my life. I tried dating, but lacking a car in sprawling L.A., and broke most of the time, that wasn't going at all well. In all, I was pretty lonely and very frustrated.

Those being the pre-pills days, few college girls were gung-ho for unprotected sex and the threat of an unwanted pregnancy (unless of course they were out to snare a husband, a fate high on most guys' list of dreads). Catching a sexually transmitted disease, though by then curable, was nonetheless worrisome and still stigma enough to turn off most girls. Condoms—then known as "rubbers"—though available, were not popular with the guys, and most girls were not adept at male masturbation. Oral sex was, of course, unmentionable in middle-class mixed company and rarely indulged in by "good girls." In fact, not yet familiar with Dr. Kinsey's report, I'd never even heard of it. All of which made my hope of any sex pretty slim. And yet, had I been more driven heterosexually, more aggressive like most of the other guys, perhaps I wouldn't have let such trivial impediments deter me. After all, many contemporaries in my predicament were making out at least occasionally, or so they claimed. So what was my trouble?

The truth is I'd been attracted to members of my own gender since boyhood, but it had taken me a long time to realize exactly what that meant. When I was a youngster back in Wisconsin, no one ever mentioned the word "homosexual." In fact, I don't recall the then-contemporary epithets "queer" and "fairy" being used until sometime late in my high-school career. Even then, I didn't know what they really referred to other than effeminate males, those boys people used to call "sissies." Though not effeminate, I didn't enjoy most sports, which was a sure sign there was something odd about me.

Resigned to the realities of my social life at UCLA, I decided to focus on my studies and try to get involved in one or another of the Theater Arts Department's productions that semester. To my delight, I was quickly cast in a small part in one of the plays being produced in Royce 170, the small theater opposite the main house, Royce Hall Auditorium. It was considered quite a coup for the regular college boys—those who had gone straight on to university from high school, ages eighteen to about twenty-two—to get cast in any of the productions and extraordinary for any to be cast in mature roles. This was mainly because of the large number of World War II ex-GIs who were studying at UCLA under the GI Bill, which guaranteed them a free education in exchange for the missing arm or leg or fucked-up head. Their ages ranged from about twenty-three to thirty-five, making most of them far more mature than the rest of us, not only in years, but also in the premature aging inevitably brought on by combat experience. At a considerable cost, they had acquired the gravitas for the meatier roles, while we callow college "boys" were generally relegated to the smaller, less manly roles, if any. To make matters even worse for me, I was almost a year younger than most in my class, having been almost a year ahead through grammar and high school. So under the circumstances, I was understandably thrilled to be cast in any part at that point.

Because rehearsals often ran late into the night, hitching a ride back to the Valley after dark took much longer than in daylight hours. Naturally, there was less traffic, and fewer drivers were willing to stop and pick up a stranger in the night, although there were some compassionate enough to take the risk. There were others, I was soon to learn, who were only too eager to do so, but for less altruistic reasons.

Gradually, insidiously, I found myself torn between sexless dates, if any, and out of near desperation, letting the occasional male cruiser satisfy me sexually. The first cautiously oblique proposal came at a time when I was both agonizingly frustrated and deeply curious. The experience left me feeling sexually relieved, but confused. Suddenly, I was in no man's land. Obviously, I was ripe for more homosexual fun and games and had been for a long time. Though it hadn't fully registered, it was certainly beginning to.

We were well into the new semester when, on the eve of May 1, I had my epiphany, the major turning point in my sexual evolution. I had gone to a movie in Hollywood by myself and intended to take a bus back to Beverly Hills, where I was sharing a guesthouse with another UCLA student in exchange for doing chores for the owners of the main house. It was raining pretty hard when I came out of the theater, so I decided it would probably be faster and drier to hitch a ride than wait for the bus. It couldn't have been more than a minute or two when a late-model sports convertible pulled up. It was pouring and no time to check out the driver, so I jumped in.

A darkly handsome young man, perhaps twenty-five, flashed a smile to kill and asked where I was headed. I told him, and we took off through the rain-swept streets. As we turned down to Sunset Boulevard and headed west, he introduced himself—first name only—and offered his hand. I told him my first name, and we shook. His hand was firm and smooth and strong, and clung to mine just a beat too long. By now, I recognized the sign.

Outside, the storm intensified, and there were flashes of lightning in the distance as we headed west out Sunset Boulevard, his warm hand now resting on my thigh. He didn't say anything until, unexpectedly, he turned right off Sunset and started up a steep, winding road above the Strip. An alarm bell went off inside my head. I asked him where we were headed. He indicated the hills above, where he lived. It was my first invitation indoors, and I wasn't sure what was expected of me.

Catching my look of concern, he gave me a reassuring smile. "Don't worry," he said. "Nothing's going to happen you don't want."

I remember his saying that distinctly, I suppose because it was exactly what I needed to hear. I was scared and new at this, but I was ready, and he sensed it.

We didn't speak as he drove me back to my place toward dawn. He didn't ask for my name or number and didn't offer his, and I never asked. The times were still dangerous, and that's what anonymity was all about.

Somewhere between the time he dropped me off and the time I crawled into bed, it hit me: I'm queer. It was one thing to let some guy service you, I rationalized, but to do what we did that night and relish it . . . ? The whole experience had been shattering enough, but the simple fact that it had revealed my true self to me was devastating. I should have put it together long before, of course. But no one had ever explained or defined for me what I might have recognized in myself and identified earlier. The subject of homosexuality itself was in the closet, along with countless millions of fearful homosexuals throughout the country. There were no television shows featuring the now trite-cute, comic, or tragic gay characters, certainly none depicting ordinary real-life homosexuals. Other than Dr. Kinsey's clinical disclosures, there were few, if any, mainstream books or films dealing openly or honestly with the subject and no immediately available realistic role models that a novice might emulate.

Suddenly, I was somebody else, and I didn't know who. Intuitively, I knew my whole life would be different from now on. But how? What does a queer do, where does he go, how does he dress, what does he think, whom does he love? I needed a role model here, some guidance. But where to find an acceptable role model in a repressive society that shunned homosexuals and legislated homosexual acts as crimes? Where were the books on how to survive as a queer in homophobic America? Where were the high-school and university counselors and all the other homosexual support groups? Where were the clubs, the dances, the Gay Pride parades, the Internet chat rooms, the Parents for Gays and Lesbian associations, the gay and lesbian branches of the Democratic and—imagine!—even the Republican parties? Stonewall, where were you when I needed you? Help was decades away.

Whatever the consequences, I knew it was too late to turn back. This was my secret, and it would have to remain so. I would confide in no one. Meanwhile, I would pretend that nothing had changed, even to myself.

Just about then, along came Joanne to help me in my pretense, unwittingly, of course. Luckily, she lived with her family in a large apartment in Westwood just off the campus and had the use of her parents' car. She also turned out to be very bright and an excellent intellectual sparring partner. But, for all her good points and advantages, I knew inside that her greatest asset was providing me with a cover for my secret vice. I was not proud of this, but I was grateful, and I genuinely cared for her.

Our attempts to consummate sex, however, had been unsatisfactory, to put it mildly. It was impossibly awkward in the car, so she'd contrived to sneak me into her bedroom late at night. It was down the hall from her parents' bedroom, several rooms away. Considering everything, each midnight visit was an extremely nervous-making and quite inhibiting adventure. Then, there was also the imperative necessity to withdraw before climaxing to avoid the ultimate disaster, then slip silently away by dawn's early light before the folks woke. Where was the satisfaction in all that?

Now, of course, there was Jimmy to consider. Because I assumed he was uncompromisingly heterosexual, living with him threatened to pose another serious dilemma. It was too late to back out of our agreement to share a place, so it appeared I'd have to be on my guard and play it very straight where he was concerned or risk losing my new "teammate."

4

Curious Teammates

My newly discovered schizoid existence neatly tucked away, I joined Jimmy for breakfast on the morning designated to find an apartment we could afford. The high ideals and fanciful dreams that he had confided to me on the bus back from Hollywood only the night before seemed remote and vague as we set forth to troll the streets of Santa Monica on foot. Unhappily, everything we looked at was either too depressing, or too expensive, or both. Our optimism faded with each disappointment. Then, just as we were about to give up, we came to a modest court-apartment complex on Tenth Street. The sign in front advertised a bachelor apartment for rent.

The landlady greeted us warmly. She was a handsome, middle-aged woman whose vitality and charm lent her a youthful air. She led us through the nicely landscaped court around which the apartments were clustered and took us into the one that was for rent. It consisted of a dark and drab main room with twin beds, a tiny kitchen, and a bathroom. We apologized and told her that it wasn't for us. As she walked us back to the street, she seemed to struggle with some thought.

"Wait a minute." She was motioning us back. "I might have something you boys would like. We wouldn't rent it to just anybody, and I'll have to ask my husband if it's okay. Care to take a look?"

She didn't say another word until we reached the top of a

narrow redwood stairway that rose from the back garden to the top of the building. "I'll have these cut back, if you want. Personally, I prefer the sense of privacy they afford," she said, sweeping aside the overhanging fronds of a palm tree that grew beside the stairway, to reveal a short catwalk leading from the top of the stairs to a rooftop bungalow.

"Our penthouse!" she exclaimed proudly.

There, aloof from the world below, stood a penthouse apartment, which had clearly been constructed only recently. Off to the left of the catwalk was a small sundeck. Standing there, one could view housetops, treetops, and, temptingly beyond, the Pacific. The entrance door to the penthouse itself was a little low, forcing a small duck and step down into the first of the three rooms of the living space. As we entered and moved through the rooms, we could see that each was artfully decorated in a sort of Santa Fe-cum-Mexican style. The slanted, beamed ceiling sloped from about five-and-a-half feet at the entrance at the rear to about ten feet at the front, which faced the ocean. On the ceiling between the beams, intricate Aztec designs had been carefully hand-painted.

Original oil paintings with Indian and Mexican motifs decorated the walls of each room. The kitchen sink and drainboard were done in hand-laid Italian tile. A small bar, where meals could be taken, separated the kitchen from the living room. There was also a large coffee table in the center of the room that could be used for dining. The bar and its redwood stools, the kitchen- and living-room cabinets all had been decorated entirely by hand and executed with the same care and taste as the rest of the décor. Clearly, a lot of love had gone into the place.

"It's my pet," our guide explained. "I have a master's in art from the University of West Virginia. I spend most of my time fixing this place up. It's sort of a hobby."

She didn't have to ask us if we liked it. I was too busy checking out the tiles, the paintings, the frescos, while Jimmy was buzzing about the rooms, touching, examining, and asking questions about everything. He tried out each piece of furniture, expanding as if it had been made for him. He sank into the alcove bed off the living room-kitchen area, appraising it for length and comfort. He flopped on the larger bed in the entrance room, rejecting it in preference for the cozy privacy of the alcove bed. He slipped out the door onto the secluded sundeck, then quickly sprang back inside to test the toilet and shower in the bathroom. He looked into the refrigerator, stuck his head into the oven. He opened every cupboard and closet door. Then, having scrutinized every inch of the place, he sat himself on the floor in the middle of the main room and announced emphatically, "We'll take it," quickly adding in an imploringly boyish tone, "I mean, if it's okay with your husband."

From his arbitrary decision, I deduced that money was to be no obstacle, neither his lack of it nor mine. While our landlady-to-be was off checking with the top man, we rationalized that, expensive or not, this place was too ideal for starting our lives of dedication to let a little thing like money stand in the way. By the time she returned, we'd convinced ourselves that the money would appear somehow. Wasn't he up for a part in that television movie, and wasn't I sure to get that ushering job at CBS? When the good lady announced that the place was ours, we hugged her gratefully and turned over almost every cent we had between us to cover the first month's rent.

Not until she'd left did my excitement turn to cold terror. What had we done? I looked to Jimmy. His fear-filled eyes met mine, and I saw his Adam's apple bob, as he swallowed hard. Then, slowly we both broke into great grins, followed by the mad laughter of the liberated that says, "Who gives a damn!"

The surprising events of the following week seemed to lend credence to our blind faith in the future. First, the impregnable walls of the Columbia Broadcasting System gave way to my persistence. With a sigh of resignation and a look of indifference, the hard-nosed supervisor of the ushering staff finally informed me that I was hired. Promptly on the heels of my triumph, Jimmy returned from his reading at the Jerry Fairbanks studio to announce that he'd read well and was up for a part in a forthcoming television movie, a principal role, no less. He hadn't been cast yet, but felt he had a good shot at getting the part. Surely, this was proof enough that his dream could work. Now, there was no limit to the future, no barrier that couldn't be overcome. With an eye on the very top rung of the ladder, we would climb, never looking back, never fearing defeat. All it would take was confidence, and, for that, Jimmy was there to bolster me and I him.

During the first few weeks in the penthouse, finding ourselves in such close proximity, Jimmy and I spent a lot of time together, moving in and fixing up and getting to know one another. You learn a lot about people when you live with them, even for a short time, and I was determined to find out as soon as possible what, if any, problems I might be in for with my new roommate. So I encouraged him to talk about himself and his background as often as possible. It proved to be easier than I thought.

He told me that, until his fifth year, he lived in Indiana with his mother, Mildred, and his father, Winton. I got the impression that his father was emotionally undemonstrative, so Jimmy became more attached to his mother. From the way he described her, she must have seemed a bit of a misplaced romantic in rural Indiana among the staid Quaker community to which the family belonged. For one thing, she read a lot, especially poetry. In fact, Jimmy believed she christened him James *Byron* Dean, not merely out of her passion for the romantic poet, Lord Byron, but more likely because it bespoke her love for her son and her hopes that he might attain similar artistic greatness.

Instead of sending him out to play with the other kids, Mildred often kept him inside to read to him and encourage his early talent for drawing, during which time she realized that her five-year-old son was nearsighted and needed glasses. Thereafter, seldom without them, Jimmy often became the object of teasing among his playmates and school chums. The ultimate eyebrow-raiser in their little farming community came when Mildred enrolled him in a dance class. Whether modern or tap, ballroom or ballet, he never made clear, although I assume it included ballet because he intimated that, though he enjoyed the lessons, they were the cause of a lot of ribbing from his schoolmates. It became a private humiliation about which he never told his mother. To the contrary, from the way he spoke of her, I could see that he worshipped his mother and that she adored him to the point of doting.

Trained as a dental technician, Winton Dean had worked at the Veterans hospital in Marion, Indiana, until Jimmy's fifth year when he learned that there was an opening at the Sawtelle Veterans Hospital in Los Angeles. He applied for a transfer and moved his family to California. They settled in Santa Monica where Jimmy was enrolled in grammar school. Less than four years later, around Christmastime, Mildred was diagnosed with uterine cancer, and it fell to Winton to prepare Jimmy for his mother's death. Jimmy confessed to me that he buried his tears in his pillow at night so she wouldn't hear him crying.

As Mildred grew worse, Winton sent for his own mother, Emma Dean, to come from back east and look after Jimmy and his ailing wife in Santa Monica while he was at work. Jimmy described how he would come home from school every day for eight long months, sit beside his mother's bed, read to her, and watch her slowly die. When she finally closed her eyes for the last time, Winton was left with the problem of caring for a lost, motherless, nine-year-old boy, while holding down a full-time job. He had requested a transfer back to Indiana, but there were no openings.

In the end, he turned to his sister, Ortense Winslow, in Fairmount. She and her husband, Marcus, owned a farm and a large house with plenty of room and had always been fond of the boy. Without a son themselves at that point, they were more than willing to take him in and look after him. It was agreed he would go to school right there in Fairmount, and Winton could come visit as often as he could get away from work.

So, in July of 1940, at the age of nine, Jimmy boarded a train in Los Angeles with his grandmother, Emma, and accompanied his mother's coffin back to Indiana where she would be buried and he would begin a new life. With evident emotion, he described to me how, on the cross-country journey, he would jump off the train at every stop and run back to the baggage car to make certain that his mother's coffin was still safely on board. How bitterly, how tellingly, he empha-sized the word "baggage," and how painfully, he tried to ex-cuse his father for not taking time off work to accompany them back for the funeral. In Fairmount, however, young Jimmy was embraced by Ortense and Marcus Winslow as one of their own. Ortense soon became "Mom," and Jimmy be-gan the process of becoming a Hoosier farm boy.

My attitude toward Jimmy softened as I learned these things about him, and I began to appreciate his sensibilities. He had few pretensions and seldom tried to impress me, ex-cept from time to time when he expanded with pride over some above-average accomplishment. One special source of pride was the fact that, while in high school, he'd won the In-diana State Forensics Contest with a dramatic reading and gone on to place sixth in the National Forensics Tournament in Colorado. Of course, this came out only after I had bragged about taking first place in the Tri-State National Forensics contest in '47 for a humorous monologue. It struck us that had I won and gone on to the national competition, we might have met in Colorado several years earlier, although Jimmy still would have bested me; humor rarely wins, I'm told.

However, when it came to sports, he inevitably won every bragging contest, being more than competent than I in most. At best, I could boast some modest ability at fencing, which I'd taken up at the University of Wisconsin. But he had yet to try fencing. So, at my suggestion, we enrolled together at the Falcon School of Fencing in Hollywood. At first, naturally, I was the better, but he soon bested me. His interest in the sport waned quickly, however, and we dropped out after a couple of months.

The only contest I won hands down was the competition over our comparative heights. Jimmy stubbornly refused to ac-cept the fact that he was only five feet, eight inches (five feet, eight-and-a-half inches at a stretch) and I was an easy five feet, nine inches, so he insisted repeatedly on measuring our heights whenever the subject came up. Bored with the contest, I finally gave him the inch, and we stopped competing altogether.

He didn't try to compete in the area of brainpower, however, at least, not at first, being convinced that I was ahead of him in that department. I, of course, didn't bother to disabuse him of that assumption. However, I was becoming aware that he was picking my brain, constantly plying me with questions about history, music, literature, and such, half of which I couldn't answer myself. Inherently lazy, I found that it was good for me to get off my intellectual haunches for a change and try to come up with some sound answers to tough questions.

The trouble was he tended to flit from one subject to another, flailing about in many directions at once. Consequently, the only activities that commanded his total concentration were sculpting, drawing, and constructing mobiles, things he could create without help and create remarkably well considering his lack of training in arts. Some of them were quite grotesque. One piece, painted in oil, portrayed a naked man, his fleshless bones stretched over with nothing but pallid green skin. Waist deep in mire that flowed through a long, sewerlike tunnel that diminished in perspective into the background, his head and one arm were raised upward as if he were pleading to be saved from slowly melting into the mire that flowed beneath him. Jimmy had titled the work "Man in Woman's Womb." I wasn't into Freudian psychology at that time, or I would probably have had a field day with that one.

Another oeuvre, a pencil drawing of which Jimmy was quite proud, depicted "Man as Ashtray." Two long elastic arms extended from a man's torso that rose from the center of the round base of the ashtray. In one hand, he held a lit cigar, between the fingers of the other, several burning cigarettes. His head, supported by a long elastic neck, consisted mainly of one huge mouth that was actually a hole right through his head. Held to the gaping mouth by one hand, the huge cigar went entirely through the mouthlike hole in his head. Freud could have probably offered some insight (or nonsense, depending on what one thinks of Freud) here, too. On the other hand, from a purely literal standpoint, it would seem Jimmy's comment on tobacco was far ahead of its time. This did not, however, keep him from smoking himself.

Jimmy would become absorbed in his artistic projects with

a concentration that I found almost eerie. This also applied to his poetry, at which I thought him remarkably adept despite his limited vocabulary. In most other areas, he appeared to lack focus and patience. Whenever I made an observation about his impatience, he would simply reply flippantly, "I don't have time for patience." On the other hand, despite his short attention span and, what to me seemed a limited education, he was possessed of an insatiable curiosity, apparently unshakable self-confidence, and unbridled ambition. And for those qualities, I secretly envied him. Perhaps that's what made our odd-couple relationship work.

We took turns reading aloud to each another, sometimes from prose, but mainly from plays and poetry. We did this partly because we both wanted to become better acquainted with theater and literature, but also because Jimmy wanted to improve his diction, and I still privately felt mine over articulate and possibly "suspect." Thus, we were able to scratch each other's artistic backs.

However, despite all the familiarizing and intimacy of rooming together, I couldn't really say that I was physically attracted to this stranger in my life. In my extremely limited homosexual experience, I had discovered that there were just some men that I found more compelling than others. Granted Jimmy might have been considered handsome, mainly due to his great facial features, penetrating blue eyes, winning smile, and boyishly innocent, heartwarming laugh. Being nearsighted, he had to wear distance glasses, but even they didn't seem to spoil his looks, only his disposition when he misplaced them. However, he did have bad posture, which tended to make him slouch and hunch a lot and made him look shorter than he really was. Although he was muscular, he was also somewhat scrawny, and, anyway, I was not yet into the finer points of male physical attributes. Where Jimmy was concerned, for me it was still just a matter of friendship and economics. What did love have to do with it?

On the downside, Jimmy's behavior left something to be desired. His mood swings made it difficult, if not impossible, to relax with him some of the time. And then, even in his more accessible moments, his efforts to share experiences, to "buddy up" or bond, if you will, often seemed awkward and bordered on the obsequious. I hoped and believed that this would change with time, which it did. In the meantime, for my part, I was determined to keep my guilty secret from him at all costs, afraid that, should he discover it, it would be the one sure way to lose my new friend. And somehow that had come to matter.

As we'd moved into the penthouse on a Friday, we were unable to get the electricity turned on until Monday. Forced to use candles for our weekend lighting, we found the effect so pleasing that we decided to use only candlelight at least one night every week. Often on "Lightless Fridays," we invited Joanne and Jeanetta and sometimes other friends over to hang out. The price of admission was either a bottle of wine or some food. The discussions get hot and heavy at times, but the mood was always warm and friendly.

A few weeks after we moved in, Jimmy introduced a new and daring piece of literature into the scene: Henry Miller's *Sexus, the Rosy Crucifixion*. He'd borrowed it from an ex-frat brother whose father had smuggled it into the country upon returning from France recently. Published by Girodias Press in Paris, across the flyleaf inside were emblazoned the tantalizing words "BANNED ENTRANCE TO THE U.S. AND CANADA," a warning that rendered the book irresistible.

In hopes of shocking the girls by its sexually explicit contents, Jimmy read aloud from it during one candlelit evening. Indeed, the girls were so shocked by even the opening passages that they refused to hear more. However, when Jimmy and I returned from the liquor store twenty minutes later with a bottle of wine, we were amused to catch them hovering over the book, their heads together, poring over its pages. The readings never led to anything sexual, however.

On the other hand, possibly inspired by the book and probably curious as to what kind of response he would get, Jimmy decided to arrange a special surprise for me one night. After I went to bed, I heard him in the other room, muttering to himself over some project on which he was apparently focused. This being nothing unusual, I soon drifted off. Shortly after dawn, roused by a sound from the other room, I woke and turned to check the time. Instead of my alarm clock, what confronted me on my bedside table was the product of Jimmy's midnight labor. With great skill and precision, he had spent the night sculpting in green modeling clay a generously detailed replica of an upturned female vulva, into which he had thrust a large candle, which had been lit and allowed to drip white wax all over his creation. Jimmy, peering at me through the curtains of the doorway that separated our rooms, tried to stifle a paroxysm of childish giggles at my reaction to the sight of the thing. He had obviously gone to a lot of trouble for that moment, and apparently, I hadn't disappointed him.

But what was his motivation in presenting his objet d'art to me in this way, this "Vagina as Candleholder"? No way was this a Henry Miller-type altar to female sexuality. Had he expected me to be shocked or repelled? What made him think I would be? Something he had observed in my nature? Had he guessed my secret, or was this a fishing expedition? Or perhaps it was merely a product of his early puritanical Quaker indoctrination, that is, female sexuality seen not as attractive but wicked and sinful, and as such, merely an adolescent "tee-hee." Or, was it possibly a veiled hint to me that we had something in common, something to share?

I watched him in the doorway, laughing until tears ran down his cheeks. Was this the Jimmy I thought I knew? For a fleeting instant, I was looking at a total stranger with a screw loose. Or, was it simply an adolescent sense of humor? Then, just as quickly, my concern passed, and I joined him in the laugh, deciding that I was too self-conscious about my secret and too concerned about his motives. Just too much Henry Miller.

So many roles. A different role for each encounter. Compartmentalizing life. Over the next five years, I was to learn that it was on this premise that Jimmy was constructing his life. Over the next fifty years, I was to discover the extent to which James Dean was effective in doing so.

5

An Actor Prepares

EACH DAY, MY JOB AT CBS BECAME MORE INTERESTING AND EX-
citing. One of my duties as an usher was to deal with the audiences that came to the various shows, line them up, chat
them up until the doors to the radio studios opened, then herd
them inside. However, being naturally gregarious and relatively new to Los Angeles myself, I enjoyed talking to the
tourists and understood their excitement at seeing in the flesh
the personalities whose disembodied voices they'd been listening to on the radio at home. For a kid not long from the Midwest, I'd experienced much the same thrill. Even after several
months on the job, it hadn't worn off.

Best of all, when I wasn't dealing with the out-of-towners,
I was interacting with radio stars of the period, like Red Skelton, George Burns and Gracie Allen, Jack Benny, Eve Arden,
Lucille Ball, Dinah Shore, Bing Crosby, Steve Allen, Bob
Crosby, Jo Stafford, the Andrews Sisters, the Modernaires,
and Giselle McKenzie. I was in Period Paradise and having the
time of my life.

Of course as studio ushers, we related to the stars in a service capacity, but it was surprising how many of them made a
point of remembering our names, took an interest in us personally, and encouraged us in our ambitions. I got the feeling
that many recalled the days when they, too, were just starting
out in show business and remembered how tough it was.

Maxene Andrews was one example, and Red Skelton another. Except for the tyrannical executive type in charge of the ushering staff, life at CBS was continuously rewarding, especially when Christmas came around. That was when the stars showered the ushers with gifts and bonuses.

Aside from the half-hour comedies and dramas that emanated from the smaller studios on Sunset, CBS also broadcast a number of major, live, one-hour musical and dramatic shows from its larger theater on Vine Street and Selma. Among them were Bing Crosby's show, which featured such top musical film and recording stars as Mario Lanza, Judy Garland, and Rosemary Clooney. Cecil B. DeMille's prestigious "Lux Radio Theater" presented one-hour dramatic re-creations of recent motion pictures featuring the original stars. Working these shows was, for me, the prize catch: The actors and directors who participated were tops in their fields. Studying their craftsmanship up close was an education in itself.

Jimmy and I found one particular broadcast truly a night to remember. MGM had just fired Judy Garland from *Annie Get Your Gun,* replacing her with Betty Hutton. It was, reportedly, a shattering blow for Garland. The story had been headlined for days, and Bing Crosby, a friend of Garland's, had invited her to appear as a guest star on his radio show as a gesture of support. Determined not to miss the biggest event in town, I contrived to get myself assigned to work the show that night and had been delegated to escort Miss Garland from her car to her dressing room before the broadcast. Jimmy was understandably eager to witness the fireworks, too, so I managed to slip him into the house before the audience was admitted and seat him in the front row of the balcony.

Garland arrived in a limousine with her husband, Sid Luft. When she stepped out of the car, I was unprepared for her appearance. Unexpectedly gaunt, she was wearing a plain black dress and little or no makeup, which accentuated her pallor and made her look like she was attending a funeral, possibly her own. She'd been in seclusion, and this was to be her first public appearance since MGM gave her the ax. As a result, I could see that she was plainly terrified. In fact, she was trembling so badly that Luft and I practically had to carry her to her dressing room.

Leaving them backstage, I hurried out front to catch the show, stationing myself next to Jimmy in the side aisle at the front of the balcony. News of Garland's appearance had gotten out, and the house was jammed to the roof with excited fans and tourists. Promptly on the hour, the show went on the air, live. Crosby crooned a couple of songs, then, after a commercial, with quiet dignity and sincere warmth, he introduced his guest star. There was a long moment before a tiny, pathetic, terrified creature in black emerged from the wings. She took a few tentative steps then faltered. Her host quickly extended a hand to help her to the microphone midstage. If it'd been rehearsed, which perhaps it was, it couldn't have played better. The studio audience rose to their feet and covered her uncertain entrance with sustained, enthusiastic applause. Standing there alone, she stared at them in dazed gratitude, as if genuinely surprised by the exuberant greeting. I fully expected her to pass out. Jimmy and I exchanged worried glances. Would she perform? Could she perform? The audience fell silent, expectant, and the orchestra played the introduction.

Garland looked up to the balcony, I swear straight at us, opened her mouth, and belted out the most exhilarating rendition of "Rock-a-bye My Baby to a Dixie Melody" I've ever heard. Why the song should have such an emotional impact, I couldn't figure. It isn't sentimental; in fact, it could be considered upbeat. But her delivery was transcendent and the emotion overpowering. I got the feeling halfway through that everyone in that audience was thinking, "My God, what have they done to Dorothy!" When the last note died, the audience was on its feet going insane. She scanned the house, as if bewildered by the outpouring of affection, then smiled wanly. The applause and cheers seemed endless. I had never seen anything like it.

All the way home, incredulous, Jimmy kept repeating, "*How* did she do that? How did she *do* that? How the *fuck* did she do that?" Actually this was the second time I'd seen him blown away by a performance. The first, very recently, was the night we'd been to see the movie of Tennessee Williams's *A Streetcar Named Desire* in Santa Monica. For days after watching Brando's performance, Jimmy had barely spoken a word. When I'd tried to engage him in discussing it, he'd refused. Instead, he'd gone back to see the picture again, alone, presumably to study Brando's performance.

In retrospect, it now seems obvious that after witnessing Brando's and Garland's performances, something had happened to him. At the time, I knew he'd been deeply affected by both, but I never guessed to what extent, dismissing his behavior as just one of his moods. However, a few weeks later, an event occurred that can, with certainty, be said to have exercised a decisive formative influence over both our lives.

Again, I had managed to get myself assigned to work a show at the Vine Street Theater, which now involved gofering, meaning being on hand to answer phones and fetch coffee and sandwiches for cast and crew during rehearsals. It was another C.B. DeMille radio production, featuring actor James Whitmore reprising his role in the recent movie, *Battleground*. During breaks, I chatted with Whitmore and learned that he was a member of the now-famous Actors Studio in New York where Lee Strasberg and Elia Kazan taught. For Jimmy and me, Strasberg and Kazan were nothing short of gods, and anyone who had studied with them was accordingly a demigod. Whitmore had recently played in the Broadway production of *Command Decision* before coming to Hollywood to play his role in *Battleground*, a role for which he had just received an Oscar nomination for Best Supporting Actor. Although he told me he liked Hollywood, he confessed that he missed the creative stimulation of New York. Most of all, he missed studying his craft at the Actors Studio. As I listened to him, the seed of an idea germinated in my mind.

Later I told Jimmy about Whitmore and the Actors Studio. He immediately came out of his funk, hungrily devouring every morsel of information I had to offer. So, encouraged by his interest, I confided my idea: persuade Whitmore to teach an acting class out here in Los Angeles, teach us "the Method," the Stanislavsky acting technique as defined in his book, *An Actor Prepares*. Naturally, I felt reluctant to ask a busy guy like Whitmore to take time out for some kids with acting ambitions, but Jimmy, now fired up by the idea himself, badgered me relentlessly at least to make a phone call and ask Whitmore to consider the idea.

When I was very young and had doubts about suggesting an idea to someone who might reject it, my mother's most frequently offered and surprisingly trenchant advice was, "Ask. The worst they can do is say no." So, I figured, what the hell, and placed the call.

To my surprise and Jimmy's glee, Whitmore invited me to breakfast the following morning at the Brentwood Country Mart, a shopping center located not far from our penthouse. Over coffee and Danish, I mustered my courage and reminded him of our conversation about the Actors Studio. I explained that I and a number of my classmates at the UCLA Theater Arts Department had often wished we could get the kind of training in L.A. that was only available at the Actors Studio in New York.

Way ahead of me, Whitmore offered to provide what we were looking for. Instantly enthusiastic, he suggested that I get together about eight or ten of the most serious theater students—he didn't want too large a class—and we could start right away. However, he cautioned, we weren't to consider him a teacher. He'd be more like a guide, showing us what he'd learned. In fact, he insisted on this. He'd be studying right along with us. He proposed that we meet two or three times a week at first to see how things went. Maybe he could even get the use of a meeting room right where we were, over the Brentwood Country Mart, for our classroom. Within fifteen minutes, it was settled. We'd have our first meeting the following week.

Jimmy was ecstatic when I told him.

Although the penthouse had become a scene of intense study and intellectual calisthenics, it was also home base for a flurry of constructive activity in career building. I was all wrapped up in the wonder of my new part-time job at CBS, and Jimmy was actively pursuing casting directors with the help of our agent, Isabel Draesemer. Yes, he'd kept his bargain by introducing me to Isabel, who had agreed to take me on, as well, although it was becoming clear that her attention was more focused on Jimmy than on me.

Since neither of us had gone the professional route before, we naturally lacked the basic equipment for the long, demanding journey. There were all the usual preparations for our careers as actors: appointments with casting directors, audition scenes to be rehearsed, and pictures for our "composites." No serious candidate for stardom in Hollywood could afford to be without a composite. For the uninitiated, this consisted of a single 8½" × 11" posed photograph or sheet of selected photos of the aspiring actor in various moods, attitudes, and, sometimes, costumes. On the back of this could be listed the actor's professional credits, assuming he or she had credits. These composites were designed to be left with casting directors, directors, and producers after auditions and interviews.

The preparation of our composites required tedious sessions with a still photographer. Isabel had recommended one who was not too expensive and lived in Whitley Heights opposite the Hollywood Bowl. Wilson Millar specialized in thirties-style glamour photos, which resulted in a John Barrymore pose of Jimmy with his sandy blond hair undulantly marcelled and his pursed lips looking painted even in black and white. My photograph was equally precious. However, no matter how much we hated those pictures, they were all we could afford, so we were stuck with them.

Unfortunately in the whirl of preprofessional activity, the relatively static processes of study and cramming for exams had to be relegated to the late, late hours when focus blurred and heads nodded. Somewhere along the line, UCLA seemed to be getting lost in the distractions. We were both cutting too many school classes in order to attend to our anticipated careers.

Since I was almost through my four-year run, this didn't bother me too much. Although Jimmy kept insisting that a degree was only a superficial means to an end, he was clearly becoming concerned as he slipped further and further behind.

Most of all, he feared his father's disapproval of his now open pursuit of acting as a profession and, more immediately threatening, the old man's withdrawal of financial support, however minimal. But now confident that he was on course for an acting career at last, Jimmy was not about to jump that particular ship for a degree, much less his father's approval. Still, the problem gnawed.

Meantime, the Theater Arts Department had been planning a production of *Dark of the Moon* in which Jimmy desperately hoped to be cast in the lead role of John, the witch boy. I thought it ideal casting. Sadly, the director didn't see it that way and passed him over in favor of someone even I considered a lesser talent. Jimmy was bitterly, spitefully disappointed. Furthermore, the injustice provided the push he needed to do just what he had been planning to do, drop out of UCLA altogether.

"Anyway," he rationalized as we drove to the Brentwood Country Mart for the first meeting of the Whitmore class, "I'll get a hell of a lot more out of this class than I will the T. A. Department."

Whitmore arrived, casual, relaxed, ready for work, and was confronted by nine tense, awed young faces. He spotted the problem immediately. Gently, slowly, smoothly, seductively, he loosened us up, coaxed us, and generally eased the strain until we were receptive. Simple conversation, a little humor, some extra personal interest, confidence, patience, these were his devices. Like the craftsman he was, he drew us out, first as a group, then individually. Within an hour, we were his, pliable, receptive, ready. Then, dropping the smiles and smooth talk, he smashed the spell with some hard realities.

Learning to act was no child's game, he warned, so we could forget the romance part. Acting was a craft, a serious profession. And in order to learn any craft, you had to apply yourself. That took time, study, practice, and patience. Most of all, it took hard work, damn hard work. And sweat. If we were after glory, we wouldn't find it learning to act. We might not even find it in an acting career. But if it was a sense of fulfillment, a sense of personal gratification we were seeking, there was no other profession that could give us more. At least, he confessed humbly, that was the way he felt about it.

If an actor were truly dedicated to his craft, he challenged, he would work until he was ready to drop, and then go on and work some more. By the time he was ready to call himself an actor, he'd be so damn tired, he probably wouldn't even care about the applause. But he'd feel good, like you feel after a good workout, when you ache all over and you're aware of every muscle in your body. It would hurt, but it would hurt good.

"We're going to work here," he concluded. "That's what we're here for. I'm not qualified to teach you, but I can pass on to you what I've learned. I'll try to explain it the way I see it. Maybe it'll make sense, maybe it won't. That's partly up to me and partly up to you. If we're lucky, we might accomplish something."

There were no lessons that first night. Instead, the time was spent getting to know one another and listening to Whitmore dispel any of the nonsensical ideas we might have had about this class being the ultimate secret to success. Then, he dismissed us and left us to ponder what he'd tried to get across. With visions of the dedicated actor's life in our heads, we left, elated and just a little daunted by the challenge. It would be interesting to see who showed up for the next session.

By morning, Jimmy and I were forced back to harsh reality. We were broke, and rent day loomed. My share would, as usual, be scraped together from the pittance I had made from Magda's driving lessons and the paltry sum CBS paid me. Mind you, I'd have stayed on at CBS for nothing if I hadn't needed to pay my rent, a fact I think they realized and took advantage of with every usher. As for Jimmy, financially drained by the photographs, rent, food, cigarettes, and with little or no help from his father, he'd been reduced to borrowing pin money from me, which made him feel guilty and beholden and finally resulted in our first row. We patched it up, but somehow it festered. However, I'd learned to tread lightly around his sensibilities, especially about the touchy subject of his indebtedness. But, praise be, just as the due date for the rent appeared on the calendar, so did the promise of funds to meet it.

It came in the form of a call—and an advance—from agent Isabel. The Jerry Fairbanks Studio had come through and cast Jimmy in a movie, *Hill Number One*, a religious film to be shot soon, for release on television at Easter. Now, instead of John the lovelorn witch boy, he would be playing John the beloved disciple. Although Jimmy had done a Pepsi-Cola commercial in which he danced around a jukebox with a girl and other aspiring young actors, including one Nick Adams, he considered the upcoming religious film as his first truly professional job. He was intensely excited, the operative word being "intensely."

Jimmy's excitement manifested itself in an unusual way. After the first burst of euphoria, he refused to talk about the job and didn't seem to enjoy the prospect of it anymore. In fact, he became moody and sullen. As the days went by and the start of shooting grew nearer, the tension in him built. He literally became incommunicado, lost in one of his drawings or poems. I got the feeling that he thought by talking about the job, or admitting that he'd even been offered one, he'd lose it. But then, a few days before he was to start the picture, he learned what he considered to be the most important lesson in his early career: focus.

As she walked around the room, circling us, the girl quickly became quite self-conscious, adjusting her clothes, not knowing what to do with her hands, occasionally blushing in embarrassment and shrugging apologetically. From our perspective, she presented an awkward, uninteresting picture of a totally self-conscious person, circling the room pointlessly, very much aware that everyone was staring at her.

We were experiencing our first class exercise. Whitmore had asked the girl to get up and walk around the room. She had asked him how she should walk. He had told her it didn't matter, simply to walk.

After she made a few self-conscious revolutions, Whitmore drew her aside and whispered something into her ear, then instructed her to walk around the room again. Gradually, she became more interesting, no longer appearing self-conscious. Instead, her eyes were fixed straight ahead, sometimes narrowed, her brow furrowed as though she were straining or struggling with her inner thoughts. Her body was poised, though she would tense and clenched her fists occasionally. From time to time, a smile would cross her lips, but then she would purse them and furrow her brow, as if straining again for some elusive thought. We leaned in to observe the inaudible muttering movements she seemed to be making with her lips, as if subvocalizing, like the elderly often do. We couldn't help but wonder what was going on in her head. Whatever it was, it was certainly compelling.

Finally, Whitmore had her take her seat and asked us to analyze the difference between her first and second walk around the room. We agreed unanimously that she was much more interesting the second time. He suggested that it was because the first time she'd had nothing to do, nothing going on inside. But the second time, she was doing something internally, there was something happening inside. As an audience, we could see it, sense it. She was no longer aware of herself or us; she was somewhere else and deeply involved in something that evoked our interest. She was struggling, and what she was struggling with was drawing us in. So, what was she struggling with? Simply, the words to "The Star-Spangled Banner." Instructed to repeat them to herself while circling the room the second time, she had been trying to remember them and get them right, focusing her attention inward on her problem, instead of outward on the class, i.e., the audience staring at her. It was a simple lesson in the dynamic force of total concentration, one that Jimmy would learn well.

The next revelation came at a subsequent session during an improvisation. Whitmore took Jimmy aside and told him that he was a college student who had stolen a wristwatch. He had taken the watch to a jeweler for repairs, but, upon learning that the police were looking for him, realized he had to leave town on the next bus, which was departing in fifteen minutes. His job was to get that watch back from the jeweler and catch that bus at any cost. Whitmore then took me aside and told me I was a jeweler who had been told by the police to be on the lookout for a young man of Jimmy's description who had stolen a watch, a watch exactly like the one such a young man had brought in the day before. If Jimmy showed up, I was to call the police and detain him until they could get to my shop. Under no circumstance was I to let him leave with the watch.

Our first tries at the improvisation fell as flat as the girl's first walk around the room. Either I would give Jimmy the watch because I ran out of reasonable excuses for not giving it to him, or he would leave, unable to figure out any more ways to get it from me. In the end, we got into a polite tug of war that became so ludicrous that it finally made us break up.

Whitmore stopped us and lectured us on the power of concentration, an intensity of concentration so deep, so complete that nothing in the world could deter us from our two conflicting purposes. He instructed us to try the scene again, but this time to focus only on our do-or-die objectives and our determination not to let anything stop us. Then, before we began, he gave us a moment to recall a time in our pasts when we felt truly desperate and told us to bring that desperation to our scene.

After a few minutes of preparation, we started again, this time digging our heels in, each refusing to give an inch. The more Jimmy insisted on having the watch back, the more I refused. He called me a bastard, a pompous one at that. From a previous incident, during a spat over whose turn it was to clean the penthouse, he knew I would react angrily at being called pompous, and I knew he would go ape if I called him a nearsighted little son of a bitch, so I made the mistake of doing so. The next thing I knew, I was down on the floor, and we were wrestling over the watch. But somehow we weren't wrestling over the watch; we were settling that unresolved dispute over the money he owed me.

Our struggle intensified, and suddenly it seemed to me that it was no longer about the watch or the money. Something else was going on, something far deeper, for me at any rate. The physicality of the situation threatened to betray something I wasn't prepared to acknowledge, and, as I struggled beneath Jimmy, I began to panic. Firmly in his grasp, I found my face millimeters from his, and for one unsettling instant, our eyes made contact. We were either going to kill one another or . . . what? We didn't have time to find out. Whitmore and a couple of the others pulled us apart.

I never heard what Whitmore said to the class after the exercise and only vaguely recall that he was pleased with the results. I was too shaken to pay close attention, still trying to figure out exactly what had happened between Jimmy and me. In that one disturbing moment, we had gone somewhere too dangerous to risk exploring. Or was it only I who had experienced that sensation? Whatever was going on, Jimmy and I didn't say a word to each other on our way home.

6

The Pearl-Handled Knife

ARMED WITH A NEW AWARENESS OF THE POWER OF TOTAL CON-
centration, the thin line between reality and acting, and the risk
of crossing that line and losing control, Jimmy took what he
had learned in class and put it to use during the filming of *Hill
Number One*. It would be Easter before the film was aired, and
we wouldn't know till then how well it had served him.

But Easter was weeks away, and the money he had earned
from the film would soon be gone. Worse yet, already facing
one economic crisis, a second, unexpected one hit the day
Magda got her license and the driving lessons stopped. Until
then we had had frequent use of Magda's car. Suddenly, we
had no transportation at all.

This time the answer to our problem came from Jimmy's
quarter. We paid a visit to his father and stepmother. Two less-
responsive creatures I had seldom encountered. The stepmother, whom I'd never met before, struck me as mousy and
shy, while Winton Dean, whom I'd met earlier on several occasions, was as reserved and monosyllabic as usual. Yet, he
tried to look interested in what his son had to say, though it
all seemed beyond him. Not even the news about Jimmy's first
television movie seemed to excite, or even please, the man. He
simply kept nodding.

I felt sorry for Jimmy as he twisted himself in knots, trying to please, all but doing a tap dance in hopes of evoking

some show of appreciation, some sign of interest in what he was accomplishing. But a cup of coffee was all he got, all we got, because he got little more than I. There was something that smelled pretty good cooking on the stove, but it wasn't to be for us. Finally, biting the bullet, Jimmy explained our transportation problem and asked if his dad could help. Winton listened quietly, nodding, until Jimmy finished. Then he mulled it over for a moment before promising to see what he could do. It didn't sound encouraging.

Within a few days, however, and much to our surprise, Winton delivered a used '39 Chevy that appeared to be in good condition. He presented Jimmy with the keys and an admonition to "Drive careful." It was truly the best windfall we could have wished for, but I got the feeling that Jimmy was more pleased that the old man had come through for him than with the car itself. I could see my roommate was starving for love and acceptance from that man. Despite that, I still envied Jimmy. I didn't have access to a father to give *or* deny me love. I didn't even know my father.

Jimmy and I made a deal: I would pay for the gas, and he would chauffeur me back and forth to work. But car or no car, we were still chronically broke, and the fact that the car turned out to be a gas-guzzler only contributed to the problem. Isabel Draesemer assured us that Jimmy would be deluged with job offers after *Hill Number One* aired. But how were we to make it to Easter?

About that time, I met a girl at CBS and struck up a friendship. At seventeen, Beverly Wills was already an able young comedienne, playing second banana on the radio sitcom, "Junior Miss." Like a number of other young working actors at that time, she was attending Hollywood Professional High School on Hollywood Boulevard near CBS, where she was in her last year. Being a "Hollywood brat," she was acquainted with quite a few other up-and-coming young performers, some who went to the same school, with names like Jane Withers and Debbie Reynolds. Although no classic beauty, Beverly was attractive, bright, and had a flare for comic antics and mugging. Her good humor and energy were a welcome counterbalance to Jimmy's moodiness. Soon we started to date, locally and, of course, cheaply.

Though her parents had long been divorced, she had kept her father's name, so I didn't know for the first couple of weeks that her mother was, in fact, star of movies and radio, comedienne Joan Davis, whom I had encountered at CBS where she had her own show. Nor did I know that Beverly lived with her mother in a Bel Air mansion and right next door to Alfred Hitchcock. In all, I was impressed and understandably intimidated.

On the other hand, Joan was not terribly impressed with me when we met. I admired her talent, but I obviously didn't possess any that was immediately apparent to her. So it took her a while to warm to me, if "warm" is what you would call it. "Tolerate" would be more accurate. I was, of course, initially suspected of being an opportunist. To me, the most appalling aspect of that suspicion was that Joan thought so little of her own daughter that she doubted any young man could like Beverly for herself, so he must be after the family fortune. Shades of Henry James's *The Heiress*. I sensed this very soon after meeting her, but did nothing to disabuse her of her suspicions as to my intentions. Instead, I concentrated on Beverly and politely avoided her mother.

Strangely, after a while, it seemed to me that Joan tried to upstage her daughter and engage my attention, not flirtatiously, but actorishly. Soon she dropped her guard and accepted me, and I became part of the scene. I was relieved and glad for Beverly's sake. I was also finally able to relax a bit around Madam.

Joan's cook-housekeeper, a Southern woman named Odessa, was an exceptional cook and had a heart to match her mighty girth. First Magda, now Odessa. I was beginning to assume that the rich and famous only hired kindhearted cook-housekeepers. Beverly adored Odessa, and the feeling was mutual. So it was relatively easy for Beverly to make it the woman's mission to see that we were shielded from Madam's vigilance. Much as I appreciated the gesture, I was uneasy with the amount of privacy this afforded Beverly and me. Given Odessa's complicity, Beverly would confirm her mother's concerns by steering us into her own bedroom at every possible opportunity on the pretext that we were going to "watch television." This was making me very uneasy, not only because Joan's bedroom was just down the hall, but also because Beverly stood little chance of turning me on. But, trouper that she was, Bev persisted, and we managed a few furtive fucks, none memorable, at least for me, all things considered.

Eventually I was invited, with Beverly, into Joan's sanctum sanctorum, the boudoir where Madam held court. It turned out to be a Hollywood movie set where Joan spent most of her time gossiping on the phone in her enormous and terribly impressive king-size bed—a rarity at that early date—propped up by great downy pillows and wearing a powdery pink-feathered bed jacket, all of which tended to make her look like a drag parody of Joan Crawford in a camp movie.

I got the impression that she rarely got out of bed, except occasionally to play golf or to be entertained by producers or studio executives courting her for a possible picture, radio series, or a guest-star appearance. At such times, in an attempt to discard her professional comedic persona, she would transform herself into a glamorous movie queen, albeit one with a rather prominent nose, and initially assume an unctuous charm, but gradually slip back into the role of Cinderella's imperious stepmother with an uncontrollable tendency to mug and flirt.

True to Hollywood tradition, the powerbrokers that came a-courting appeared to be so charmed that the little gold stirrups on their Gucci loafers fairly jingled with glee at her every jest. Anything for a deal. Besides, as I was to learn from Beverly some time later, Joan had had affairs with many a mogul, not to mention leading men, among them Eddie Cantor, and had a reputation for being pretty hot stuff.

One of her current gentlemen friends was Johnny Mercer, the noted songwriter. Early that New Year's Eve, he arrived at the house to pick up Joan, but had to wait for her because she'd been delayed at the studio. Beverly and I were there with her sexy blonde girlfriend, Sue, waiting for Sue's sexy blond surfer boyfriend, who was going to drive us to a party. We offered Mr. Mercer a drink, and, after one sly glance at the delectable Sue, he accepted.

It would not be inaccurate to say that, for an hour or more, he sat at the piano and played for us one after another of his hit songs—"You Must Have Been a Beautiful Baby," "Laura," "Lazy Bones," "That Old Black Magic," "Goody, Goody," and on and on. Gradually it became clear that he was playing not so much for us as for sweet Sue. Nonetheless, it was a treat. When Sue's beau finally arrived, we left "Johnny," as he had earlier instructed us to address him, to wait for Joan alone. As I walked out the door, I turned and caught him gazing after Sue, a wistful look in his eyes. He was only about forty-five or so, but in the company of four vital, attractive youths, sad to say, he was obviously feeling ancient at that moment.

In an effort to amuse my increasingly depressed roommate or, unlikely as it seemed, even cheer him up, I tried relating my show-biz experiences over at the Davis mansion to him. But Jimmy was so involved in his anxiety over the upcoming television release of *Hill Number One* that it seemed only to make him more irritable. I gave up trying, believing that Beverly and her famous mother were of little or no interest to him. I was soon to find out how very wrong I was.

Suddenly it was Easter, and *Hill Number One* was aired and greeted by favorable reviews, some singling Jimmy out for praise. There was a brief moment of euphoria and relief. Agent Isabel reacted as if Jimmy had become a star overnight.

It was not to be.

Her phone did not ring off the hook with offers. Instead, there followed an ominous silence, and the longer it persisted, the deeper and darker Jimmy's moods became. From past experience, I knew there was no way I could penetrate his gloom, so I respected his need to retreat into himself and became a silent spectator. During what seemed an endless wait, Jimmy would spend almost every day in silence, sometimes drawing, sometimes writing poetry, always unreachable. If I had thought it difficult to communicate with him at times before, now I found it impossible. Often he would sit in his nook, just sit there and stare into space for hours. Any attempt to reach him was usually met with a grunt or an absent look. Sometimes he just wouldn't see me, as if I didn't exist. Cats do that, but not being a cat person then, I didn't know how to handle it.

One night, returning late from a party, as I was getting off the bus on Santa Monica Boulevard, I spotted him heading toward Ocean Avenue and the beach. I tried to catch up with him, but he was too far ahead, so I decided to just follow him instead and see what he was up to.

I watched from a discreet distance for a while as he prowled the Santa Monica amusement pier then settled on a bench. He was studying a young couple as they tossed baseballs at milk bottles and won a cuddly toy, then wolfed "one-footers" at the hot-dog stand next door. The boy gently licked the mustard from the girl's cheek. She turned her lips to his, and they kissed. Then they strolled together, hand in hand, to the end of the pier to gaze out into dark infinity where the stars met the sea. Jimmy turned and ambled back toward the street, hands thrust deep into pockets, head down, hangdog style, then halted to observe some young hoods trying, with little success, to provoke a fight with a couple of black kids. At that point, he let a vagrant wino bum a cigarette from him and listened, sometimes nodding, sometimes laughing, as the guy presumably told him how things were coming down.

I left him chatting to a chubby hot-dog stand waitress over coffee and started back to the penthouse, realizing that I had just witnessed Jimmy in the act of doing his homework. After all, didn't Konstantin Stanislavsky's definitive work on acting, *An Actor Prepares*, propose that it was an actor's task, nay duty, to experience as much of life as possible in order to be prepared for any role he might be assigned, and hadn't that now become Jimmy's bible?

Many nights thereafter, Jimmy would slip out after I'd gone to bed, then return hours later and sleep till noon the next day. At first, I figured he was prowling the Santa Monica pier again or other haunts of the night people. Then it occurred to me, in the wee small hours, the pier and the boardwalk were pretty deserted of characters to study. So where, then, was he going? Having no way of knowing how serious Jimmy's bouts of depression were, I began to worry that he might be going through troubled times. In the end, my concern would keep me awake until I heard him finally come in.

Then one night, around midnight, as I was walking back to the penthouse after a movie and coffee with friends, I saw Jimmy ahead of me, just leaving our building. I was about to call out to him, but he turned without seeing me and headed in the opposite direction, toward Wilshire Boulevard. I hesitated for a moment, then gave in to my curiosity, and followed him once again. When he reached Wilshire, he sat down on a bench by a bus stop and lit a cigarette, apparently waiting for a bus. From the shadows of a darkened doorway up the street, I waited and watched. I knew buses could be few and far between at that hour, and I was too tired to hang around long. I began to feel stupid and a little guilty for spying on him again. Still, something told me not to leave.

I was just about to go back to the penthouse when a bus appeared. The driver stopped and opened the door for Jimmy to board. I could see Jimmy shake his head, declining the offer. The bus drove off, but Jimmy stayed put, now posing himself on the bench, arms spread out along the back, butt slid forward to the edge of the seat, legs stretched out in front and crossed at the ankles. The better to display his wares, it appeared. In that instant, I thought I knew what he might be up to. But was he hitching, hustling, or was he just waiting for a blow job? Or was it something more involved? I was about to find out. A car came to a stop at the red light, idling next to the bus stop. The driver leaned over, lowered the passenger window, and said something to the sexy young man posed on the bench. From past experience, I could imagine what. It would go something like: "I'm headed into Beverly Hills. Hop in. I'll give you a lift."

Jimmy got up casually, slipped his hands into his jacket pockets, stepped off the curb, and bent down to look inside the car. He made no move to open the door, but just studied the driver for a second or two through the open window. I couldn't make out whether the driver said anything more, but Jimmy didn't appear to speak at all. Instead, he withdrew something from his jacket pocket and revealed it to the driver. I caught a flash of the streetlight reflected briefly off a steel blade as it flicked out from his hand. It wasn't a switchblade, but a knife that snaps open like a jackknife at the touch of a button on the handle. I knew this because the knife was mine. Jimmy must have borrowed it for the occasion. The car took off, burning rubber. He watched it go, then closed the knife, put it back into his pocket, and sauntered off toward the beach. Suddenly I was afraid, afraid for Jimmy . . . and afraid *of* Jimmy.

Back at the penthouse, I immediately checked the drawer in which I kept a small box of my most prized possessions, such as they were, my special treasures. No knife. It was mine, all right. It had been my grandfather's. I'd admired it since I was a kid. He'd given it to me some years before, and I treasured it. Jimmy had spotted the knife among my things when we moved in, and I had let him examine it. Flicking it open and shut again and again, he had seemed fascinated. At the time, I had no idea how fascinated. Now I only hoped he wouldn't actually put it to use. I didn't even want to think about that.

Not wanting to face him if he came back unexpectedly, I undressed quickly and slipped into bed. I lay there wondering what I'd seen. I had been too far away to see his expression when he scared off the driver, so I had no way of knowing what he might have been thinking. Why use a knife to intimidate somebody who was just offering a ride? A sadistic game? Hang around waiting for a queer to offer a ride, then get your kicks watching the terrified guy burn rubber? As far as I'd been able to observe, the driver wasn't threatening him. Of course, there was always the possibility the driver had provoked the action by something he said. But to flash a knife just because somebody says something you don't like? It seemed a bit extreme, to say the least. Besides, wasn't Jimmy's pose deliberately provocative? Wasn't he inviting a pickup? Or was that the game, the reason he took the knife? Was he simply getting off on scaring fags?

I tried to avoid speculating about the reason I feared most: that Jimmy had a thing about homosexuals, a loathing so profound that it compelled him to seek them out, threaten them, terrify them. Or, was it only Stanislavsky again? *An Actor Prepares*. Prepares for what, though? In any case, I decided, he must never learn my secret. Torn by questions I couldn't answer, I fell asleep and didn't hear him come in that night.

The next morning, the knife was back in my drawer, and I never confronted him about it. The truth was, I didn't imagine he would give me an honest answer. Anyway, I preferred not to know, although the incident would continue to haunt me and do lasting damage to my trust in him.

7

Mother's Day

JIMMY'S PERIOD OF INSULATION ENDED ABRUPTLY WITH A PHONE call from Isabel. I assumed it was good news about a job. No such luck. But to him it was something almost as encouraging. A group of teenage girls from Immaculate Heart High School near Griffith Park had been required to watch the Easter airing of *Hill Number One*. Apparently, they had creamed over the young actor who played John the beloved disciple and promptly formed the first-ever James Dean Fan Club. Having tracked down his agent, they begged her to persuade their new heartthrob to make a personal appearance at their next meeting.

Jimmy was tickled. What a gas, an honest-to-god fan club! He told Isabel to accept their invitation. But as the moment of truth approached, he grew endearingly nervous and looked to me for moral support. In fact, he wanted a chaperon, and I was elected.

As we drove to the address provided by Isabel, we tried to imagine the scene awaiting us. Would they be hysterical bobby-socks screamers like Sinatra fans or prim and proper parochial schoolgirls with white-collared uniforms and patent-leather shoes? We pulled up in front of a modest bungalow in the Los Feliz area. Before we got out of the car, he hesitated at the wheel, nervous again. What should we do if they started coming on to us? After all, these girls were "jail bait." It would be their word against ours. Now he was making me nervous. We agreed to play it cool, keep our distance, and avoid anything that might even be construed as "suggestive."

Inside the modest home, everyone was nervous, the dozen or so girls between the ages of fourteen and sixteen on one side of the living room, Jimmy and me on the other. No sign of parents or any adults. However, to our relief, the girls were polite and proper, giggling among themselves a lot. They offered us coffee and cake, then bombarded Jimmy with a stream of prepared fan-type questions, taking it for granted that he was already a star, if only on television. Jimmy donned his most modest, unassuming attitude and answered in soft, self-effacing mumbles, forcing the girls to lean in closer, eagerly straining to catch his shy responses. Later, as they lined up, autograph books at the ready, you could almost hear their little hearts beating behind their budding breasts. I thought a couple of them might even faint. Signing each book obligingly, Jimmy pressed it back into its owner's hands with a smile, his eyes telling her that her autograph was singularly special. I was impressed by his amazingly polished and suave technique. By the time the ordeal was over, I figured Jimmy had secured himself at least a dozen fans for life, even if he never made another television movie.

I wonder how many of those girls remember that experience today. Every one of them I suspect; after all, they were his first fans. As for Jimmy, he would have to cling to the memory of that night for a while yet. Although there would be tens of thousands of adoring fans in his brief future, there would be hundreds of millions long after he no longer had a future, after he had realized his dream of immortality, but he was never to know that. And that's the sting in the tail: In the race for immortality, you have to live long enough to know you've made it to the finish line.

A week before Mother's Day, I received a letter from my mother, announcing that she was arriving from Milwaukee by train and would grace us with her presence for ten whole days. Bee, for ten days! First, I panicked, then sank into a minor depression of my own. I wasn't ready for Bee at that time—at *any* time, for that matter. Not that I didn't love my mother. It was just easier at a distance.

I broke the news to Jimmy as gently as I could. To my surprise, instead of disturbing him, he reacted positively. He really seemed to be looking forward to her arrival. He said he was sure it would work out just fine. He even offered to let her have his bed in the front-room alcove, which was only big enough for one. He would bunk in with me. Besides, he anticipated, she'd have money for food and gas and stuff. Best of all, she could cook and help clean the place. Cook? Clean? Bee? How could I tell him? How did you explain Bee? In the end, I didn't even try. He would find out for himself soon enough.

Bee, short for Bernice (inappropriately spelled, yet aptly descriptive of her temperament) was, as my grandmother used to say ruefully, too beautiful for her own good. Not well educated, but instinctively shrewd and an incredibly resilient survivor, she was born a party girl and died a party girl. However, in her early years, she was also an unmanageable hellcat with a wild temper. On her third marriage, with a number of lovers in between, she seemed to have settled down at last, except for her uncontrollable habit of flirting with anything in long pants, which sometimes resulted in violent marital arguments. I stress, *seemed*. With Bee, you never knew which row might terminate another union with her favorite line: "The door swings both ways, Brother, so don't let it hit you in the ass on your way out!" My grandfather, a gentle man of stoic patience and an abiding love for his family, once, at the end of his tether, proclaimed to the heavens that his misbegotten daughter ". . . couldn't be happy with Jesus Christ himself."

Jimmy and I picked her up at Union Station downtown. She looked great, if a tad overdone—but then, she always did, and she always was. As for her luggage, she had restrained herself; it only filled the trunk of the car and half of the backseat. She complained about the train trip all the way to Santa Monica. Oddly, Jimmy didn't seem to mind, which I found strange, until I remembered that she occupied a sacred status in his lexicon: She was a mother, of which he had none.

"It's so small" were her first words on entering the penthouse. "You didn't tell me it was this small."

We dined out that night, Mexican, on Bee. All through dinner, I kept thinking what an unlikely trio we were, Jimmy and Bee and me. Still, it was the first real meal Jimmy and I had had in weeks, so we were grateful. Besides, Bee and Jimmy were hitting it off remarkably well, so I relaxed and began to cheer up after a couple of beers and some green-corn tamales. Bee had several margaritas and was asleep before we got her home.

I awoke in the night with a full bladder. I was on my side, facing the curtained doorway that separated my room from the main room where Bee was sleeping in Jimmy's alcove bed, the room I would have to pass through to reach the bathroom. I could hear her snoring softly beyond the curtain. As I started to get out of bed, I realized I'd probably have to wake Jimmy to get up. He was curled up behind me, one arm draped over my waist in his sleep. So I made a careful move to slip out from under his arm, but as if in response, he tightened his hold around me. It was then that I felt his erection pressed against me.

Was he asleep or awake? I couldn't tell from his breathing. Asleep, no problem, I'd make my move for the john. Awake was a different matter; we were suddenly in another place completely. He would have had to know what was he doing and why. In which case, did he want me to wake, acknowledge what he was up to? And if that, what if I were to respond? I had a vision of that knife flashing in his hand. My bladder was bursting, but I waited anyway. I had to know what, if anything, was going on. Then he moved closer, his arm sliding further down my body, his hand nearer my erection, his own now pressed more firmly against me. I stared at the curtained doorway and considered the options. As I saw it, there weren't any.

So I remained motionless and waited, ignoring the frantic messages from my bladder. After what seemed an eternity, he grunted, withdrew his arm and turned over, his back to me. He was asleep. Not knowing whether to be relieved or disappointed, I gently slipped out of bed and peeked through the curtains to check on Bee. She was lying on her back, her mouth open in a silent scream. I tiptoed across her room and into the bathroom.

Back in bed, I lay awake, trying to sort out my new feelings about Jimmy. What had I expected to happen? What had I *wanted* to happen? The truth is, my attitude toward Jimmy had changed over the short while we had lived together. My present concern over what may seem such a trivial incident should have been indication enough to me of this fact. From being oblivious at first to any sexual charms he may have possessed, I had moved to a place where, not wanting sex to complicate our living arrangement, I tried to avoid thinking about Jimmy in a sexual context. As it happened, the knife incident had certainly reinforced my resolve.

But I now found myself wondering where Jimmy was coming from. Had he been awake and conscious of what he was doing? Had he thought I might wake? Had he wanted me to wake? Was it, in fact, an overture? And then there was also the chance that he had been faking sleep, not wanting to embarrass himself should I disapprove of his "gesture," assuming that was what it was. Maybe when I failed to respond, he gave up, figuring I was either asleep or sending a negative message. After all, he didn't know about me, did he? I'd carefully kept my secret from him. Was he keeping a similar one from me? How would I ever know now that I'd let the opportunity pass?

Bee started to snore softly in the other room, and I realized that I had a whole nine days more to find out the answers to my quandaries, should there be other such incidents. There weren't, however, all the following week, so I was left in my state of confusion.

Meantime, there was Bee, as in, "busy as a . . ." For a few days, Jimmy and I took time out to entertain her, show her some of the sights that were new since she'd left Los Angeles. But a time came when Jimmy needed a break and I had to work. I couldn't just leave her sitting in the penthouse all day with nothing to do but drive Jimmy nuts. There was nothing else for it but to take her along to CBS and park her in some of the shows. Mercifully, she loved it. Problem solved, so I relaxed. Should have known better.

Our head usher was a tall, blond guy, named Bob Butler. Slightly older than I, Bob was a young man of few words, good at his job, fair minded, but a conscientious taskmaster. On this particular day, having parked Bee in the audience lineup for Latin band leader Desi Arnaz's radio show, I was assigned by Bob to change the marquee for another show. The job took a bit longer than I expected, and by the time I returned, the audience had been ushered inside the main studio, and the show was on the air. The Latin music of Desi's orchestra, which was now being piped in from the studio, filled the main lobby.

There, to my astonishment and embarrassment, another audience had gathered to watch a different show that was going on right there in the lobby. Instead of being in the studio watching the performance, Bee was in the lobby doing one of her own, dancing to the beat of a hot little mambo in the arms of Harry Ackerman, president of CBS-KNX. I had never even spoken to the exalted Mr. Ackerman, and there was my mother, shaking her bottom with my boss while dozens of people, including my fellow ushers, looked on. Although I find it amusing now, at the time, I was mortified.

When the number ended, the onlookers broke into enthusiastic applause, and Harry took mom and me to lunch at Nicodell's, the watering hole nearby where the CBS brass hung out. It was, of course, only an innocent flirtation, if that, but I felt like I was pimping for her. And apparently, from their attitudes, so did the rest of the ushering staff. Were they jealous? No way. I remember feeling rather defensive, as in, "Hey, bring your own moms down, and see how far *they* get."

Not one to let the grass grow, a few days later, Bee excused herself for the evening, informing Jimmy and me that she had a dinner date. This time it was with Bill Goodwin, a top CBS Radio Network announcer, who also had a role as a character on the Burns and Allen television show. When I reminded Bee that she was a married woman and he was a married man, she replied dismissively, "It's only dinner, for chrissake."

Meantime, tension was mounting at the penthouse. Jimmy's dream of job offers after his good reviews for *Hill Number One* had not materialized. He was losing patience with Bee's incessant buzzing and becoming less and less communicative each day. He began retreating into himself once more. The crisis struck one rainy day shortly before Bee left. She had decided to stay home and "clean this pigsty." When I returned from work that evening, I found her near tears. Jimmy had not spoken to her all day. In fact, he had totally ignored her, concentrating all his attention on a mobile he was constructing.

"Not one word!" she whimpered. "I even made him lunch and not so much as a thank you. He just sat there, the whole damn day, making that . . . that thing. It was like being locked up with a zombie!"

I tried to explain that he was under a lot of stress about his acting career and worried about money.

"It's not natural, treating people like that," she insisted, too hurt to care about his so-called career.

How could I explain that he didn't know how to behave when people did things for him? Making him lunch, doing the dishes, cleaning the place, buying the groceries, taking us out to dinners had finally made him uncomfortable. Living with him, I had learned that he hated the sense of obligation that goes with the acceptance of a favor, from anybody. (Not that he had ever refused a favor, to my recollection.) He knew he was in no position to repay Bee for her kindness and generosity, and he resented feeling beholden. I hadn't quite put it together at the time, but I was learning that he was almost pathological about being indebted to others. When it came his turn to be generous to me, he would somehow make the gesture of giving attractively seductive, and I couldn't escape the feeling that he considered my act of receiving a submission of some kind. But being beholden to anyone for anything was a status Jimmy resented. I was yet to find out how profoundly.

Wondering how I would ever resolve the friction between them, I took Bee out to dinner and left Jimmy with the mobile he was constructing. When we got back, the completed mobile was gently twirling over Bee's niche bed, and Jimmy had gone out. I immediately went to check my drawer and breathed a sigh of relief to find my knife still in its place. I returned to find Bee, contemplating the mobile, which was, in fact, quite charming. It seemed to mollify her wounded feelings. Later, while I studied for an exam, she slipped into bed and watched it spin slowly round and round above her until, mesmerized, she drifted off to sleep.

It must have been nearly three in the morning when Jimmy quietly crawled into bed beside me. I pretended not to wake. I wondered how we were going to make it through the last couple of days until she left. I figured I'd just have to keep them apart. I finally drifted off into a fretful sleep, his arm around me once more. I was getting used to it by then and found myself regretting Bee's imminent departure and Jimmy's return to his own bed.

Two days later, we drove Bee downtown to Union Station and got her luggage aboard the train. She was still a bit wary of Jimmy, but they seemed to have struck a polite détente. With less than ten minutes before the train was due to depart, Jimmy excused himself and ran off, leaving us on the platform.

"Isn't he even going to say goodbye?" Bee sighed in dismay.

A few minutes later he was back, breathless and presenting her with a box of chocolates he'd bought, probably with the last of his money, and a manila envelope, which he'd obviously retrieved from the car. In the envelope, Bee found an autographed picture of him, one of the thirties John Barrymore-like numbers taken for his composite. It was signed, "To my second mother. Love, Jimmy." That literally took Bee's breath away. At first utterly confused, then, overwhelmed by the sentiment, she tried to fight the tears, burbling, "Oh, that's the sweetest thing!"

I watched, astonished, as they embraced. Jimmy's eyes were closed, as he burrowed his face deep into her fox fur, clinging to her, as if savoring the moment. He was sharing my mother. It was the only time I ever saw them touch, and they were never to meet again. As for Bee, she cherished that photo until her dying day.

8

Surviving

FOR MONTHS, IT SEEMED I'D BEEN LEADING A TRIPLE LIFE, SEEING less of Joanne and more of Beverly, while keeping a furtive eye out for possible anonymous sex with guys who were signaling with their glances that they were interested. Because of my job, school, the two girls, acting classes, and the fact that I now had Jimmy providing transportation most of the time, those kinds of encounters were fewer and farther between. Then, early one evening, as I was dealing with the audience lined up outside one of the CBS radio shows, I came face to face with a Marine, tall, blond, blue eyed, and *muy simpatico*.

Possibly twenty-four or twenty-five, he was a Nordic knockout. A great build, a gentle smile, a quiet, intimate voice, and a compelling air of sensitivity about him. I wasn't exactly picking up the usual signals from him—he was too guileless for that—but I was definitely reading something in those eyes. When I gathered my wits, I managed to ask him the routine questions I generally put to all the out-of-towners. I learned his name (I shall call him Craig), that he was from Minnesota, and that he was stationed at the Camp Pendleton marine base, about sixty miles down the coast near Ocean-side. This was his first visit to Los Angeles, so he had rented a convertible for the day to drive around and see the sights. Trouble was, he didn't know where to drive or what he was looking at, in any case. I suggested that he not try to see everything in one go, but save some for his next weekend pass. He explained that there wouldn't be another as he was shipping out to Korea the following Monday.

More than sympathetic, I offered to show him the sights myself if he cared to stick around after the show while I changed out of my uniform. I explained that I also played tour guide between semesters at UCLA to pick up money toward my fall tuition and proposed my Special Grand Tour, but on the house, of course. Regretfully, he explained that he was due back at the base by morning, so he'd have to return the rental car by midnight in order to catch the last bus back to Pendleton that night. That wouldn't leave much time for a tour. I immediately suggested my famous Quickie Tour, which would get him back in time to catch the last bus. He smiled and accepted the invitation.

It was a warm, balmy night with a spectacularly clear view of the city as we drove around Hollywood and up into the hills along Mulholland Drive, taking in the sights along the way. Craig told me about his life in Minnesota, his parents and younger brothers and sisters, all of whom he loved dearly. Strangely, he was reluctant to share his dreams, explaining only that he had given up dreaming for the time being. I was beginning to realize that I was more than just sexually drawn to this person. It wasn't just his looks and sexuality that were tapping a disturbing new emotion in me, but something inside, some need, some loss perhaps, but certainly a sadness.

We headed for Westwood where I directed him to drive through the Bel Air gates and up to my most private and special spot at the very top of Bel Air: communications tycoon Atwater Kent's idyllic, Italianate estate, Capo di Monte. On all my previous visits as a tour guide, no one ever seemed to be in residence, and the gates to the magnificent grounds were invariably, inexplicably, left open. I was relieved to find this night no exception. For me, this special spot was more than just *il capo di monte*, the top of the mountain, it was the ideal Italian villa, perched on the top of the world, secret, private, and aloof from the mundane life that buzzed and flickered far below, and I wanted to share it with someone who might appreciate it as much as I. That night, it was perfect. From its majestic perch, it commanded a breathtaking view of the unusually smog-free city, a carpet of multicolored lights scattered on inky darkness all the way to the Pacific. We sat there a while with the car's top down, quietly taking it all in. Then, in this tranquil and beautiful setting, Craig confided to me the nightmare that was haunting him.

Immediately upon graduation from high school toward the end of World War II, he had been drafted and assigned to the Marine Corps. After basic training, he was trained as a medic and shipped to Europe. The catastrophic Battle of the Bulge was raging in Belgium, and he wound up in an area where the casualties were highest. As a medic, it was his duty to go out onto the battlefield, unarmed, during the fighting and retrieve the wounded. The survival rate among medics being the lowest in the corps, each day he fully expected to die, each night he thanked God he was still alive. When the war was over, he was one of the few medics in his division to return alive or unscathed. Now a new war was raging in Korea, one even more savage than the last. Ironically, he had been drafted again and was being sent overseas, once more as a medic. This time, however, he was resolutely convinced that he would never return.

My only exposure to the horrors of war had hitherto been through newsreels and movies, which paled beside the things Craig described. His vivid, yet unemotional, account of the harrowing battlefield scenes he had somehow survived left me appalled; but it was his resignation to a fatalistic conviction that he wouldn't make it back alive this time that upset me most. I tried to persuade him not to think like that. He had come through it once, and he would come through it again, I insisted, but he remained unconvinced. Instead, he gave me a sad, appreciative smile, then reached over, drew me to him, and kissed me on the lips, long and intensely. I felt that he was trying to absorb my promise and keep it with him.

Until then, I had never been kissed by a man, certainly not like this, and the desperate, hungry kiss of this fine, doomed soul had an overwhelming impact on me. I think we stayed there almost an hour, just talking. There wasn't any sex. That didn't seem important.

By the time we turned in Craig's rental car, he had missed the last bus back to Camp Pendleton and now risked being AWOL. We took a taxi to the penthouse where I woke Jimmy from a sound sleep, introduced Craig, explained the situation, and asked to borrow his car to drive Craig back to Camp Pendleton. Craig offered to pay for the gas. Totally sympathetic, Jimmy insisted on driving us himself.

As Jimmy had dumped Craig's stuff on the front passenger seat, Craig and I were obliged to sit in the back, which allowed us to clasp hands in the darkness. But I felt that even the night couldn't hide our feelings and was sure Jimmy sensed something, too. I can still see his eyes searching mine in the rearview mirror as he drove down the Pacific Coast Highway through the night. The expression in them seemed a strange mixture of curiosity and—could it have been—approval? Was it all, was I, so obvious? Had Jimmy deliberately put Craig's stuff in front so that we would have to sit in the back, where he could observe us in his rearview mirror?

Still, at that moment, I was beyond caring what Jimmy knew or thought he knew. Craig was convinced he was going off to war to be killed. Deprived of words and open expressions of comfort, I could only convey my need for him to believe that he was wrong by clasping his hand hard and repeating to myself my unspoken mantra: "You will come back alive, you will come back alive!" I had only his grateful look to tell me that he understood.

We dropped him off at the entrance to Camp Pendleton, and I slipped into the passenger seat beside Jimmy. As we made a U-turn and started back up the coast, I looked back and saw Craig standing at the roadside, watching us go, growing smaller and smaller, until he disappeared in the predawn sea mist. Jimmy didn't press me, but I owed him an explanation, so I told him Craig's story and explained that he didn't think he would make it this time. With only UCLA standing between us and the draft (Jimmy had not officially dropped out of school yet), we could identify only too well. We drove the rest of the way in silence, realizing that Craig's fate could and probably would soon become ours.

It was nearly dawn by the time we got back to the penthouse. I undressed and flopped into bed, physically and emotionally wrung out. Outside, the damned mockingbirds' incessant mating calls echoed in the predawn world. I could only think of Craig. After a moment, I felt Jimmy slip into bed beside me. He put his arm around me and held me until I fell asleep. We never spoke of that night again, which left me wondering exactly what, if anything, he had deduced from it all.

As a result of Bee's visit, Jimmy decided that he had grown accustomed to the finer things in life, like regular meals and reasonable food, so he decided to take a job. That is to say, he decided that I should get him a job at CBS. So, after much persuasion, I finally convinced my dour boss to hire him as a part-time usher.

Despite the fact that Jimmy had briefly held down a job when he returned to L.A. from Indiana, a job as an athletic instructor at a local military academy, which he claimed to have enjoyed, he now found it impossible to conform to the comparatively minor regimentation of a studio usher's life. He openly objected to the "monkey suits" we had to wear, presumably to identify ourselves as ushers to the general public, and he consistently refused to take head usher Bob Butler's directives seriously. As a result, unprecedented as it was at CBS, Butler fired him after only one week, during which period Jimmy had managed to provoke almost everyone on the staff. I, of course, got the fallout. "About your friend Dean . . .!" was an accusation that dogged me for weeks, whereas Jimmy accepted his dubious notoriety with some kind of perverse glee and gracefully lapsed into the status of being unemployed once again.

Some financial relief came from Beverly's direction, thanks largely to her movie-star mother. I had introduced Bev to Jimmy, and she had quickly introduced him to a girlfriend for the obligatory double-dating ritual. As Jimmy and I were broke, we spent most of our time swimming in Beverly's (or, more accurately Joan's) pool; eating Beverly's (or, more accurately, Joan's) food; drinking (quite definitely Joan's) booze; and watching Beverly's own personal television in her bedroom, a rarity in the average home at the time.

Having little else to occupy his time, Jimmy was only too willing to pick up Beverly after school for me, then collect me at CBS after work. From there, we would all drive back to Joan's Pleasure Trough for drinks, dinner, and a swim. What could be nicer? This went on for some weeks, until, one hot night when we stopped at a drive-in on Wilshire Boulevard for a burger after a movie, I noticed something strange, a strain, a heaviness in the air.

"Bill, there's something we have to tell you," Beverly finally broached uncomfortably. "It's Jimmy and me now. We're in love."

Beverly was young and saw a lot of movies, not all good ones.

"We didn't plan it this way," she explained, "but there was nothing we could do. It just . . . happened."

It just "happened"?

Beverly then asked me to understand, especially for Jimmy's sake, because he didn't want to lose my friendship. I remember thinking that this wasn't a very clever way to hold onto it, and why did *she* have to say this for him anyway? I looked over at Jimmy, but his gaze was fixed on the steering wheel. I had never seen him so uncomfortable. So I decided to say nothing. Let him stew. Beverly blathered on as the tension blossomed.

I could have laughed off the whole thing, reminding her that there was nothing really serious between us anyway. But I figured no girl wanted to know that the guy she has just thrown over for another is relatively unaffected. In truth, I suppose my male ego was only ever so slightly bruised, whereas my trust in my "teammate" was seriously shaken. I was hardly in a mood to laugh that off. So, I put on a sober face and went along with the drama. The three of us fell into an awkward silence as Jimmy drove to Bel Air and dropped Beverly off at her home, then continued on to Santa Monica.

It wasn't until we were about to go to sleep that night that Jimmy finally spoke out. A bit too defensively, he offered to forget the whole thing with Beverly if it meant that much to me.

I panicked. I suddenly realized that I had in some ways actually been relieved by the new turn of events. I had been aware for some time that my relationship with Beverly was becoming an onerous burden. The longer it had gone on, the more was expected of me, and I didn't want to have to fulfill anyone's expectations, especially Beverly's. I had too many other personal matters to resolve before I could think of handling that. I didn't want her back, even if she would have been agreeable to such a ludicrous trade-off. What was she, a baseball mitt?

And where was Jimmy coming from, offering to bow out? Surely he had given her the idea that he was at least interested—"We're in love," she had said, clearly believing it meant both of them, with each other—yet, here he was backing off. Certainly Beverly was no siren. In fact, compared to Jeanetta, with whom I had assumed Jimmy had broken up, she was, proverbially speaking, chopped liver. My friend Dean, it was suddenly clear, was ambitious. Obviously Beverly's lure had been Joan Davis and the world of fame and fortune she could open to him, albeit at my expense. On the other hand, where did I get off being so high and mighty? What exactly had I been after with Beverly? It sure wasn't sex. If I were honest, I would have to admit that I'd been after the same advantages to some extent. But I was damned if I would admit that to Jimmy. I, at least, hadn't taken Beverly away from anybody and wouldn't have, certainly not from my closest friend. Anyway, the prize didn't matter. He had broken a trust. That's what hurt most.

Still, I couldn't help feeling privately ashamed. So I told Jimmy that it honestly didn't matter and pointed out that he must have known that Beverly and I weren't really serious. He nodded, almost, but not quite reassured, returned to sit on his bed, and spend half the night sketching and mumbling to himself, justifying his treachery no doubt. As for me, I lay awake for a while, listening to the indecipherable mutterings from the other room, his apparent guilt giving me some slight satisfaction.

• • •

A few days later, I had another chance to watch my friend Dean operate. Some months earlier, he had gotten a ticket for speeding, which he had never taken care of. Consequently, the original fine of ten dollars had soared with each letter of warning to the staggering sum of twenty-five dollars. The final reminder had warned him that a warrant for his arrest would be issued were he to fail to appear in court within ten days. This had impressed him. He had to appear, but, because he didn't have the twenty-five dollars to pay the fine, there was a chance he might have to spend some time in jail. With that possibility in mind, I would have to go along to drive the car back.

We picked up Beverly, now in her new role as Jimmy's girlfriend, from her home in Bel Air and drove to the Van Nuys Municipal Court. I had hoped the penitential mood of guilt and gloom would have lifted, but it persisted, compounded by the prospect of Jimmy going to jail and, worse, sticking me with the entire rent. Inside the courtroom, we waited anxiously through the trials of several other traffic offenders and a Peeping Tom. The judge, we noted dismally, was straight out of the Inquisition.

Finally Jimmy's case was called, and he stepped up before the bench. As he had no lawyer, the judge asked him if he had anything to say in his own defense. Assuming an appropriately humble demeanor, Jimmy spoke softly. It went something like this:

"Your Honor, I know I did wrong by not taking care of this ticket by now. But I was afraid."

"Afraid?"

"Yes, sir. You see, I'm a student at UCLA, and I've been having a rough time of it. I mean, with money. I don't have much, and what I have goes mostly for food and books. I know twenty-five dollars doesn't sound like much to most people, Your Honor, but to me it could mean food for a whole month or books for a whole semester."

"I see. But you were speeding, exceeding the thirty-five mile limit by ten miles. You broke the law. There's no excuse for that, now is there?"

"No, sir, there isn't," Jimmy admitted, hanging his head in shame.

That was it, I figured, and wondered how much time he would have to do.

"I knew it was wrong," he went on, mumbling in shame, "and I never would've done it, if . . ."

The judge leaned forward. "You'll have to speak up, son. I can't hear you."

"I said, I never would've done it, if I hadn't promised my father I'd return his car by noon. He let me borrow it so's I could go on an interview for a part-time job I needed. Guess I just didn't want to let my . . ."

He wasn't going to say, ". . . my poor old . . ." was he?

". . . my father down. He's a good man." He lowered his eyes and hung his head even further in abject shame.

The judge pursed his lips and frowned. "Did you get the job?" he probed.

"No, sir," Jimmy replied humbly. "I'm still lookin'."

"Five dollars!" pronounced the judge with a crack of his gavel. "Pay the bailiff. Next case."

As Jimmy turned to pay the fine, he actually threw a wink in our direction.

We whooped all the way back to Bel Air, where, by the time we had had lunch and a swim, it appeared we had put aside our little problem. However, it only appeared that way.

Within a couple of days, the ugly subject of rent money arose again. Jimmy shrugged indifferently and suggested I borrow some. I had put the touch on friends at UCLA so often they were beginning to avoid me. So I countered by suggesting that it might be refreshing if he hit some of his friends for a change. Maybe then I might even be able to repay mine.

I had fallen into the trap. I had pressed the Obligation Button.

He turned on me, and I suddenly found myself confronted by a new Jimmy, not the old friendly one. "This is about what I owe you, isn't it?" he challenged unpleasantly. "Well, don't worry! You'll get it all back, every fucking penny!"

Of course, I was worried about what he owed me, but

right now, I just wanted the tiger back in its cage.

"Who said anything about that?" I protested.

Wrong again. It wasn't the Obligation Button this time. It was the Guilt Button.

"You're still pissed off about Beverly," he accused bitterly. "That's it, isn't it?"

You bet it was. But not in the way he meant. "That's your problem, buddy, not mine!" I countered as I slammed out, my patience finally exhausted.

Among the teenage Hollywood set, Beverly Wills's annual birthday fete was considered a major event. Each August, the cream of the town's most talented youngsters would turn out for the lavish party that Joan would throw for her only child, not to mention a bit of publicity. This year promised to be more glamorous than any previous year. The guest list included such up-and-coming teens as Debbie Reynolds, who had just wowed them with her interpretation of Helen Kane's "Boop-boopee-doop" in *Three Little Words*; Carleton Carpenter who, with Debbie, would create a small sensation with their "Aba Daba Honeymoon" number in *Two Weeks With Love*; and Lugene Sanders and Bobby Ellis of CBS Television's new *Meet Corliss Archer* teen comedy series. Usually Joan made all the preparations for the party, but this year, Beverly had her finger in the pie, as well. It promised to be interesting.

Jimmy had taken up archery, and Beverly had been joining him at an archery range several times each week to watch him practice. There, they had befriended his teacher, a national archery champion, and the three of them had come up with the inspired idea of giving an archery demonstration at Beverly's upcoming party.

I got off work at CBS late and turned up at the party just in time for the main event. Everyone had settled on the sprawling lawn that swept down to the pool to watch the exhibition. A lounge chair was placed in a strategic spot for Joan, who gave the signal for the games to begin.

After showing off his mastery of the sport, the archery champ asked Joan to participate in a demonstration. Being a natural clown, she got some laughs out of playing the coward, but finally gave in. Nervously poised beside a tree, she was given a huge balloon to hold in front of its trunk at arm's length. The archer was enough of a showman to miss his target by a foot or so, first above, then below the balloon, giving Joan the chance for some more clowning. With the third arrow, he burst the balloon, whereupon Joan did a slapstick faint, and the spectators cheered enthusiastically, calling for more.

Jimmy then stepped forward, announced that the champion would next shoot the proverbial apple off his head, produced an apple, and placed it on his head. But, as the archer raised his bow and arrow and took aim, Joan stepped into the scene. Enough was enough, she declared, though I sensed from her expression that she was tempted to let the shot go astray and rid herself of one James Dean. The archer respectfully lowered his bow, and Jimmy, thwarted, glared venomously over the rim of his glasses at the dominant Miss Davis, who barely suppressed a little smirk of satisfaction as she took a bite out of the apple.

I doubt that any of the guests perceived as much, but I had picked up a number of hints from Joan's housekeeper, Odessa, and glum confirmations from Beverly about the animosity building between Joan and Jimmy. Apparently, Joan was becoming increasingly antagonistic toward him. On several occasions, Jimmy had joined her and Beverly on the golf course, only to unnerve Joan by making unwelcome comments about her technique. If there was one thing Joan prided herself on, it was her golf, and comments from a non-pro upstart, she definitely did not appreciate. Adding insult to injury, he had further incurred her disfavor by beating her at her own game. There had also been flareups over his table manners and general attitude. Trouble was definitely brewing in Bel Air, and, I must admit, I quietly relished the prospect.

In truth, I hadn't been holding a grudge so much as feeling deserted. I had lost two playmates at once, not to mention the cozy setup at Villa Joan. I had grown to like Jimmy enough to feel possessive, a realization that made me only slightly uneasy. Now I realized that I resented him, as well, not only for estranging himself, but also as a competitor. I had never shied from friendly competition, but I was discovering that, to my "teammate," life was just another sporting event to be played and won at all costs, even friendship it seemed. Somewhere inside, I was vaguely aware that, for me at least, there was more than friendship at stake.

After our confrontation, Jimmy's disposition had gone from bad to worse, and his moods around the penthouse were really getting on my nerves. His guilt had turned him into a mean-spirited bore. I found this ironic considering that it was I who had a right to be bitter and resentful. Suddenly, the game had become unpleasant, and I wasn't into unpleasant. As a result, I found myself avoiding him a lot of the time. Whenever he stayed home evenings, I would take long walks and mull over what to do about the situation. There seemed no way to relieve his sense of guilt. It was on one such walk that I decided I needed somebody I could talk to about the problem. Some time earlier, Jimmy's former girlfriend, Jeanetta, had taken an apartment nearby. She would listen.

Indeed, she did listen, with sincere interest and sympathy—until I got to the part about Beverly. Apparently Jimmy had neglected to tell me that, despite his new commitment to Beverly, he was continuing to string along Jeanetta. Her reaction to my unintentional slip—which was, after all, a major part of the problem I was having with Jimmy and needed advice about—was, to put it mildly, explosive. I hadn't meant to spill any beans, but, consciously or subconsciously, I had done just that. I had come to seek solace and wound up administering it.

After her initial outburst and a dose of sympathy, Jeanetta calmed down and seemed to be taking the bad news more in stride. As I was leaving, she mentioned that she was moving the following morning. She had found a flat closer into Hollywood, closer to a job she had taken, and wondered if I would lend her a hand to move. I agreed and left, no clearer in my head about my own problems than when I arrived. I never imagined that I'd just created an even greater one.

The next morning, I was wakened from a sound sleep by insistent tapping at the penthouse door. It was Jeanetta. I had overslept. Letting her in, I signaled silence to her, indicating that Jimmy was still asleep in the next room after one of his late nights. I then tiptoed across his room and into the bathroom to shave and dress. When I came out, I found Jeanetta hovering over Jimmy's sleeping form, shredding something into bits, and sprinkling them over him.

"The picture," she whispered in response to my puzzled frown. She was referring to a photograph of Jimmy and herself taken at a fraternity dance months earlier. It was one of Jimmy's favorites, which he'd pinned to the wall over his bed. I winced, wondering what his reaction would be when he woke. She gave me a triumphant smile that said, "I have a pretty good idea," and headed for the door. Another good idea, I thought, following her out.

After helping her move into her new Hollywood apartment, I let her buy me breakfast, during which she shredded Jimmy's character into even smaller bits than the photo. She reminded me what a snake he had been in taking Beverly away. I admitted that it hadn't bothered me as much as he apparently thought it did, mainly because I wasn't really emotionally involved with Beverly. Of course, he hadn't known that.

"There you go, makin' excuses for him again!" she pounced. "For all he knew, what he was doin' was gonna hurt you, but he went right ahead and did it anyway. Honey, considering what he's done lately, you're a damn fool if you don't move out."

The thought had crossed my mind.

Sensing a weak spot, she brightened. "As long as we're here in Hollywood, why don't we look around? Maybe you'll find somethin' you can afford by yourself. No harm in lookin', sweetie."

The harm in looking, I discovered, is finding. After checking out a couple of really grim little apartments with rents I couldn't afford, we came across a prospect in a small residence hotel on Gower Street, only a block from CBS. It consisted of one drab room, plus bath, with a window overlooking the rear of the American Legion Stadium, famed for its televised Friday and Saturday night wrestling matches. Of course, the place didn't hold a candle to the penthouse, but it was cheap and would suit my needs, such as they now were. Tired and dejected, without considering the ramifications of what I was doing, I put down a deposit on the place and called the penthouse landlady to advise her that I was moving.

We drove back to Santa Monica to move my things out of the penthouse, Jeanetta chirping merrily about how healthy my decision had been, while I sank into a deep depression over my precipitous action. Not only was I walking out on Jimmy, probably terminating the closest friendship I'd ever had, I was also letting down our landlady. Over the phone, I could tell how upset she was when I told her. She had always been kind to me, and now I was leaving the rent to Jimmy, which she and I both knew he wouldn't be able to manage on his own. In all, I wasn't very happy with myself.

As Jeanetta's car pulled to the curb across from the penthouse, we could see Jimmy, standing in the walkway that led to the penthouse, arms folded, glaring at us, radiating rage. Obviously, the landlady had already told him what was up. I advised Jeanetta to wait in the car. As I approached, Jimmy took off his glasses and flung them on the lawn. Coward that I am, I was trembling as we came face to face.

He grabbed me by the shirt front. "I trusted you" was all he said. He was so furious he choked on his words. He yanked me close to him, within focus, ripping my insides apart with the hate in his tear-filled eyes.

All I could think was "My God, what have I done!" But all I could manage was "If it'll make you feel better, go ahead, hit me."

However, never to be upstaged, Jeanetta had come running and was tugging at his sleeve. Jimmy tried to shake her off, but she persisted.

"If you're gonna hit somebody, why not somebody who won't hit back? That's your speed, isn't it?"

"This doesn't concern you!" he shot back.

"Oh, yes it does! I talked him into it!"

He loosened his grip on me, refocusing his rage on her.

"Go ahead!" she taunted. "I can't defend myself."

"Just shut up, or . . .!" He couldn't finish.

"Or what? C'mon, get some real kicks!" she goaded. "I dare you!"

In a flash, he had released me, whirled, and backhanded her across the face. She staggered backward.

"Oh, you can do better 'n that!" she challenged, clearly hurting. "Big, tough guy like you!"

Before I could restrain him, he lashed her face twice more, this time drawing blood. I grabbed for his arms to hold him back. He didn't resist. The sight of her blood seemed to drain his rage.

Somehow I managed to get them both upstairs into the penthouse. Jeanetta got sick and rushed into the bathroom where we could hear her throwing up. Jimmy fell apart, almost weeping in shame, apologizing to her through the door. Shaken, I started throwing my clothes into a suitcase. When Jeanetta emerged, Jimmy became totally unstrung, offering her handkerchiefs, aspirin, anything he could think of to help. She rejected it all.

"Hot tea!" he exclaimed and ran downstairs to borrow a tea bag from the landlady.

The minute he was out the door, Jeanetta looked up at me, suddenly pulled together again, confiding with a smile, "Don't worry, I'm not really sick. Let him squirm a little."

I was shocked by her callousness. "You'd better lay off," I advised unhappily.

"Lay off? Honey, I'm enjoyin' this!"

Jimmy returned with the tea bag and slammed a kettle on to boil, all the while keeping up his litany of apologies to Jeanetta, groveling, comforting her, trying to explain himself to me. I found it extremely painful to watch. In fact, the more he apologized, the more I hated myself. All I wanted to do now was to get out of there. I grabbed my things and started taking them down to the car. On the last trip, I grabbed my suitcase and informed Jeanetta I was ready to go. Jimmy began to cry. Whoever said revenge was sweet had no heart.

"So long, Bill." He offered his hand.

I just looked at it, unable to speak, shook my head numbly,

and left with Jeanetta. As we drove off, I had to turn and look back. He had come down and was standing on the lawn out front, still in tears, pointing after me and shouting, "I trusted you! I trusted you!" I presumed it hadn't occurred to him that I had trusted him, as well, but his accusation was still the most painful I had ever faced. It pains me now even to recount it.

We had driven less than a mile back toward Hollywood when I told Jeanetta to turn around and go back. She was stunned and told me not to let him fool me. It was all an act, she assured me, a plea for sympathy. But I insisted. She made a U-turn.

We sat in the car across the street from the penthouse for almost an hour, watching the windows for signs of movement. I was tempted to go back up to the penthouse, but I knew if I did, I would change my mind. I was so torn. Finally, we saw him moving past one of the windows, and I told Jeanetta to head for Hollywood.

That was the end of the penthouse and, I figured, a friendship.

9

Enter Svengali

I MIGHT HAVE SPARED MYSELF ANY ANGST ABOUT LEAVING JIMMY in the lurch. Beverly bailed him out. She lent him enough to meet the rent that month, and he set about finding a part-time job. Within a matter of days after I moved out, he was well on the road to recovery, at least monetarily. I wasn't to know until later how difficult the split had been for him emotionally. I only knew that for me it continued to be painful and destined to get worse, but in a way I never could have guessed.

While Jimmy had been so briefly employed by CBS, he had befriended Ted Avery, another would-be actor briefly on the ushering staff. The three of us would hang out together occasionally but, after the blowup, I dropped out. Jimmy, having few if any other friends now, started spending more time with Ted. Ultimately, this would serve him well.

Ted had also recently left the CBS ushering staff and had taken a job as a parking attendant in the lot adjoining the studios. His new boss had agreed to allow him time off to play the occasional bit parts he was managing to snag in movies. Recognizing the wisdom of the move, Jimmy angled for a job in the parking lot, too. He was hired on Ted's recommendation, with a similar promise of time off to pursue his own acting career. To that end, the parking lot was doubly ideal. The CBS executives, producers, directors, and stars who used the lot were big tippers, and this padded Jimmy's salary almost enough to equal that of a full-time job. More importantly, there was always the chance that one of them might spot him and give him a shot at an acting job.

At the end of the month, I learned that he had moved out of the penthouse and was temporarily staying at the Averys' apartment in Hollywood with Ted, whose wife was out of town. On weekends, Ted, an accomplished horseman, was teaching Jimmy to ride and rope, skills Jimmy hoped would increase his chances of being hired for Westerns, which were Ted's mainstay. After riding sessions on rented horses in Griffith Park, the two took to showing up in cowpoke getups and clowning around in the corridors of CBS. This was largely to annoy their former bosses and, on Jimmy's part I suspect, to show me how well he could get along without me. I must admit the point was hitting home with me. Even with Jimmy's black moods at the penthouse, I wasn't having nearly as much fun, friendless and on my own in the bleak little room at the Gower Hotel.

To my relief, Jimmy and I began speaking again only a few weeks after our split. Avoidance was difficult in any case, both of us being anchored to CBS Columbia Square by our respective jobs. Casually, we started comparing notes on how our lives were progressing, or not, as the case may have been. Like Jimmy, I too had been angling, specifically to get off the ushering staff and into a production job on any of the early television shows that were then being broadcast from CBS, and I was finally making some headway.

The one thing we avoided discussing, of course, was Beverly. She, however, filled me in on the details of her brief relationship with Jimmy later, long after their breakup. Indeed, she took some pleasure in describing to me how, when Jimmy took his parking-lot job, Joan finally had her fill of him and banished him from the house, forcing Beverly to see him on the sly. They took to escaping to Paradise Cove where Beverly's father, Si Wills, Joan's early vaudeville partner and ex-husband, had been reduced to living in a trailer. The Cove was then basically a poor man's version of the Malibu Colony, that exclusive settlement of beachfront property inhabited mainly by stars and the Hollywood elite, located only a couple of miles down the Pacific Coast Highway.

According to Beverly, on weekends, she would drag Jimmy off to the Saturday night dances in the Paradise Cove pavilion. She was crazy about dancing, but Jimmy was not at his best on the ballroom floor and wouldn't risk making a fool of himself in front of guys who were far better dancers than he. I knew this was highly probable because I had previously seen him soldier bravely through a dance at UCLA, after which he grumbled to me how much he hated dancing. Beverly said she offered to teach him and repeatedly tried to coax him out onto the dance floor, but he stubbornly insisted on sitting out most of the numbers. Not one to tap her toes idly on the sidelines, Beverly soon found any number of willing partners among the other young men on hand. In fact, she confessed, she rather enjoyed catching glimpses of Jimmy from the dance floor as he looked on, alone at their table, sulking while she danced with one guy after another. Then, predictably, one Saturday night, unable to take any more, Jimmy stomped onto the dance floor and accosted her. According to Beverly-the-movie-buff, he shouted (rather uncharacteristically, I thought), "Go on! Dance your fool head off!" then turned and stormed out of the dance hall and out of Beverly's romantic life.

As Jimmy had hoped, his CBS parking-lot job brought him into contact with a number of producers and directors on a personal, one-to-one basis. Foremost among these was one Rogers Brackett. A director of radio drama employed by the then formidable ad agency, Foote, Cone and Belding, Rogers was directing one of their shows at CBS Hollywood. As fate would have it, he would park his car in the very lot where Jimmy was now working. In his midthirties, Rogers was of medium height and a slim, if not skinny, frame, which he carried with an almost militarily erect posture. The first time I met him, he struck me as an arch, foppish villain out of Dickens or a haughty Max Beerbohm dandy. His unusually long neck supported what I can only describe as an avian head, on the thin beak of which he would perch large, horn-rimmed glasses, giving him a somewhat owlish look. Obsessively vain, he maintained a tan that had rendered his skin prematurely leathery, rather in the style of those elderly Hollywoodites who had retired to Palm Springs to bake in the sun, turning the fashionable desert town into a necropolis inhabited by living mummies. In Rogers's case, however, as he was still relatively young, agile, and only half-baked, the look merely lent him what I perceived as a taut, aloof air. I was soon to learn firsthand, however, that the cause wasn't the tan, but the man behind the tan.

It took little time for Jimmy to fall prey to this well-schooled chicken hawk, not because Rogers was so adept or so winning, nor because Jimmy was in any way a masochist, but because Jimmy was, under the circumstances, an opportunist. He was in that car lot for that very purpose, after all, and he jumped at the first overture Rogers made. At that point, had it been Dracula himself—with Hollywood connections, of course—I suspect Jimmy would have become a voluntary donor at once. But, compared to Mr. Brackett, Dracula would have been child's play. Jimmy had not bargained on Rogers. But then Rogers had not bargained on Jimmy, who would ultimately come to play Rimbaud to Rogers's Verlaine.

At first, over coffee at the local diner, Jimmy seemed to derive special satisfaction from telling me how "great" Rogers was, how Rogers had taken an especially keen interest in his career, given him excellent advice, taken him to a couple of parties, and even introduced him to some of his show-biz friends. If envy was what Jimmy was looking for, he got plenty from me. Although, observing Rogers from a discreet distance, even I, in my relative naiveté, perceived his true motives. However, despite my envy of Jimmy's windfall, I quailed at the thought of swapping places with him. I had already developed an aversion to affected bitchy queens. They intimidated me, and I resented the way they put people down. I could consider a Sugar Daddy, perhaps, but never the Wicked Bitch of the East.

Although Rogers was considered by his intimates to be witty and possessed of a keen intellect (about which I felt they exaggerated), others did allow that he could be perceived as somewhat supercilious. A meticulous dresser, his wardrobe appeared to be fashioned almost exclusively by Brooks Brothers, a must for the "in" Madison Avenue queen of his day. At first, I thought his haughty indifference was reserved especially for me, possibly on Jimmy's behalf because I had run out on him, but as time passed, I began to think that the man was purely and simply pompous and affected. When Rogers condescended, he deigned to observe you from some vast distance, indeed from the stratosphere, an unattractive trait he managed to keep in check when in the company of his peers or on the make.

Not that I doubted that Jimmy also recognized Rogers's intentions, exploited them, in fact. But, I found myself wondering, was my friend putting out already? Possibly. He could also have been stringing Rogers along for all I knew. At that time, neither of us ever confided any of this to the other, not even obliquely. To admit to as much would have taken an act of considerable courage, certainly on my part. Instead, we persisted in our self-protective pretenses, neither willing to change the rules of the game by revealing his alter ego.

Then, quite unexpectedly, Ted Avery's wife returned to L.A., and Jimmy found himself evicted from his temporary roost. How fortuitous that Rogers just happened to have a spacious apartment on Sunset Plaza Drive, above swingin' Sunset Strip, where Jimmy could stay until he found other accommodations. I half-wondered if Rogers had anonymously sent Mrs. Avery a plane ticket, encouraging her to return to her pining husband in Los Angeles as soon as possible. And so, Lucky Jim moved in with Rogers, and life was never the same again for any of us.

Overnight there was new excitement and glamour for Jimmy, and he had to share it with someone, someone, he clearly felt, who wouldn't find his new situation demeaning or embarrassing. Because he knew me better than anyone else and obviously got little satisfaction out of rubbing my nose in his newfound good fortune, I became his receptacle. Every day when we met for coffee, Jimmy would confide all the exciting things that were happening in his new life. Almost everything, that is. Any intimacies between Rogers and him were judiciously edited out, at that point, anyway.

Was I disturbed? Of course I was. We hadn't had time to work things out, time to find the courage to be honest with each other, when suddenly this interloper was diverting Jimmy's attention, luring him away from me, giving Jimmy even more of a chance to make me regret walking out on him. It hurt, and I'm sure Jimmy knew it.

However, painful as it was, I soon came to understand that in his role as mentor, Rogers was introducing Jimmy to more than the glamorous life of a kept boy. After all, if the boy were to fit in, he would need some polish and at least some exposure to rudimentary social behavior and sophistication. To give the devil his due, Rogers did manage to facilitate the metamorphosis of James Dean from an unsophisticated shit-kicker into an urbane and polished bicoastal sophisticate, or at least a good facsimile thereof. In truth, however, Jimmy never fully shed the art of plain ole shit-kickin' nor did he ever embrace urbanity, except for effect.

Suddenly Jimmy was holding forth in restaurants on all manner of fashionable and esoteric subjects: the French Impressionists, the Cubists, the genius of Cocteau, Picasso, Chagall, the delights of Colette, the challenge of the new Existentialism, the brilliance of Stravinsky, our debt to Diaghilev, and so on. With what seemed to me dizzying speed, he seemed to be absorbing a great deal. Maybe he was skimming the surface, but doing it with an amazing facility and dishing it out with impressive confidence. I was eventually to recognize this shortcutting as a special talent of his. However, in his effort to impress me with his glib new erudition and the dazzle of the new social life into which Rogers had thrust him, he was buying into Hollywood's most notorious game: name dropping.

Often he would regale me with tidbits:

"Had the greatest weekend. Drove down to Tijuana for the bullfights with Davey Wayne and his wife. You remember Davey. He starred with Hepburn and Tracy in *Adam's Rib* last year. Davey's the greatest, a real wit. We were having lunch in this terrific restaurant in Laguna on our way down the coast . . ."

Or, "I was sitting beside the pool yesterday, when Barbara Payton came out in a bikini—you know, Franchot Tone's latest sex kitten. This kid's got more body than a Renaissance Madonna. So, after a while, I went in and got my sketch pad . . ."

Or, "Finished *Moulin Rouge* last night. The end! You've got to read it! I understand it's been optioned for a movie. It's about Lautrec's life. Rogers flipped over it, too. In fact, we picked up the phone and called Pierre La Mure—you know, the author—just to tell him how terrific we thought it was. We're going to meet him for lunch."

I used to sit and listen to this uncharacteristic chatter, numbed. Who was this person, and why was he talking like a gossip columnist? I was actually embarrassed to listen to him at times. But, of course, I wasn't listening to Jimmy. I was listening to Rogers and his cronies. Jimmy was merely parroting their style, and it didn't suit him one bit. Oh, he did it well enough, but he lacked conviction, and it rang hollow. It was hollow. And shallow. And I think he knew it. In time, I hoped, he would abandon it, and he later did—except when it was useful. By then, of course, being an actor, he had smoothed off the rough edges, made it sound more casual, more off the cuff. To disguise it even further, he found a way of mocking himself as he performed, with a kind of East Coast lockjaw delivery, in which he managed to drop the names, yet ridicule the process at the same time. Still, it never sounded right on him. Not to me, it didn't, and he knew it.

Jimmy finally managed to get Rogers and me together for more than just a perfunctory greeting. One weekend, he twisted Rogers's arm and got me invited along to Tijuana for the bullfights—no Davey Wayne this trip, however, just Jim and Rog and little me. It seemed to me that Rogers tried, rather successfully, to overlook the fact that I was along. Maybe he felt that I posed a threat to him, although just what kind of threat I'm sure he hadn't yet figured out. I also felt sure that Jimmy hadn't told him about our relationship, our actual relationship, at that point. Knowing Jimmy, I suspected he had told Rogers just enough to leave him wondering and wary. Knowing Rogers, as much as I ever came to, that is, I don't believe he would ever have believed the truth anyway, no matter how innocently, and honestly, Jimmy protested. To me, Rogers appeared profoundly insecure in their relationship—and for good reason. So I guess it was only natural for him to consider me, to some extent at least, his competition.

But I wasn't as interested in Rogers that day as I was in Jimmy. I had never seen him so avidly absorbed in anything, bar acting, as he was in the bullfighting. In fact, he insisted on dragging us to the bullring outside town early so that he could observe, and if possible, learn the whole gory process from beginning to end. Somehow he managed to con his way backstage at the ring to study the preparation for the fight at closer range—the picadors, traditionally unpopular horsemen armed with lances used to stab and weaken the neck muscles of the bulls so that they are less able to rear their heads and gore the matador, who shows off his (or now occasionally her) cool mastery of the beast with a series of elegant, but daring, close-call passes made by taunting the bull to charge, using a *muleta,* a red satin cape draped over and concealing the sword with which he administers the final death blow.

Just prior to the fights, we stopped by the bull pens so Jimmy could study the mighty animals, corralled and waiting for almost certain slaughter (for rarely does the crowd ever give the bull the thumbs-up sign for its courage and resilience, thus allowing it to go free, wounded but alive and sent to pasture, usually crippled). One of the handlers there confided to us that the bull's rage is often enhanced as it is released into the ring by shoving a lit firecracker up its ass. Hemingway or no Hemingway, if that weren't enough to put me off bullfighting forever, nothing would be.

But not Jimmy. His fascination and appetite for the "sport"—I use the word reluctantly—seemed to intensify during our tour until neither Rogers nor I existed for him. He remained like that through the entire afternoon as we watched from our seats on the shady side of the bullring while, one by one, six beasts were butchered. That day, Jimmy grew from a mere aficionado to determined aspirant. He would never become a true matador, but he would never give up the dream.

Some weeks later, however, for one glorious afternoon, Jimmy came close to realizing it. He returned to L.A. on a high from a weekend in Mexicali where he and Rogers had visited a bull-breeding ranch outside of town. He told me that Rogers's friend, film director-cum-bullfighter Budd Boetticher, had arranged for him to practice his *veronicas* on a two-year-old bull, which he was, of course, not meant to kill, but merely taunt. He had come back with a practice cape of his own, made of red felt in this case, and a practice pair of real bull's horns, gifts from Boetticher for his impressive "initiation."

From that day on, Jimmy was never without those damn props. They adorned the walls of every place we lived together and, later, those he inhabited alone. At every possible opportunity, he would whip them down to practice his *veronicas*, enlisting the help of any unfortunate friend or acquaintance who happened to be on hand at the time to handle the horns and play *toro* to his *matador*. Each time I saw Jimmy reach for his gear and hand me those inevitable horns, I would silently curse the name of Budd Boetticher.

Budd Boetticher, no less! From the sidelines, I marveled at Rogers's impressive assortment of Hollywood contacts, most far outreaching him in talent, which deepened the mystery even more for me. What did they see in him? Of course, at that point, I hadn't yet heard of the so-called "Homosexual Mafia," whispered for years to be widespread in the film and budding television industries. Mafia, indeed! Except for their sharp wits and rapier tongues, most gay men in those days were armed only with a simple, double-barreled weapon: deception and networking, both learned at a tender age out of necessity. How else to get along in a generally hostile society and the viciously competitive environment of Hollywood? Eventually new generations both hetero and homo, male and female, would refine those same talents, deception and networking, until today they are considered essential tools, certainly in the cutthroat worlds of filmmaking, television, and investment brokering, to mention only a few arenas of ex-

treme competition. A presidential campaign being a prime example, hasn't life in America, after all, become one gigantic
corrida? Watch out for the firecrackers!

By this stage of Jimmy's transformation, Rogers had begun
to come through with the goods in return for the satisfaction
he was now presumably deriving from the relationship. Initially, he cast Jimmy in a few bit parts on the CBS radio shows
he was directing, such as "Alias Jane Doe" and "Stars over
Hollywood." But as time passed, between Ted Avery's and
Rogers's contacts, Jimmy was also picking up a number of bit
parts in feature films: a nonspeaking locker-room bit in the
Dean Martin and Jerry Lewis comedy, *Sailor Beware*, at Paramount, or a one-liner in *Fixed Bayonets* at Fox. To Beverly's
professed amazement, he even did a little dancing in *Has Anybody Seen My Gal?*, a Universal-International musical, starring Rock Hudson and Piper Laurie.

It was after his first day of shooting on that picture that
Jimmy confided to me his contempt for Mr. Hudson, based on
nothing more than Hudson's hypocritical pose as straight on
the set while privately trying to hit on him. Even at the time,
this struck me as a case of the slightly scorched pot scorning
the kettle's black bottom. Of course, I said nothing of the sort
to Jimmy, as he was yet to admit to me the intimate details of
his game with Rogers.

Although the occasional jobs Jimmy was getting were not
important per se and had been secured through friends with
contacts, they were providing him with much-needed encouragement. Yet, despite that and all he was garnering from his
rapid-fire urbanization on the fringes of Rogers's Inner Circle,
he was not happy with the scene or his role in it as Rogers's
apparent trick. In fact, he was making it increasingly obvious
to me that the game was beginning to sour.

"You know, it gets sickening," he sneered one night over
a bowl of chili at our favorite Mexican restaurant. "The other
day at the pool, I made a bet with Rogers that the names of
La Rue or the Mocambo [chic Sunset Strip nightclubs of the
time] would be dropped at least fifteen times within the next

hour. We kept count, and I won. What a pile of crap!"

He then proceeded to complain that he was listening to too many inane conversations, too much catty chatter from the same empty people. During the Barbara Payton/Tom Neal/Franchot Tone scandal, it was kind of kicky to get the inside dirt on the latest cunnilingual developments, sensational as they were back then, details the public at large would never know. Furthermore, while sketching, Jimmy enjoyed having the voluptuous Payton pose for him in her bikini at poolside. But listening to the clever, snide remarks about her afterward, remarks that would later titillate Rogers's table at the Mocambo, would turn his stomach. Bitterly mimicking the gossips, he repeated for me one bit of dirt that particularly seemed to gall him: "Dahling, did you know that Paulette Goddard went down on Otto Preminger under the table at Ciro's the other night? My dear, Otto Preminger, that Hun!" This was followed by a sickened expression and forefinger down his throat. It had been great fun knowing who was screwing whom at first, he admitted, but, as he put it rather aptly, "Once you know, who gives a shit?"

There I sat, listening enviously, as he complained about his inside look at a lifestyle from which I was excluded. Yet, as I listened, I could understand his distaste for the scene he had gotten himself into, even if I couldn't entirely sympathize. Frankly, I wouldn't have minded having a crack at it myself. On the other hand, I hadn't been subjected to it, but I could imagine how it would fast begin to wear on me, especially under the auspices of someone like Rogers. More importantly, I hadn't paid the price he apparently was paying in return for the experience, so how could I question his revulsion? Neither did I have a Quaker conscience about sexual matters to bother me nor a conflicting ambition like Jimmy's to further entrap me.

Obviously, the whole scene had palled for him, and he felt that there were more important things for him to do. I could sense that something inside was goading him on. Perhaps, as he had explained to me so earnestly that night on the bus to Westwood, he still had that impossible ultimate goal to achieve: immortality. It seemed to be nagging, and he seemed to be in a hurry.

"I'm beginning to understand Caligula," Jimmy said a week or so later.

He and I were dining in a dim, faux-medieval Scottish inn near the stables where, that afternoon, we had rented horses and gone riding in Griffith Park. The Tam-o'-Shanter was a place where Jimmy apparently felt at ease and could throw off pretense.

"You know, Caligula, the mad Roman emperor," he prompted.

He had taken to explaining such things to me, apparently assuming I wouldn't have the faintest idea about them. I felt it would have been unkind of me to call him on it, mainly because I knew that, aside from trying to impress me, he was also trying to be generous by sharing some of his newfound knowledge and insights with me. It was somehow touching. In a strange way that I couldn't quite understand, we were getting closer on a new and peculiarly significant level.

"In his madness, Caligula thought he was a god," he went on. "Just to satisfy a whim, he'd command a man to do something totally degrading, something that would strip him of his dignity, completely humiliate him. If the man did his bidding, Caligula would have his head cut off in disgust, reasoning that any man who would allow himself to be so debased was not worthy of life. If the man refused, dared to oppose his emperor's command, Caligula would have his head cut off anyway, as punishment. But at least he'd respect him.

"That's what it's like with these people. With all their power and wealth, they've got it in their heads that they're gods. I've met enough of them now to know. Town's full of them. They get poor saps like me, make them perform, you know, like court jesters, trying to charm the pants off people they want to impress, people they want to use. So, the poor jerks put on a good show. Why shouldn't they? They think by turning a few somersaults, they'll keep themselves in the emperor's good graces. What most of them don't know is that all they'll probably get in the end is a swift kick in the ass, right out the door."

Did I detect trouble in paradise again, this time on Sunset Plaza Drive? Oh, I did hope so! But was my schadenfreude for

Jimmy's sake or mine? Was my envy getting the better of me, or did I simply miss Jimmy and our days back at the penthouse and want him back in my life?

"I guess, in a way, you can't blame them," he went on. "That's how the game is played. And maybe, just maybe, once in a while, the show will pay off, and the poor sap'll get a screen test or an audition for a good part. But out of the handful that lucks out, how many'll have the stuff to make a break like that pay off?"

Then, pausing, he looked me in the eye and confessed, "I did a little dancing myself."

I wondered where this was going and leaned in.

"I was dumb," he mused. "I thought it might pay off. But it doesn't take long to find out it won't. I'm not performing for them anymore."

"Them?" I thought to myself, reluctant to challenge him out loud. Why always "them"? Can't you please be more specific? Rogers! C'mon, say it! "I'm not performing for Rogers anymore." It would be such a relief, and we could stop this game-playing and get real. Maybe I could even dump my problems on you for a change. God knows, I've got a lot to dump! But, of course, I didn't say any of this. Besides, he was talking to himself, not me, wasn't he?

"If I can't make it on my talent, I don't want to make it at all," he asserted, avoiding the issue I hoped we could share and unaware of my impatience. "I know I'll never work in this goddam town, but at least I'll preserve some dignity. If nothing else, the bastards'll respect me—even if I do get the boot."

There! I seized on his words and assured myself that, even though he wasn't being specific, he meant Rogers. After all, who else could give him the boot?

I wondered if old Rog knew that he was becoming his own worst enemy. It sounded like his latest trick had finally perceived that there were no allegiances owed by people like Rogers and himself, only temporary ties that, once made, were easily broken and dropped for some cuter trick—or better opportunity—as the case may be. In short, did Rog know that *he* could be replaced?

Of course, there was the possibility that Rogers had some-how allowed his infatuation with his protégé to become too serious and therefore put himself in a precarious position. Had he allowed himself to fall in love with Jimmy? If so, could Rogers be the one in for the nasty surprise? Did he even sus-pect? Would Jimmy actually walk? I didn't think Rogers un-derrated the kid's guts; I just figured he counted on his vulner-ability, his ambition. I could almost see it coming: *Sunset Boulevard* revisited, but I hoped without the gun.

"I can't stomach this dunghill anymore," Jimmy an-nounced, with some finality, a few weeks later.

He and I were concluding a late-night snack at Barney's Beanery.

"I've had it," my friend went on. "A guy could go on knocking his brains out, getting nothing but bit parts for years. There's got to be more."

Maybe this was my opportunity to find out?

"What about Rogers?" I probed. "He's been a big help, hasn't he?"

"I paid my way," Jimmy grumbled into his coffee, a bit too defensively, I thought.

So it was a fact, I reflected. But a fact of which he clearly wasn't proud. How could he be? Here was a kid who, only a few months ago, had pulled a flick knife on a guy who had of-fered him a ride, a guy he had led on by posing provocatively on a bus bench at two in the morning. Or had that all just been some kind of rehearsal for a future role, another exam-ple of Jimmy's "Method" homework? Even so, putting out for some other guy, Rogers in this instance, and, in effect, being kept, surely had to produce some kind of internal conflict for a Quaker-bred Indiana farm boy. "Love thy neighbor as thy-self" doesn't really work when thee doesn't love thyself. And if and when thee stops loving thyself, and starts actively loathing thyself, watch out neighbor!

"Rogers took off for Chicago," Jimmy finally announced.

"Oh, yeah?" I blurted happily. Things were looking up.

"The agency sent him back there to do some shows, I

guess. Before he left, he told me I should get my ass to New York if I expect to accomplish anything. I called Whitmore to see what he thought. He said the same thing. Easy for them! How the hell am I supposed to get to New York?"

How, indeed?

"Anyway, I asked around, and one of the television directors over at CBS gave me some names to look up. One's a guy named Jimmy Sheldon, directs the Robert Montgomery show back there. Picked up a few other contacts, too. But I don't know. What do you think?"

"Start packing." I was talking to myself now, but Jimmy overheard. If only he would wait for me. But I knew instinctively he couldn't. Any more than I could wait for him, had I the chance to go.

And so, one miserably hot fall night a week or so later, I dragged myself up the stairs of my hotel and let myself into the drab little cubicle I called home. The manager had slipped a phone message under my door: "Mr. Dean called. Gone to New York."

I flopped on the sagging mattress, the crumpled message in my fist, and lay there, staring at the cracked ceiling and listening to the shouts of the spectators coming from the American Legion Stadium across the alley where the wrestling match was reaching its peak of rehearsed brutality. Sometimes, when it was earlier in the evening, I would hear them sing "The Star-Spangled Banner" before the fights began. Not that night. I had come in too late for that treat. Instead I got, "Kill the son of a bitch!" "Break his neck!" "Tear him apart!"

I was alone, trapped in a savage, not to say indifferent world, and Jimmy was gone.

10

How I Didn't Join the Marines

AT CBS, I HAD MANAGED TO SHED MY USHER'S UNIFORM FOR civvies, for I had now moved up to a job assisting floor managers on television shows. At last, it seemed I'd be able to afford a more amenable place to live. On the other hand, I reasoned, if I could suffer the dreary pad I was presently stuck in, I could save money faster and leave for New York sooner. Getting back to New York had long been number one on my list of dreams, dreams based on an earlier, magical time I had once experienced in that city. Now I had another, reinforcing reason to get myself back there. Jimmy was there.

However, in the meantime, it was almost inevitable that I would start seeing Beverly again. She was still working at CBS, now cast in a running part on a television sitcom, and we would run into each other from time to time. Over dinner one night, she described how Jimmy had disappeared after their Paradise Cove breakup. The last she had heard of him, he had run off to New York "with a friend." It didn't take much probing to realize that he never told her about Rogers. But then, how could he, and why would he? By now, she had graduated from high school, was enrolled at UCLA, had her own car, had pledged a sorority, and was living on campus. Of course, the sorority house was less than a mile from her mother's Bel Air house, so at least she wasn't under Joan's thumb night and day, yet free food and a pool were only a

stone's throw away at home. It wasn't long before I was seeing her again. Actually I liked Beverly a lot, though sadly, not
in the way she would have preferred.

Simultaneously, in keeping with my schizoid lifestyle, I
was being wined and dined by an art decorator for one of the
shows I was working at CBS. Because he was disarmingly unpretentious and deceptively straight in looks and manner, I recall being somewhat surprised, although pleased, when he
asked me out to dinner. I forget his name, but I will never forget his car. He drove the most sexy, yellow MG convertible I
had ever seen, and I enjoyed shamelessly sporting around
town with him in it with the top down.

It had been a gradual seduction—admittedly mutual—
probably not unlike how it had gone with Jimmy and Rogers,
but I suspect more relaxed and uncomplicated. After all, I
wasn't in it for the opportunity. In fact, my first public fling
with a male was actually turning out to be fun. Perhaps
Jimmy's escapade with Rogers had somehow given me permission, as well as a road map to potential pitfalls. At any rate,
because I actually liked the guy, I was learning to let myself
enjoy the sex, free of any furtiveness or guilt, although the relationship lacked the emotional involvement that might have
elevated it into something special, something I hadn't experienced since my brief encounter with Craig.

About that time, I also struck up a friendship with a young
actor—definitely straight—who was the co-star of the CBS
television series "Meet Corliss Archer." After rehearsals, we
would sometimes have a drink or dinner at Nicodell's or
Naples Restaurant, a friendly Italian restaurant across from
CBS on Gower Street in Hollywood. Often he would bring
along his girlfriend, soon to be his wife. To my shame, I con-
fess I have forgotten her name, but not her warmth. His name,
however, I will never forget. Bobby Ellis would, quite soon,
and very unexpectedly, be instrumental in launching my career as a television writer.

But for now my new job in production at CBS was providing me with a valuable learning experience. I found myself
working on the hottest new shows on television, which were

all live at the time. I learned everything I could and became friendly with many of the performers, directors, and other crew members. Ralph Levy was one of the most prolific of the directors. Imported by CBS from the East Coast earlier, his forte was comedy. Only in his thirties, he was already directing the top shows on the air, among them Burns and Allen, Jack Benny, Edgar Bergen, Red Skelton, Ed Wynn, and Alan Young. I greatly admired his technique for directing live comedy. Getting the right shots at the right moment was an art all in itself. However, it was Levy who directed the pilot of the very first "I Love Lucy" show, which I believe was to be the first sitcom ever shot on film and would mark the beginning of the end of live television.

Of all the performers I befriended at the time, the comedian Alan Young was probably the most special. A young Canadian with a friendly disposition and a happy smile, he started by treating me with a rare kindness and ease, never condescending, never patronizing. As the holidays approached, he and his wife, Ginny, invited me to share Christmas and New Year's Eve with them and their young children. In fact, it was at their New Year's Eve party that I first fell under a Gaelic spell.

As midnight approached, I was suddenly taken by surprise when all lights save the candles were extinguished and the guests fell silent. I became aware of the enchanting, ethereal sound of bagpipes, coming from outside the house. It was Alan in kilt and full Highland regalia, playing the pipes while circling the house in what, I learned later, was an ancient Scottish rite to ward off evil spirits. At the stroke of midnight, a bowl of steaming hot chocolate was ceremoniously carried across the threshold and into the house to ensure a year of prosperity ahead. Alan was a Canadian of Scottish descent, and his heart was definitely still in the Highlands. The pipes were a part of his heritage, and he played them like a true Highlander. Noting my fascination, he encouraged me to take up the pipes and made me a gift of a practice chanter (the flutelike component of the bagpipes). However, unlike Jimmy, who was eventually to master the recorder through pure determination, I soon realized that I was not destined to be a piper, but merely an enthusiast, and finally admitted defeat, much to my landlord's relief and, frankly, mine. Still, pipes or no pipes, I'd made a dear friend in Alan, a bond that would eventually change the whole direction of my life, far, far from Hollywood.

Meantime, because of my double life—dating my CBS art director while still seeing Beverly—I was back in No Man's Land. To make matters worse, Beverly started angling to know when we were going to "make it official." She figured once it was a done deal, there would be little her mother could do about it. As for my concerns about my prospects, she pointed out that we wouldn't have to get married until she graduated from UCLA, by which time I was sure to be prospering. In the meantime, we would have some relief from Joan, who was characteristically disapproving of the arrangement as it stood.

Quite insanely, I went along with Beverly's madness, never truly believing it could work out, but going along because in those days, it was the thing to do. I had yet even to imagine that homosexuality could be considered a viable way of life. We picked out an engagement ring, "modest" in Beverly's terms. On my CBS salary, I could hardly afford the indulgence, but at least Joan was mollified and promptly arranged to have the news blazoned abroad by columnists Hedda Hopper and Louella Parsons. As for me, I felt trapped by my own duplicity.

Probably because of the stress involved in this reckless decision, I was suddenly struck with abdominal cramps. I'd suffered from a bout of spastic colitis when I was fourteen—the cause, as diagnosed by the doctor at the time, being nervous tension. As diagnosed by me, however, the cause was strictly parental mismanagement. Life had become unusually stressful at home, but I had managed to get my nervous gut under control fairly quickly with medication, diet, and practiced indifference to the home scene.

However, when Beverly found out about the recurrence of my abdominal complaint, she mentioned it to Joan, who promptly insisted upon making an appointment with her own doctor, one Morley J. Kurt. Dutifully, I presented myself at Dr.

Kurt's clinic in Beverly Hills and was thoroughly examined. To my relief, the good doctor didn't seem overly concerned. He prescribed some medication, told me to watch my diet for a while, and assured me I would eventually "grow out of it," a cryptic remark which puzzled me, as I was pretty well grown by then. Sure enough, as promised, the problem went away in short order, doubtless thanks to Dr. Kurt's prescription. It was only a minor incident, but it was soon to prove a monumental blessing in disguise.

About this time, my grandparents moved back to Los Angeles from Wisconsin and took an apartment in Hollywood, not far from CBS. Fortunately, there was room for me, so I sacrificed my privacy and moved out of my grim apartment-hotel and in with them. I also started saving my money, theoretically for the day when Beverly and I would wed, but secretly in hopes of eventually joining Jimmy in New York instead. The problem would be finding a graceful way to break my engagement to Beverly and spare her the pain I knew I would eventually cause her. Night after night, I would struggle with my unresolved dilemma, kept awake by the incessant howl and bashing of bulldozers outside my grandparents' apartment block, as they gouged a giant trough for the new Hollywood Freeway that would soon link downtown Los Angeles to the San Fernando Valley.

Then one morning, something arrived in the mail for me that reduced all my other worries to the category of minor irritations, the one piece of mail every young man I knew at the time feared most: a draft notice. As I had long since completed my courses at UCLA, I was no longer protected as a college student and therefore was considered fair game for the Korean death mill. Craig's letters to me had graphically contrasted the horrors of that particular "theater of combat," as the U.S. government so euphemistically referred to it, as far worse than those he had experienced in the war in Europe. Now I was being ordered to report for my physical within a few weeks and instructed to be prepared to leave the same day for basic training, if inducted. From there, I would probably be sent to meet my fate on the killing fields of Korea, along with countless other unprepared young men.

Jimmy and I had briefly toyed with the one surefire gambit for avoiding the draft so often debated by fellow male classmates at UCLA: claiming to be a "practicing" homosexual. While I had been living in the dorm off campus, many a bull session had been devoted to the subject of conscription, particularly disturbing because the older men who had served in Europe or the Pacific during World War II would participate and fill us in with the unspeakable details of warfare. Some of them were still feeling the effects of their traumatizing wartime experiences, while others bore grimly obvious physical scars and disfigurements. In fact, some were amputees, which lent the discussions a certain gravity, to say the least. Interestingly, most of them weighed in on the side of duty to country, despite their experiences. Only the most traumatized swore, despite being straight, that they would rather have "worn drag" back home till the war was over.

The debates were never settled one way or the other, of course, but most of the undergrads were worried about being stigmatized for the rest of their lives by playing the "homosexual" card. They feared being unable to get clearance for important jobs later on or being exposed as shirkers and publicly humiliated years down the road. None of them were willing to take the chance, including me, of course.

In the end, the choice was left hanging until the dreaded day might come: declare yourself a queer or take your chances on the battlefield. I can hardly believe now that anyone would have hesitated. But we didn't know then what we know now. In those days, facing death or being stamped a queer was a tossup. Death, not necessarily a certainty, seemed the better bet.

So, dutifully, as advised in my notice, I quit my job at CBS—so long pursued and so hard won—sold my first and only car, put my affairs in order with a view to my possible demise, and braced myself for what I was convinced would be the end. Beverly tried to convince me that we should promptly get married, which might qualify me for a deferment. After all, she joked, doing battle with her was better than doing it with the Koreans. How could I tell her that both prospects were almost equally terrifying, though on balance, Beverly did have the edge.

On the appointed day, Beverly and one of her girlfriends volunteered to drive me to the induction center in downtown L.A. and wait to see me off to boot camp. Once inside the induction center, I was directed to a small indoctrination area, told by the gruff sergeant in charge to strip to my shorts and join about twenty other young men, who were also stripped to their shorts, in the next room. The sergeant then called us to attention and started to explain the process of the physical we were about to go through when, unexpectedly, a recruiting officer in a Marine uniform entered and interrupted briefly. He informed us that there was room in the Marine Corps for ten recruits from this group and asked any of us who wished to volunteer to step forward. No one made the slightest move. Clearly annoyed, the officer then instructed us to count off and ordered all the even numbers to step forward. My number was eight, so I stepped forward along with nine others.

"Welcome to the Marine Corps, gentlemen," he announced with a hint of sadistic pleasure. "You have just volunteered. When you've finished your physicals, you'll board the buses and be transported to Camp Pendleton to start your basic training. Good luck."

I was going to be a Marine? This had to be somebody's idea of a joke. I had been enrolled in the Reserve Officer's Training Corps at the University of Wisconsin because it was a draft deferment, but after six months of training, I still had trouble keeping in step on the drill field. I did, however, manage to distinguish myself as a marksman with an M-1, but I was shooting at a target, not another human being. In truth, I was a full-fledged coward, and, per force, a dedicated pacifist. I would disgrace my uniform. I was, in effect, already dead. How had this happened?

Still numb with disbelief, I was herded along with the others through the interminable physical. Finally, still in a benumbed state of disbelief and dread, I shuffled up to a long table where several examining doctors were interviewing the prospective inductees. A bored young doctor in a white smock took my form and, never looking up, read off a list of diseases and physical problems for me to indicate whether or not I'd had any.

When he got to, "Ever have any stomach or intestinal disorders?" I was about to say no automatically, when I realized my spastic colitis qualified as an intestinal disorder.

"Spastic colitis," I informed him dutifully.

"When was that?"

"When I was fourteen. The first time."

"First time?"

I informed him I'd had a little bout again recently, but was now okay.

"Who's your doctor?" he inquired routinely, pen poised for my response.

"Dr. Kurt."

He looked up instantly, as if alerted by the name and asked pointedly, "Morley J. Kurt?"

"Why . . . yes, sir," I replied, taken aback that, of the thousands of doctors in Los Angeles, he actually knew my doctor's whole name, including his middle initial.

"We'll need X-rays. You want us to take them or Dr. Kurt?"

Still thrown by the coincidence, I didn't focus on the question.

"The X-rays," he repeated. "You want us to take them? Or Dr. Kurt?" I couldn't swear to it, but I was, and still am, almost certain he stressed the right answer.

"Dr. Kurt?" I answered, scoring an A on that test.

With that, he stamped something on my forms, shoved them into my hand, and said, "Give these to Dr. Kurt. He'll know what to do. Get dressed. You can go."

Not quite sure what had just happened, I looked at the stamp across my papers. In large, bold letters that jumped out at me, it announced: "TEMPORARILY REJECTED."

So, a week or so later, I found myself in a Beverly Hills radiology lab. I, of course, never saw my X-rays. That privilege was Dr. Kurt's alone. Whatever they proved went with his diagnosis to my draft board. He did not even confide his findings to me, so I was left not knowing what might be the final determination of my "temporary rejection" status. I was only told that I would receive notice of my draft status by mail. How soon, no one could say.

Convinced for some reason that I would not be inducted, Beverly now decided she didn't want to wait two years. She definitely wanted to get married right away. I freaked and tried to reason with her. I was out of work and could be called into the service any day. There couldn't be a worse time to get married. She wouldn't listen. Fortunately, when Joan learned Beverly's plan, she insisted, quite reasonably, that Beverly finish her studies and get her degree first. Everybody was in disagreement, which caused considerable tension and ended, to my huge relief, with Beverly petulantly breaking the engagement.

There followed two excruciatingly anxious months. Having quit CBS and invested in a relatively expensive engagement ring that wound up at the bottom of Joan's swimming pool after one final row between mother and daughter, I was nearly broke and had to find some way to make a living. I had sold my car and now, denied the use of Beverly's, I once again found it hell trying to get around town to apply for jobs. In any case, I couldn't commit to a permanent job knowing I might be called up at any time. Who would want to hire me?

Fortunately, my grandfather came to my aid. A life insurance salesman as far back as I could remember, he had retired several years previously with a gold watch, a handshake, and a meager pension after twenty-five years of dedication to the Prudential Insurance Company, and had left Wisconsin for California, where the living was easy and the weather bearable. To supplement his pension, he had decided to go back into the insurance business, specifically hospitalization insurance this time. Through his good offices, he was able to get me a job as a salesman with the company then employing him.

How I envied Jimmy way off in New York, furthering his chosen career. Since he'd left, I'd had one brief note from him shortly after he had arrived and one phone call to let me know he was living in a midtown YMCA. Even that sounded enviable, compared to my present position.

Each day, I approached the mailbox with dread, waiting for my new draft classification. Days became weeks, and still nothing arrived from the Selective Service. It wasn't until the seventh week of purgatory that, among the bills and letters, there appeared a simple postcard, no envelope, just an open notice for all the world to see. It declared that I was classified 4-F, unfit to serve, or die for, my country. In this way, I learned the delirious joy of abject shame. I was unfit. It hadn't occurred to me before, although it eventually would, that the usual treatment for colitis involved a special bland diet, something the armed forces were not interested in providing. From that day to this, I have never had another colitis attack. God bless you, Morley J. Kurt, wherever you are!

Winter was giving place to spring now, and I found myself still combing the outlying burbs of L.A. for insurance prospects. I had forgotten my great good fortune and was cursing my fate like an ingrate. I had tried to get my old job back at CBS, but of course there were no openings now. They knew I'd quit because of the draft, so obviously they had figured out why I'd come back. I was UNFIT. They weren't going to have any weaklings, any shirkers, at their network, certainly not in one of their proud usher's uniforms.

I was at an impasse. I had to get out, out of L.A. So I became more determined than ever to squirrel away every penny toward buying my freedom. Jimmy had recently phoned again from New York and extolled the glories of the big city, encouraging me to get my ass back there. Having quit the YMCA, he had moved into an apartment, and he gave me his new address and phone number. What was I waiting for? All I had to do was get there, somehow. But come April, after two more months of scrimping and saving, I figured I only had enough to get about as far as Topeka. It looked hopeless, until one morning, when another of those what I can only regard as semi-miraculous strokes of good fortune that seem to have attended my life over the years occurred. To account for it will require only a brief digression into my past.

11

"The Rich Are Different From Us"

WHEN SCOTT FITZGERALD POINTED OUT THAT THE RICH ARE DIF-
ferent from us, he certainly slobbered a bibful. In the summer
of my sixteenth year, 1947 to be precise, I was unaware of his
astute observation, but about to be enlightened through firsthand experience.

That first, amazing trip to New York occurred while I was
still living with my mother and her latest husband in Kenosha,
Wisconsin. As a member of what was known as "Junior
Achievement," then a relatively new national organization
dedicated to helping young people "learn business by doing
business" and underwritten by an impressive list of major national corporations, I had started two junior "companies."
One was a half-page insert, *The Teenage Review*, published
every Friday in the *Kenosha News*, the town's only newspaper;
the other was a weekly half-hour radio show, "Over the Rainbow," which broadcast dramatized fairy tales for the local
kiddy audience every Saturday morning over the town's only
radio station. Both earned modest profits from advertisers and
were relatively successful, on a very minor scale, of course.

That summer, Junior Achievement was sponsoring another
of its annual national conventions, this time to take place in
New Jersey, just across the Hudson from New York City. Having entertained dreams of someday living in that exciting magical metropolis, preferably in a skyscraper high above the

throngs, I even then nursed an ambition to get there, and here was my chance. By hook or by crook, I would go to that convention. So I managed to get myself sent as an alternate delegate and made my first trip outside America's Dairyland.

I took the North Shore Line interurban to Chicago, where I caught a New York-bound train. My eyes were glued to the passing panorama of an America I had known only in the movies. We left behind the endless suburbs of "Cow Town," as Chicago was still called by envious Wisconsinites, and were soon crossing the Illinois border into Indiana. Somewhere out there, beyond the fields of corn and wheat that stretched endlessly southward, on a Winslow Homer-perfect farm, owned appropriately by a family named Winslow and situated outside a small town named Fairmount, lived a boy my own age with dreams much like my own, who would one day shake up my life forever.

With the other young delegates from all forty-eight states (that's all there were back then), I was met at Grand Central Station with a few other delegates and whisked through Manhattan, across the George Washington Bridge to New Jersey. There we gathered at an encampment on the banks of the Hudson River for a week of proselytizing (DOING BUSINESS IS GOOD!) proffered by the industrialist-backed organization's leadership. They didn't have to sell me; at sixteen, I had two prospering "companies" and enjoyed being involved in both. I doubt that many of the other young delegates absorbed any more of the propaganda than I did—we were all having too much fun. But on the last day of the convention, something quite extraordinary happened.

One of America's leading industrialists, S. Bayard Colgate, chairman of the board of Colgate-Palmolive-Peet Inc., as it was then known, came to address us, accompanied by his wife, Beatrice. I was utterly awed (my God, I use their toothpaste!). After Mr. Colgate's speech, the couple mingled with the young delegates, most of whom were rendered inarticulate in the presence of such capitalist royalty. When it came my turn, they asked my impressions of the convention and seemed genuinely interested in whatever it was I burbled in response. Learning that I was from Wisconsin, Mrs. Colgate asked if this was my first visit to New York. I explained that it was, but that I had come directly to the convention without stopping to see the city just across the Hudson River, something I definitely intended to do the day before I took my train back to Wisconsin. Mrs. Colgate protested that it was impossible to take in all the wonders of New York City in one day. No, she insisted, I must come and stay with her and Mr. Colgate for a week or two. That way I could really get to see the city properly. Mr. Colgate concurred enthusiastically, apparently delighted with the idea.

They didn't have to twist my arm. I placed a long-distance phone call to my folks to inform them that I was sticking around New York for a while.

The Colgates' chauffeured car skirted the city and headed northward toward their home in Connecticut. Not wanting to appear too provincial, I resisted the temptation to crane my neck and gape back at the towers of Manhattan as they receded behind us. That is, until Mrs. Colgate—Beatrice, as I had by then been instructed to call her—drew my attention to them. Gratefully I turned to take in, certainly to me at the time, the most exciting view in the world. It brought a lump to my throat. Beatrice caught my eye and smiled. Apparently, she understood my reaction.

The Connecticut countryside seemed voluptuously verdant in comparison with the flat farm country of southeastern Wisconsin. In less than an hour, we arrived at the entrance to the Colgate estate outside New Canaan. As we drove onto the grounds, I found myself confronted by lush, sweeping lawns flanking us on either side with a backdrop of dense woodland. Horses and cows grazed in a pasture. An impressive house appeared ahead on the right. As I was about to comment on their beautiful home, Bayard identified it as their farmer's house. Yes, he confirmed, the horses belonged to the estate, the cows and chickens, too, so I could expect fresh milk and eggs every morning for breakfast. We rounded a bend, and a mansion rose before us. Turrets, and it could have been a castle, at least from my naïve perspective.

I later learned it was the home Bayard had shared with his previous wife, which may have explained why Beatrice wasn't enamored of it, though she blamed her bad hip on the mansion's many stairs. Perhaps it was her Mandalay, I remember speculating to myself at the time. In any case, Bayard was planning to build another house for them on a tiny island called Contentment, snuggled along the shore of Long Island Sound near Darien. But for now, Beatrice and I would have to put up with the family pile, which didn't bother me one bit. In fact, as it turned out, it would be my home for the next two months.

From that first moment, almost every aspect of my stay with the Colgates was new and amazing. Meals were served by staff; beds were turned down at night and made in the morning by invisible elves; wrinkled or dirty clothes vanished to be laundered or cleaned and returned as magically as they disappeared; and, indeed, the milk and eggs at breakfast were fresh every morning, and, best of all, so were the blueberries. It was all very grand, certainly in my limited experience, yet, due mainly to the unpretentiousness of my host and hostess, not at all inhibiting, and I never felt uncomfortable.

I was treated like a member of the family. We breakfasted together each day, explored the gardens and farm, walked through the woods, went horseback riding, had drinks each evening before dinner—ginger ale for me, of course, "spritzers" for them, half wine, half soda, which, Bayard confided from personal knowledge, had been Franklin Roosevelt's customary drink in public. Later, we would sit out on the veranda, listening to Beatrice play Chopin and Schumann on the piano as we watched the fireflies (my first) dance and flicker in the summer twilight. On Saturday nights, the three of us would dine at the yacht club, and on fair-weather days, Bayard would take me sailing on Long Island Sound and, with remarkable patience, try to teach me to sail. I can still hear his repeated admonition, whenever I was at the tiller, to keep the red buoys to the right when returning to port. "Remember the three Rs: Red, Right, Returning."

Bayard also introduced me to his study, where the bookshelves boasted the most impressive library I had seen outside a public library, and invited me to browse and borrow any book that interested me. While exploring the collection, I came across his diary of an archaeological safari he had made across China's Gobi Desert in the thirties. Delighted by my interest, he produced albums of exotic photographs he had taken at the time and showed off some of the lesser artifacts he had collected on the expedition, the major ones having been donated previously to various museums, I believe.

He also enlisted my help in testing new formulas for his company's toothpastes. This was not done condescendingly; he genuinely wanted my input. Although his attitude toward me never indicated it, he doubtless considered my tastes fairly "average," which they indeed were. Lined up on the counter of his vast bathroom, he had a dozen or so sample tubes of the various new pastes his research department had developed for potential marketing. Each day, he would ask me to join him in trying a different one, after which we would compare opinions as to its taste, aftertaste, and consistency. Its efficacy would be left to the experts and, ultimately, the buying public. He made me feel a part of a very important corporate decision-making process, and I was both flattered and proud. Separated at age three from my real father and subjected to indifferent stepfathers since, I began to wish Bayard were my father.

Most mornings, Bayard and I would catch the commuter train into New York. Once onboard, he would read and prepare notes for his day while I took in the scenery. From time to time, he would enlighten me on subjects that he considered of national or international consequence. I was all attention. On one such occasion, he passed me a document the size of a short novel, explaining it was a special report that had been commissioned by President Roosevelt just prior to his death. It dealt with the depletion rate of America's natural oil supply and was prepared by a select committee of which Bayard was a member. What I gathered from my skimming amazed me; I had no idea that America's oil would ever run out, but apparently it could and would if we continued to consume it at our ever-increasing rate. The report implied that we would eventually have to rely on the Middle East until we finally became its oil-dependent captive. Those train rides proved to be most educational.

Bayard's office was near Grand Central Station in the heart of Manhattan, and from his thirty-fourth-floor window, you could see all the way to New Jersey. He pointed out the spot where the Hindenburg had gone down in flames ten years before and told me how he had stood right there and watched the whole horrible spectacle. Some days, I was on my own to explore the city; others, he would show me the sights around town and treat me to lunch near his office at the Yale Club. Once he took me on the boat trip around Manhattan, explaining every point of interest in detail with great enthusiasm, demonstrating that he was still very much in love with the place himself. Upon learning that I had never been to Radio City Music Hall, he eagerly introduced me to that most awesome movie palace for a matinee performance of the spectacular stage show. Even then, it featured the Rockettes, the famous block-long line of chorus girls, all kicking their legs in perfect synchronization. Noticing how Bayard's eyes were riveted to them the whole time, I surmised that the treat wasn't solely mine.

But if I thought my extraordinary adventure might begin and end with the Colgates, how wrong I was. There was still more of New York for me to experience, still further heady heights to be explored. During the Junior Achievement convention, I had befriended a delegate named Danny O'Keefe, I believe. Slightly older than I, he was a precocious high-school graduate from right there in New York City, who moderated his own weekly, teen-oriented, half-hour radio talk show, which aired on a local New York station every Saturday morning. The format was simple. He would pose a teen-slanted political or sociological question to two prominent experts with opposing views and encourage them to go at each other.

Over lunch on one of my forays into town, Danny confided his problem to me. He had just won a Rhodes Scholarship to Oxford University and only that week learned that he would have to leave for England before the end of his radio show's season. Knowing that I had some experience producing a children's broadcast back in Kenosha, he asked me to moderate the last few shows for him. He assured me that it would be no problem as he had already worked out the topics and set the guests for the remaining few shows. Though feeling somewhat out of my depth, I accepted.

Of course, it would mean extending my stay in the East. But where to find a place in the city for a couple of days each week during the show's run and how to pay for it? Once again, the Colgates came to my rescue.

Beatrice's mother, Mrs. Shaw, an heiress in her own right as it turned out, owned an apartment on Park Avenue, which she wasn't using during the summer, preferring the relative cool of New Canaan to the sweltering heat of the city. To my utter astonishment, she offered me the use of it. So, for several weeks, at the age of sixteen, I found myself moderating a weekly radio show on WNYC in New York City while living on Park Avenue and commuting on weekends to a mansion in Darien. Wasn't I the hotshot!

The bubble burst shortly after the final broadcast, of course, when it was time to return to Kenosha for my last year of high school. The Colgates sensed my dejection at the prospect of leaving—not too difficult, I imagine—and offered a simple solution: stay with them and finish high school right there in New Canaan. I was ecstatic and promptly phoned my mother and stepfather to tell them what I wanted to do. They were cool to the idea, however, and so I bid the Colgates a painful good-bye at Grand Central Station and boarded the train back to Kenosha and normalcy.

But, that is how miracles happen.

My grandmother woke me early one morning a month or so after my draft status had finally been determined. There was a phone call for me. Still half-asleep, I couldn't place the voice at the other end of the line at first. Then, the sun came out and filled life once more. It was Beatrice. She and Bayard were coming to Los Angeles. They invited me to lunch at the Huntington Hotel in San Marino, near Pasadena, where they were staying.

Neither of them had changed, or if they had, they seemed to me as youthful and warm and wonderful as they had when I first met them. Over lunch, I told them the story of how my colitis had got me turned down by the draft. They wanted to know my plans now that I didn't have to go into the service. I was understandably vague about the future. All I could say for certain was that I wanted to get myself back to New York where I felt there would be more opportunities, although I had no specific ideas what they might be. Bayard said he had friends who were top executives at New York advertising agencies and offered to give me introductions. I was naturally most appreciative, but without even considering the consequences of my words, blurted out that I simply didn't have the money and that it might be some time before I could save up enough to make the trip. Of course, they offered to help.

I wondered in disbelief at my good fortune. Who were these people? How did they find their way into my life? And why had they chosen to bestow so much kindness on me? My grandmother decided that someone was surely watching over me. At the risk of sounding disrespectful to her, I insisted that I didn't subscribe to such notions. However, in my heart, I now knew that I had two guardian angels, both of whom were very real and very much back in my life.

So, for better or worse, I packed my bags, bought a plane ticket, and took off for New York, my wonderful, magical New York, and, inevitably, Jimmy.

12

A Small Hotel

IT WAS TEN O'CLOCK ON A MUGGY MAY MORNING WHEN I stopped in front of what looked like an abandoned office building on New York's West Thirty-eighth Street. I climbed the creaky, increasingly sloping wooden stairs warily until, sweating and exhausted, I reached the fifth floor and knocked on the only door. Slumping against the wall to catch my breath, my body was heavy, my clothes sticking to it. I had forgotten about New York humidity and knew nothing of fifth-floor walk-ups; Mrs. Shaw's Park Avenue apartment had had a doorman and an elevator, of course. I knocked again. The door opened a crack, and two squinting red eyes peered out at me, Jimmy's. When I'd phoned and wakened him earlier, I'd figured he'd go back to sleep after inviting me over. Apparently nothing had changed. The door opened further. He was still only wearing his undershorts. He grunted, swung the door wide, and motioned me inside.

I found myself in a loft apartment, which was mercifully air-conditioned, almost cold, in sharp contrast to the heat outside. Heavy drapes had been drawn across the ceiling-high studio windows, and the only sound was the hum of the air conditioner. I had spent my first night in New York in a dismal room at the Midtown YMCA only a short walk away, but even in the semidarkness, this seemed a palace by comparison.

While Jimmy gathered clothes strewn from one end of the

room to the other and disappeared into the bathroom to dress, I checked the place out. Opening the drapes, I found myself in a surprisingly spacious studio apartment, expensively furnished and designed for comfortable midtown living. It was a far cry from the penthouse in Santa Monica, although hanging on one wall were the familiar bullfighting practice cape, sword, and bull's horns. That certainly hadn't changed. Scanning the other walls, however, I was confronted by several unfamiliar paintings, which upon closer inspection appeared to be originals by artists of note. That definitely was a change. There was even a small, signed Chagall. I was impressed.

"Only be a minute," Jimmy burbled from the bathroom, brushing his teeth.

Suddenly I wanted to get out of there before he came back.

Even before phoning him earlier, I had hesitated. After all, the détente we had struck in Hollywood had at times seemed to me more an excuse for Jimmy to boast about his glittery new friends than a genuine reconciliation. Similarly, his protest about "paying a price" for his exciting new life was, I suspected, a perverse way of gloating disingenuously. On the other hand, maybe I had just interpreted it that way because I was still guilty about walking out on him, despite the fact that he deserved it. Anyway, here I was, about to find out, one way or the other, whether we were truly friends or not, whether he would trust me and I could trust him.

"Nice place," I commented, when he reappeared, now dressed. "You must be doing okay."

"It's Rogers's," he mumbled without looking at me.

"Everything?" I asked, meaning the valuable artwork, as well.

"Not quite," he replied, misunderstanding and assuming I was being arch, and threw me a narrow glance over the rim of his glasses. We still spoke elliptically. That hadn't changed either. He opened the apartment door, suggesting we get some coffee.

Over breakfast in a midtown coffee shop, he filled me in on the missing months and his sudden disappearing act. After letting him stew in L.A. for a while, Rogers had finally called from Chicago to tell him that he was soon being transferred to New York. He'd offered to pay Jimmy's train fare to the big city if he wanted to join him there. Did he not! But Rogers wanted him to stop off in Chicago en route to New York and spend a few days with him. That had turned out well because Jimmy got to meet some interesting people while there, notably an actress named Maggie McNamara, who was appearing in a play there, and her husband, writer David Swift.

Then, because it was so close to Chicago, he'd made a side trip to the farm in Fairmount and spent a few days with his aunt and uncle, Ortense and Marcus Winslow, and their son, Markie, Jimmy's five-year-old cousin. Having not seen them in three years, he was afraid it might be his last chance to do so for another three. I could sympathize with that. After all, they were the only real family he'd known since he was nine, and he cared for them too deeply to let the opportunity pass.

When I told him I was staying at the Y, he groaned sympathetically. He'd been forced to stay there himself when he finally arrived in New York ahead of Rogers. But things weren't all bad. While waiting for Rogers, he'd contacted a director to whom he'd been referred.

"Jimmy Sheldon," he reminded me, "you know, the guy Ralph Levy referred me to back in L.A."

"Ralph Levy?" I reacted, not so much puzzled as surprised.

"At CBS," he confirmed. "The director? Burns and Allen Show, Jack Benny . . . ?"

I reminded him in turn that I knew Levy very well, having worked his shows. However, I was almost positive Jimmy had never mentioned that Ralph Levy had given him any introductions. I would have remembered. "I didn't even know you knew Levy."

"Yeah, Rogers introduced me," he dismissed lightly.

"Guess you got to know Levy pretty well, huh?" I probed.

"Had drinks a couple of times, dinner maybe." He shrugged it off casually, a bit too casually, I thought. "You know."

Yeah, I knew. He was being evasive, and I was sure it was because he was embarrassed to admit he had gotten cozy with Levy. Levy was rumored to be bisexual, a balletomane with a

notorious foot fetish. Maybe Jimmy was afraid I'd heard the
stories about Levy, which, as it happened, I had. Now, as I
watched him avert his eyes uncomfortably, I couldn't help wondering whether any of Jimmy's own little piggies ever went to
market. In any case, it shouldn't have mattered to him whether
I did or didn't know about Levy's alleged tastes, now that it was
tacitly—and only tacitly—understood that I knew the truth
about his relationship with Rogers. When were we ever going
to get real? Not that I was going to go first, of course. It seemed
a runaway carousel that neither of us could get off.

As Jimmy wiped his plate clean of egg yolk with bread, he
explained that, aside from getting him his first job on television in New York, Sheldon had called a few other people in
the business for him and introduced him to a new, crackerjack
actor's agent, Jane Deacy. Deacy had agreed to represent him,
which was, to him, the best thing that could have happened.
In the short time since becoming her client, he had been cast
in a number of major television shows, including "The Web,"
"Studio One," and "Lux Video Theatre." Things were definitely looking up careerwise. In fact, he had managed to save
enough to move out of the Y and take a cheap little apartment
on the Upper West Side for a short time, that is, until Rogers
turned up and invited him to move in with him.

Finishing his food, he shoved his plate away and removed
his dental bridge, a replacement for the two upper front teeth
he had lost playing basketball in high school, and started cleaning it with a paper napkin. How often I had seen that stunt before: Jimmy nonchalantly whipping out the bridge to delight in
the onlooker's reaction. He had even developed the knack of
flicking it out with his tongue, which had an even more star-
tling effect on the unsuspecting. As a veteran, I was inured.

"You know, thith town'th the end," he lisped, now tooth-
less. "It'th got everything in the world. I mean, if you let
thingth happen, there'th no telling where you can go."

I wondered to myself exactly what "thingth" he meant for
me to let happen, and I had a suspicion I knew.

He slipped the bridge back into place and rinsed his mouth
with coffee. "It's not like L.A. You don't have to put up with all

that crap here. It's talent that counts, period." After only a few months in town, he was already talking like a seasoned pro, a bit prematurely perhaps, but I was encouraged, nonetheless.

Then it was my turn. He was itching to know what I was doing in New York. I reminded him that he knew very well I had always wanted to come back.

"Sure, sure," he allowed, suppressing an I-know-more-than-you-think grin. "But by now I figured you'd be married and spending Joan Davis's money back in Hollywood."

Embarrassed and annoyed that he was getting such pleasure baiting me, I said I was surprised that he even knew about the engagement, it had been so short.

He laughed, reminding me that the whole world knew—it was in the trades and all the columns. Joan had seen to that. He then disclosed that Beverly had shown up in town with Joan, who had been doing a radio broadcast with Tallulah Bankhead. He and Beverly had gone for a hansom ride in Central Park, and she had flashed the engagement ring I had given her. Naturally, he was curious to know what had happened to end it all. I filled him in—briefly.

"Got out of that by the skin of your teeth," he teased. "Aren't you a crafty one."

"Yeah," I grinned back, "I also got out of the draft."

Instantly sobered, he leaned in intently. How had I managed that?

"I didn't," I replied honestly. "It was just incredible luck." I told him the whole story and produced my 4-F classification card.

Jimmy slumped back in his chair, studying it and shaking his head, obviously envious. He confessed he had no idea what he was going to do if he got called up. He had already made inquiries. They would definitely not turn him down for being nearsighted.

"Just have to pretend I'm queer, I guess," he concluded flippantly, yet searching my eyes as if were running the idea past me. I could see he was looking for a reaction.

I let the "pretend" part pass. But I did say that I thought he'd be crazy to try a stunt like that. If it ever got out, he could forget about an acting career. Jimmy nodded solemnly as if already very much aware of that little problem.

"It's a bitch," he grunted, genuinely troubled. "A real bitch."

Then, shaking off the concern, he jumped up to make a phone call. When he returned a few minutes later, he slapped some cash down on the table for the check and said he had to stop by and see his new agent for a few minutes. After that, he wanted me to meet a friend.

Jimmy walked into the Shurr Agency like he owned the place and introduced me to Jane Deacy, who seemed strictly no-nonsense, yet warm and accessible. I liked her at once. Of course, Jimmy called her "Mom," his surefire Older Woman charm. In the end, he would leave an army of "Moms" behind, each probably convinced that she was the one-and-only. Yet, I never doubted the genuine need behind his compulsion to make up in numbers for his early loss of the real thing. It was easy to see that Jane was already hooked, although canny enough not to let him know how deeply. She took special pleasure in telling him that she had him up for a terrific part in some television show and would let him know when they wanted him to audition. Jimmy's step was noticeably lighter as we left and headed for Central Park.

On our way up Broadway, he announced that he was taking me to meet someone named Dizzy. Her real name was Elizabeth—although she used "Liz" professionally—but most of her friends called her Dizzy. He explained that she was an aspiring dancer, the daughter of a concert pianist named Frank Sheridan. Implying that there was "nothing serious," he assured me that she was just great fun and posed him no serious challenge like so many other "females" he knew. From the way he put it, I took this to mean both matrimonial and sexual challenges. They had met accidentally in the reception room of the Rehearsal Club, a chaperoned boardinghouse in midtown that catered to young women aspiring to theatrical careers in New York. He had taken to her spontaneous sense of humor at once and was sure that I would, too.

The minute I saw her, I knew he was right. Tall, lithe, and supple, with a mane of tawny hair that cascaded to her waist, Dizzy was attractive, though not what you might call a conventional beauty. But she had the captivating, free, open, and spontaneous charm of a child. Her smile was radiant and her laugh infectious. With no pretensions to sophistication or erudition, she seemed totally without guile and was, like so many other Broadway "gypsies" I later came to know, chronically, if indifferently, broke. In fact, she existed somehow on the twenty-some dollars she picked up weekly as what was then called an "usherette" at the Paris movie theater opposite the Plaza Hotel on Fifty-eighth Street. Despite this, like the rest of us, she dreamed that one day her career would blossom and get her out of uniform and more profitably onto the stage. As Jimmy had promised, I found her both fun and funny and within five minutes understood perfectly why Jimmy felt she posed no threat to him and how she got the nickname "Dizzy."

The three of us strolled through Central Park, chattering and laughing, like carefree kids. We lolled on the grass, frolicked in the meadow, and finally strolled over to the zoo where Jimmy and Dizzy immediately rushed to the monkey cages and began to clown.

"Look at the monkeys!" Dizzy cried.

"No, look at the people!" Jimmy contradicted, mimicking the gawking onlookers.

Our romp in the park made me forget my concerns briefly, but one thought began to nag: I had to get out of the Y. I announced that I had to take off and find someplace to live before the end of the day. Blithely, Dizzy made the suggestion that Jimmy and I find a place together. The idea dropped like a heavy brick. I shot a look at Jimmy. Clearly he was entertaining the same thought, the memory of our ugly parting at the penthouse only months earlier. In the moment of awkward silence that followed, I found myself wondering if she knew about Rogers and was actually angling to get Jimmy out from under his influence. However, Dizzy looked from one of us to the other, utterly puzzled.

"I say something wrong?"

Jimmy broke the tension first. He started to giggle, then lost it completely, falling to the grass and laughing uncontrollably until tears streaked his face. The penthouse incident and everything that had happened in L.A. suddenly turned farcical. I began to laugh, too, more out of relief than amusement. Dizzy had no idea what was so funny, but joined in anyway. Without a word, the past had been set right or at least set aside. The ties of friendship binding us were stronger, it seemed, than the pain we had inflicted on each other. And so it was settled; Jimmy and I would find a place together again.

As any New Yorker may recall, there was a science to finding an apartment in the city in those days. And the formula started with: "Buy the Sunday *Times*, study the rentals, pick your targets, take plenty of money, and add two parts determination and a hefty supply of stamina. And be ready to settle for less, far less." Realizing that neither of us had enough cash for security on an apartment, nor anything with which to furnish one, let alone rent in advance, our only hope lay in finding a cheap, centrally located residence hotel, preferably rent payable weekly, with maid service included.

With no Sunday *Times* (it was midweek) and no plan of attack, the three of us spent the afternoon working our way downtown, zigzagging from West to East Fifty-seventh Street downward, checking out each likely prospect. By the time we reached Forty-fourth Street, our hopes had dimmed considerably. Everything we looked at was either too expensive or too seedy. Then Jimmy remembered that he knew someone who lived at the Royalton, an apartment hotel just east of Sixth Avenue.

As we entered, I could tell from the elegant lobby that we were definitely out of our league. The weekly rates posted at the desk proved me right. We were beating an embarrassed retreat when we ran into an acquaintance of Jimmy's, actor Roddy McDowall, a resident at the time, who was just entering the hotel. Roddy had come to New York from Hollywood where he had been a major child star at MGM. Sadly, his voice had changed, but, fortunately with it, his career. He had moved to New York, determined to establish himself as a serious adult actor in the theater, an ambition he was fast realizing.

Having known Jimmy since they both appeared in Jimmy's first television movie, *Hill Number One*, he stopped to chat. We told him what we were looking for, and he suggested the hotel directly opposite. Thinking he meant the Algonquin, that awesome theatrical landmark made famous in the thirties by drama critic/actor Alexander Woollcott and such notorious Algonquin Round Table habitués as Dorothy Parker, Robert Benchley, Hayward Broun, Tallulah Bankhead, and George S. Kaufman, we quite naturally demurred. Instead, Roddy directed our gazes to a more modest hotel just a couple of doors east of the Algonquin. It bore the name of another regional tribe, the Iroquois. As conveniently located as her nominal sister next door, though lacking her polish and history, she was certain to be cheaper.

A poky single room with twin beds and bath for ninety dollars a month was, I was assured by my exhausted friends, a real bargain for midtown Manhattan. As I scanned the drab little room, I could only remember how much larger and more atmospheric our penthouse had been, and how much cheaper. But since it was getting late and we were weary, I agreed to give it a try for a month. Besides, now reunited with my teammate, surely anything was possible. Or was "teammate" still the word for it?

13

Bill and Jim: Together Again

JIMMY NEVER TOLD ROGERS HE WAS MOVING OUT. HE AND I SIM-
ply hurried back to the studio apartment before Rogers got
home from work and, like a pair of pack rats, moved his
things out of there and into our new quarters at the Iroquois.
It all happened so fast that I couldn't help wondering if he was
that anxious to flee Rogers or that eager to move in with me.

Fortunately, Jimmy had accumulated very little in the few
months he had been in New York. The first and most prominent installation was the hanging of his prized bullfighting
practice gear on the wall beside his bed. The rest consisted of
some books, which were lined up on the one and only desk,
and his clothes, which went into the one and only closet beside mine. Luckily, we both traveled light. All I had was a
small suitcase full of clothes and a shaving kit, so it appeared
we could just manage in the cramped quarters, at least for the
time being.

What worried me, however, was how Jimmy was going to
adjust to his new circumstances. No more Rogers to pay the
rent, buy the food (and probably the clothes), and provide the
social and business contacts. But Jimmy seemed confident that
he would manage on his own and visibly relieved of the onerous burden of being beholden: aside from utter penury, his
least tolerable circumstance. Besides, earlier that morning he
had obliquely led me to believe he knew his man. From the

way he referred to Rogers, it now appeared that there had been somewhat a reversal of roles, and Jimmy was in a position to call the shots. However, despite our "tacit" understanding about his relationship with Rogers, Jimmy had yet to acknowledge it openly, specifically, as sexual. The game was: Rogers was a friend and mentor, that's all, his role strictly paternalistic. The allusions were: Rogers was a predator whose appetites Jimmy satisfied in return for everything Rogers did for him. Okay, so he wasn't ready to discuss it forthrightly, only euphemistically, as in, "I did a little dancing myself," and "I paid my way." Nonetheless, I now wondered about his relationship with this girl, Dizzy. On first seeing them together, it had seemed apparent that there was nothing serious involved, no kissing, no hugs, not even handholding. When I put it to him, he had shrugged dismissively and said that "she makes me laugh." More obfuscation? Never mind. I was used to it by now. Anyway, if I'd tried to pry further, I knew he'd only clam up and turn irritable or sullen. In any case, I didn't care at that moment. I had my friend back.

Starting our very first day together, Jimmy put me through a rigorous orientation program, dragging me all over town, animatedly explaining everything, making the rounds of the casting directors and production offices, introducing me to the favorite hangouts of his acting friends and acquaintances, which were also usually the most friendly—and cheapest— places to eat.

There was Cromwell's drugstore on the ground floor of the awe-inspiring RCA building, where other actors, writers, and directors hung out between jobs, drinking endless coffees or grabbing a quick bite during breaks in rehearsals for television shows, some of which were broadcast from the NBC studios above in the same building. The place had a kind of clubhouse atmosphere, where familiar faces like Marty Landau, Billy Gunn, Barbara Glenn, gentleman John Newland, and Billy James would congregate daily and exchange tips and gossip. Just up Sixth Avenue, a few blocks from our hotel and near the old Ziegfeld Theater, there was also Jerry's Bar, another show-biz hangout. They served the best manicotti around at out-of-work-actor prices. Because of our cramped quarters and the lack of a kitchen at the Iroquois, Jerry's became our dining room and living room, where we could bring or meet friends, eat and drink and talk till closing time, night after night. Remarkably, we were always welcome, no matter how little we spent.

Forced to eat all our meals out, aside from Jerry's Bar, we sampled everything within a radius of one mile, from the Automat to the various other inexpensive diners Jimmy had vetted during his penniless, pre-Rogers days in the city. In the coffee shop a few doors from the Iroquois where we breakfasted each day, we befriended a sympathetic counter waitress named Marie, who would serve us orange juice, bacon and eggs, toast, and coffee, and charge us only for the toast and coffee. Marie was a saint.

Afternoons, we would sometimes escape the early heat wave that was scorching New York by taking refuge in the merciful cool of the air-conditioned Forty-second Street movie houses. Best of all, Jimmy introduced me to the joy of theater signs that read, "SRO," Standing Room Only. For a fraction of the price of the cheapest seat in the house, we would stand at the rear of the orchestra section, lean on the chest-high partition, and quite comfortably catch the latest Broadway hit. Over the next year, I would manage to see almost every production on Broadway while on my feet, some several times.

By the end of a few weeks, I was thoroughly indoctrinated and had my survival techniques down pat. Disconcertingly, however, during the course of that process, one thing had become increasingly clear to me: Our relationship had done a complete about-face. No longer, as in L.A., was I the one who led the way while Jimmy turned to me for guidance. Now I was following his lead, which, although helpful, at times made me feel slightly patronized about a city I'd once considered my own special domain. The shoe was on the other foot now, and it was pinching. Still, I was extremely touched by his eagerness to share with me this exciting new world he had discovered. He'd known from our days in the penthouse about my love affair with New York and my early experiences there, and now he was helping me realize my dream of returning. "Here it is, for your delectation," he seemed to be saying. "Come feast with me!"

Of course, it was a New York quite different from the one I had known five years before. Then I'd been a kid, now I was an adult—or liked to think of myself as one. In the end, Jimmy's generosity won out, and my slightly hurt pride gave way to gratitude. In fact, when I thought about it, I realized that he was the only man, aside from my grandfather and Bayard Colgate, who had ever cared enough to look after me, not out of obligation, but what? Friendship? Something more? I wasn't sure, but whatever it was, it gave me a new sensation of security, and I found myself feeling closer to Jimmy than I ever had before. Unlike our more naïve days in the penthouse, I now felt a subtle undercurrent of emotional attunement in our renewed friendship and closer physical proximity. Although he had shared mine several times, our beds had never been so close. A hand stretched out could touch the other.

Inevitably I found myself wondering how much of the mentor act he had picked up from Rogers, whether I was going to be expected to play Jimmy's role in the game and, more importantly, to what extent. Or, were I to make a move first, would I take Rogers's place in his eyes? Looking back on it, I wonder now if that concern was based on apprehension on my part or wishful thinking. In any case, I wasn't prepared to ask myself that question then. Dangerous waters could lie ahead, and I wasn't a good enough sailor to risk that voyage. Not yet. Red, Right, Returning.

Indeed, I experienced a subtle, unsettling reminder of the flick-knife incident one night when Jimmy was out and I had just returned to the hotel room early. While readying for bed, I noticed his sketchbook lying on the desk and happened to glance at it. Staring at me from the page was a grotesque sketch of a lizard, that is to say, a lizard's body supporting a man's head. The head was unmistakably Rogers Brackett's, horn-rimmed glasses, arch expression and all, and the caricature was decidedly uncomplimentary. From my perspective, I could appreciate such a negative assessment of the man. But this was Jimmy's perspective not mine, and it revived my old concerns about his inner conflict. Whom did he find more loathsome, Rogers or himself, Rogers for being a lizard or himself for consorting with one? Was this how the Quaker within him perceived someone who performed homosexual acts? If so, how would he perceive me if and when I allowed myself to be honest with him? Time to go back inside my clamshell once more.

Obviously it came as something of a surprise to learn shortly afterward that Jimmy and Rogers, having made some sort of accommodation, were seeing each other again, albeit, Jimmy maintained, on a strictly social basis. Apparently, this was an acceptable arrangement as far as Rogers was concerned; at least Jimmy was back in his life socially, which spared Rogers the humiliation of total abandonment before his circle of friends. In return, presumably having held back some of the more interesting and influential of these friends for future use, Rogers now started doling them out to Jimmy in measured portions in what appeared to me a calculated attempt to lure his lost prize back to the fold. And to some extent, it seemed to be working. Rogers took to organizing his own little version of the Algonquin Round Table, gathering together a circle of bright talented folk to meet each week in the "Algonk's" lounge or bar for drinks and banter, folk whose number included Maggie McNamara; David Swift; composer Alec Wilder and lyricist Bill Engvick; Sarah Churchill, the "dipso" (as Jimmy described her) daughter of England's legendary prime minister; and soon-to-be Broadway producers Lemuel Ayres and his wife, Shirley. And into their midst Rogers had brought Jimmy.

Each and every member of the cabal, as I came to see them, embraced the fair-haired, well-mannered (!), motherless boy with open heart and, in a few cases, as it transpired, open arms. They took him to their collective bosom as the earthly personification of the Little Prince, straight out of Antoine de Saint-Exupéry's treasured book of the same name.

According to Jimmy, so important to them was that particular book that it had almost become a bible in which they individually and collectively placed their secular faith. To illustrate this fact, he told me how, when he first arrived in New York, not knowing the degree to which they held the Little Prince in reverence, he had, in his words "almost given Alec Wilder a heart attack." Provided with the phone number by Rogers, he had phoned Wilder and, assuming his most innocent voice, announced, "Hello, Mr. Wilder, this is the Little Prince." Wilder later told him that he thought he was having an epiphany.

To the delight of his new audience, Jimmy played his role to perfection, as I witnessed on the rare occasions when Jimmy invited me along. On those occasions, I found myself back in my old position of being not only overlooked, but uncomfortably having to watch Rogers bask in the reflected glory of his protégé's performance. It was like old times in Hollywood. Was I embarrassed for Jimmy? Definitely. Was I jealous? Not a bit. Well, perhaps a smidge. My consolation came at the thought of the price Jimmy was paying: putting up with, if not out for, Rogers.

Jimmy seemed to thrive on being the center of so much attention, attention that bordered on adulation. But more, and wisely so, he reveled in his elite audience's perspicacity, their talent, their wit, their breadth of knowledge, and, not entirely coincidentally, their potentials as steppingstones to success. Over the past year, he had learned well the value of being aware, informed, of knowing as much as possible about everything, and, especially, knowing who was worth knowing. He recognized that he had started out an ignorant kid fresh off the farm, but was fast making up for lost time, and these people were fodder for his ravenous hunger to grow and get ahead. Consequently, with the same ruthless determination I had witnessed him display whenever he entered into physical competition, he now attacked every source of information, of knowledge, of sophistication, seizing on each morsel with the rapaciousness of a starving beast.

Whatever the price, he owed Rogers an enormous debt for opening his narrow world to greater sources of knowledge, experience, and awareness, as well as valuable contacts. Sadly for Rogers, what he failed to recognize was his protégé's almost pathological abhorrence of indebtedness, that Jimmy could not merely bite, but eventually devour the hand that fed him.

A couple of weeks after we moved into the Iroquois, the Colgates invited me up to Connecticut for the weekend. Jimmy knew about my relationship with Beatrice and Bayard. I hoped he wouldn't feel slighted by not being asked along. Although they knew I was sharing a place in town with my old college roommate, they hadn't invited him nor had I suggested it. Frankly, it struck me as ill advised. In the first place, it wasn't his scene. Aside from that, I think I feared a repeat of what had happened when I introduced him to Beverly and Joan and felt justifiably protective of Bayard and Beatrice. In effect, they had become my foster family, and considering Jimmy's unpredictable behavior and tendency to move in and help himself, I didn't want to risk losing them or even, like a jealous sibling, sharing them. Fortunately, he had other plans that weekend, and by the next time I was invited, he had gone off himself with Rogers and his friends, Lemuel and Shirley Ayres, who had a house somewhere in the Hudson Valley, to which I was not invited. In some areas, it would seem we were mutually self-protective.

By that time, Beatrice and Bayard had finally built their dream house outside Darien on that small island appropriately named Contentment. Situated on a promontory facing Long Island Sound, the property backed on a lagoonlike inlet across which the Charles Lindbergh estate was situated. You approached by a country road from town, snaking along the inlets, then across a little wooden bridge and up a private drive past a woodland pond and quaint old icehouse. Approaching from the inland side, the new house appeared to be one story, long and low, which lent it a much more humble look than the family mansion in New Canaan. It had been built mainly on one floor to make life easier for Beatrice who had a hip that was giving her trouble. However, the promontory on which the house was perched sloped down to the Sound on the waterfront side, which allowed for a lower floor on that side of the house where the guest and service rooms were to be found. Both floors enjoyed views of the Sound from almost every room.

There was a small, private beach protected by a breakwater, in the lee of which Bayard kept his new thirty-five-foot catamaran. Whenever I visited, weather permitting, he would take me sailing and risk all trying to make a sailor out of me, as he had done before on his smaller, less-daunting sailboat. With stoic determination, he almost succeeded.

Over various weekends that summer, I learned to love Contentment Island. Each day at dawn and dusk, the call of the loons echoed across the inlet. Sometimes, after dinner, we would sit out on the veranda under the stars, listening to Bayard's records of classical music while a company of fireflies would dance their nightly ballet with the ink-black Sound as their backdrop. Sometimes we would play word games, and on occasion, the Lindberghs or other friends would come by for bridge. Leaving the foursome to their game, I would often adjourn to Bayard's library and read, and read, and read. Later, the gentle lapping of waves against the breakwater and rhythmic foghorn of the lighthouse just offshore would lull me to sleep. In the morning, in season, just as Bayard had promised in Darien years before, there were fresh blueberries for breakfast.

The contrast between my new life in town with Jimmy and my weekend life with the Colgates could not have been more pronounced. In fact, it was downright schizoid, a condition by then familiar to me. True to his promise, Bayard arranged a series of job interviews for me with several New York advertising agencies. None went well, however. I suspect the ad men were unimpressed by my non-Ivy League education, my theater arts major, and possibly with my draft-worthy age. I, of course, made no mention of my draft status, and no one bothered to ask. After all, had I been called up, I would have already been in the service or, heaven forbid, 4-F, which in those days would have made me detritus on Madison Avenue. I also began to realize that I was probably interviewing badly because I basically didn't want a job in the advertising world. This was the era of the Madison Avenue Ad Man, the uniformed *Man in the Grey Flannel Suit*. Having narrowly escaped one army, I wasn't keen on joining another. I found the regimentation, the conformity, the rigid wardrobe requirements, and the Old Boys Club atmosphere as stuffy and repellent as I had the prospect of fraternity life. Naturally, I couldn't very well confide such feelings to Bayard. And so I began declining invitations to Contentment Island on one pretext or another, hoping to avoid probing questions about my job-hunting progress, at least until I was gainfully employed somewhere else. This meant, before facing Bayard again, I would have to find a job on my own. The question was, where?

The answer came as I was walking down Madison Avenue after yet another dismal interview at an ad agency. Suddenly I found myself confronted by old, familiar, and comforting initials: CBS. Without hesitation, I entered the unprepossessing office building and applied for a position. To my great surprise and relief, I was hired. I was to start in the mail room and "work my way up."

In effect, this turned out to be exactly the opposite of what I did. I learned that my job was to deliver and pick up mail and telexes at the reception desks of each of twenty-three floors on an hourly basis. However, I immediately figured taking the elevator one floor at a time and then waiting for its return would be far too time consuming if the deliveries had to be made on an hourly basis. So, expeditiously, I took the stairs, spiraling down each flight, dropping off and picking up at each reception desk, then down the next flight, and so forth, to the ground floor. Then back up to the mail room on the top floor in the elevator where I could sort the new batch of incoming telexes and briefly relax, only to repeat the same process again at the beginning of the next hour. Within the first week, I became a whiz, making the round trip in less than twenty-five minutes. By the end of the first month, I was developing vertigo. But at least I had a job.

14

The Little Prince

AT FIRST, JIMMY EXTENDED HIMSELF BY OFFERING ME A PRACTI-
cal guide to New York life as he'd found it, then gradually by
trying to share his newly garnered treasures of intellectual enlightenment as he perceived them. I say trying because he had
difficulty articulating abstract ideas. Among so many other
things, he seemed to want to convey the idea that there could
be, between like-minded people, a powerful link, deep friendship, or love, which could only be achieved by putting aside
all extraneous trivialities, the mountain of petty preoccupa-
tions and prejudices that generally kept us all apart. Only in
this way could "true unions of mind, spirit, and body," as he
put it, be achieved. I tried to decipher his meaning, again wondered where all this might be leading.

"You're running so fast, it's all passing you by!" he would
insist impatiently. "People. You've got to learn to give and receive. You've got to bounce the ball."

I felt like a dunce. Everything he said sounded so ambigu-
ous, and yet he seemed to find it all profoundly meaningful. I
was too much of a pragmatist and he too much of a skeptic to
embrace such cryptic double-talk. So what was he on about?
He certainly sounded sincere and seemed mightily frustrated
not being able to get his message across, yet he refused to let
it go. Apparently, this was something too important to him
not to be imparted.

One night, catching my glazed stare of mystification, he stopped in the middle of trying to explain, shook his head in frustration, and heaved what I thought might be his final sigh of exasperation. For one brief moment, I was overcome with relief. Either he was going to give up or come to some kind of point. Instead, he reached for a little book on the dressing table and handed it to me. It was his copy of *The Little Prince*. He asked if I had ever read it. I hadn't. What I didn't say was that I did know a bit about the author, Antoine de Saint-Exupéry. A French commercial and wartime pilot, he'd been declared missing and presumed dead after a flight to North Africa in World War II. Whether he'd been shot down or crashed in the Sahara Desert or Mediterranean Sea had yet to be established. What was rumored, was that he was homosexual.

Slipping into his jacket, Jimmy instructed me to read the slim volume then and there, assuring me that it would explain everything better than he ever could, upon which he left, saying he'd be back in a while.

I opened the book dutifully and began to read. The pages were well worn, and Jimmy had underlined in pencil certain lines and passages that appeared to be the most meaningful to him. For those not familiar with the book, it's a romantic and touching fable about a pilot whose plane crash-lands in the Sahara Desert. Here he encounters a fair-haired little boy, the Little Prince of the title, who has come from a tiny distant asteroid. The Little Prince teaches the pilot how to "tame" him, that is, befriend him by slowly building a trust between them. Then, sadly, after the pilot has tamed him and opened his heart to his companion, the Little Prince announces that he must leave him to return to his tiny asteroid, where a single, vain rose, which has long ago tamed him, needs his care and attention. But before he goes, the Little Prince leaves his new friend with a simple message: "It is only with the heart that one can see rightly. What is essential is invisible to the eye." Then, because his small body is too heavy for the interplanetary journey, the Little Prince deliberately allows himself to be bitten by a poisonous desert snake, whereupon he dies, allowing his spirit to return to his tiny asteroid in the heavens.

That little book reached me, as it has millions through the years since it was first published. Perhaps I somehow associated the sad little tale with my friend, Craig, off somewhere on the killing fields of Korea, from whom I had not heard in a while. I also now understood the appeal of the book to Rogers and his set, to Alec Wilder, and now to Jimmy. When Jimmy returned to the room, he immediately perceived how moved I was, sat down on the bed beside me, and put an arm around me.

"Didn't think you'd dig it the first time," he said gently. "I didn't."

And then he smiled and kissed me softly on the lips. My surprised reaction made him smile.

"Haven't you ever been kissed by a guy before?" he asked.

"Have you?" I challenged, still mortally afraid to reveal anything before he did.

"Sure." His delivery was easy.

I knew I had to push for more.

"But you never . . . you know?" I couldn't quite say it.

"Made it with a guy? Why not? Got to try everything once."

At last. Time to put it on the line.

"You mean, Rogers, right?" I said.

He shrugged noncommittally, meaning yes. But that wasn't good enough. If we were going to level with each other, we were going to level with each other.

"Were there others?"

He looked over the rim of his glasses puckishly and smiled.

"Who?" I pursued.

"Remember the television director I introduced you to last week?" he reminded.

"Of the show you just did?"

He nodded. "Invited me up to his apartment for a drink after the show."

"So . . . ?"

"We were sitting on the couch. He reached over and started fooling around."

"And then . . . ?"

"He went down on me."

I reacted, more impressed than shocked. "Did you . . . ?"

"I just lay back and watched this fly walk across the ceiling."

I remember him searching my eyes intently, looking for my reaction. "It's no big deal. Didn't you ever want to try it?"

I hesitated a moment, embarrassed by my own game, then allowed only, "I guess."

"So?"

I wanted to challenge him, say, "I'm not an actor. I don't have Stanislavsky as an excuse," or, "Of course I have, a hundred times. What do you think, I'm totally square?" Instead, I shrugged and said, "I don't know."

Here was my chance, the perfect opportunity to put an end at last to the game playing, but now I was being evasive. Why was it so damn hard for me to take the plunge and open up? Was it my inherent distrust of him? Was I afraid he'd eventually use it against me or, worse, if I became fully emotionally engaged, reject me? Instinct told me he had it in him to do just that. How could I let down my guard? I had to know first where this was leading us. I wanted to get there, but wanted *him* to get us there. I couldn't take the reins myself. How could I survive his rejection; how could *we*?

Before I could persuade myself to confide anything, Jimmy suddenly jumped up, grabbed my clothes off a chair, flung them at me, and told me to get dressed. Confused, I asked where we were going.

"I'm not going anywhere. You are." He grinned. "Just do what I tell you. Get up, and put your clothes on."

With some reluctance, I obeyed and started dressing. It was past midnight after all. I had to be up early for work. But I was far too curious about where this might be leading to refuse.

"You have to make sacrifices for your art," he insisted, fussing and adjusting my outfit, tossing aside one shirt in preference for another. My God, I thought, he's sending me out to cruise! Now was the moment to stop it, but I couldn't. For some perverse reason, I wanted it to play out his way. I was actually enjoying it.

"What art?" I retorted. "I'm not an actor."

"You want to be a writer, don't you?"

"I have a good imagination. If I write a murder mystery, do I have to go out and kill someone?"

Ignoring all my protests, he gave me my marching orders and shoved me out the door while I was still buckling my jeans, adding, "Call me if you run into trouble."

Fifteen minutes later, as instructed, I was standing at the bar of the Astor Bar in Times Square. I was to leave myself "open to experience." Without saying so specifically, he seemed to be expecting me to get picked up, get laid, and then report back on it. All the way to Times Square, I'd felt more and more foolish. Why this game? Why was I going through with this? Why hadn't I just told him that I knew the Astor Bar from past experience and get it over with? Clearly, he knew the place from personal experience, as well, or he wouldn't have dreamed up this absurd exercise. It was with that thought that the penny dropped. He *knew* the place. Was this his way of telling me that he was leading the same double life I was, not only putting out for Rogers or other potential benefactors opportunistically, but actively seeking sex with men because he *wanted* it? If only I could be sure.

The Astor Bar was what passed for an uptown gay bar in those days. No giddy chatter, bitchy queens, cooing young lovers, or preening musclemen there, however. This was more for the Closet Brigade, a smart, dimly lit room, where mostly middle-aged men skulked in dimly lit corners or posed at the oval bar, nursing drinks, their eyes furtively cruising the handful of younger men in the room, yearning to approach one, but too wary. These were serious hunting grounds. I already knew about its reputation, of course. On desperate nights in the recent past, I'd stopped by for a drink, in the unfulfilled hope of connecting with someone even remotely desirable. Sadly, the place didn't usually attract my type, and I'd always been too nervous to approach anyone anyway. Like everyone else there, I never knew who might be a vice cop. It was galling to realize that only one street away, on Forty-second Street, dozens of straight guys were picking up prostitutes without a qualm.

On this particular night, it was late and the pickings even slimmer than usual. Toying with a drink I didn't want, my mind was in turmoil. I felt like an idiot and now wondered why I had allowed myself to go through with this crazy charade. Was I really so determined to remain in the closet as far as Jimmy was concerned? Bizarrely, he seemed to be trying his best to force me "out." But why like this? Why didn't he just take the initiative? After all, he'd been dangerously close to it with that kiss. For the first time in our relationship, I had felt susceptible to his intimacy and would have gone along with anything he wanted. Considering the tenderness of his concern and our closeness at that moment, I'd felt no trepidations for once. But, instead, he'd backed down and sent me on this fool's errand, and to make the situation even more ridiculous, I went. Maybe it was my fault for not having been forthright with him. Still, how could I be? Memories of the brandished flick knife and the caricature of Rogers-as-lizard still lurked in the back of my mind. On the other hand, didn't he have reason for caution, too? How well I recalled his searing accusation, "I trusted you! I trusted you!" as I skipped out on him and the penthouse that bleak day back in L.A. My betrayal must have left some kind of scar. Or maybe this was just his diabolic way of leveling the playing field? If I knew about Rogers, now Jimmy would know about this, whatever it turned out to be. That is, if it turned out to be anything at all.

I was still trying to sort this all out over my drink when a stocky, older guy with nervous sweat dotting his upper lip sidled up and asked if he could buy me another. Borrowing a line from almost all of Ida Lupino's movies, I told him one was my limit. Apparently not a film buff, he didn't take the hint, but persisted, trying to engage me in conversation. By this time, I was constructing my own scenario. Sadly, he wouldn't stick to the script, and it got out of hand. Mistaking my tolerance for interest, he asked me to go home with him. I invented a story about a friend who was expecting me. He promised it wouldn't take long and urged me to phone my friend and say I'd be a little late. He even gave me the damn nickel.

The phone conversation with Jimmy was as loony as the situation. I told him some guy was trying to pick me up. He asked me if I was attracted to him, and I replied with an emphatic, "Are you kidding? Anyway, that's not the point. What the hell am I doing here, Deaner?" I had taken to calling him Deaner in retaliation for his calling me "Willie." I hated Willie.

There was only one thing I wanted him to say, and he did. After a thoughtful pause, he replied, "You're right. It ought to be somebody you've tamed first." I realized that this was an allusion to *The Little Prince*. "Sorry, Willie," he continued. "My mistake. You don't belong there. C'mon home."

An invitation, I assured myself. After all, hadn't we "tamed" one another over the past couple of years? Yes, it was definitely an invitation. Even the way he said "Willie," so gently, so affectionately, was inviting. Besides, he didn't say, "C'mon back," he said, "C'mon *home*." Apologizing to my would-be pickup, I left the bar and hurried back to the Iroquois.

I might as well have taken my time. Jimmy was gone when I got there. I had momentarily overcome all my fears and trepidations and rushed back at his summons, expecting the walls of Jericho to come tumbling down, and he was gone. Was he trying to torture me? Or, was he as frightened as I to test the safety net of our friendship by taking the final plunge? And was I really ready to overcome my fear of him? More unanswered questions. More complications.

Then, I saw it. On my bed, propped against my pillow, was Jimmy's copy of *The Little Prince*. Fastened firmly to the top left side of the dust cover by a paper clip was a note. It read, "For a gift one is always beholden," which I took to be a quote from the book. It turned out to be a line from *The Moon Is Blue*, an early fifties Broadway comedy and subsequent Otto Preminger movie about sexual mores. As I'd neither seen nor read the play, I didn't understand Jimmy's (and indeed the play's) message, which actually precedes the line in the scene, namely that it was okay to cast aside innocence in favor of sexual fulfillment. The note itself was unsigned, but printed in Jimmy's unmistakable, childish hand. Reading it, I experienced this sudden, unfamiliar aching sensation in my chest, in my heart, almost physical. Wondering, I looked around the bare hotel room. Why did he leave? I started to remove the paper clip that held his note to the book jacket, wanting to put the note somewhere safe and keep it. But the clip was tight and threatened to tear the jacket or, worse, the note. So I left it fastened, an incidental, fleeting decision that would one day return to haunt me.

He didn't return that night until long after I had fallen asleep, atop the covers, still fully dressed and clutching the book. Nor did he wake me when he came in.

A couple of weeks later, I returned to the hotel one afternoon, barged into the room, and stopped short to find Jimmy sitting on the floor with an attractive young blonde girl. Since the day we had first looked at the room with Dizzy, to my knowledge, he had never brought anyone there before, least of all a girl, not even Dizzy. In fact, after Jeanetta and Beverly, I never knew him to "date" girls, period. As for Dizzy, he seemed to regard her simply as a playmate to hang out with. In fact, in all the time we lived together, I don't recall him ever telling me he'd had sex with any girl. He never talked about girls in a sexual context, generally or specifically. He never checked out a pretty girl when she passed. In fact, I had never heard him express any sexual interest in women, never heard him comment on or allude to any girl's looks or anatomy, neither "tits," nor "ass," nor any other physical attribute—with the one exception of the grotesque *Vagina as Candleholder*. The only time I heard him tell of a female sexual encounter was once, later in Hollywood, when he was trying to impress a particularly boring macho actor who'd been bragging about his own sexual exploits with a number of starlets. Jimmy tried to outgross the guy with an allusion to ". . . winding up with pubic hair between my teeth."

As I stood there in the doorway, taking in the scene on the floor, I must have looked stunned because Jimmy quickly reacted, clearly clued by the expression on my face.

"Hi, Willie! This is Chris White. We're rehearsing a scene." He waved the slim few pages of script in his hand as evidence. "Chris wrote it," he clarified. "We're going to audition for the Actors Studio."

It turned out that he'd met Chris in the outer office of the Shurr Agency, where she was also a client. She'd borrowed the receptionist's typewriter and was reworking her scene when Jimmy came in and spotted her. Looking over her shoulder, he'd started kibitzing. Annoyed at first, she'd grudgingly considered incorporating some of his suggestions. When she'd told him the scene was intended for her Actors Studio audition, Jimmy promptly took an even more active interest. A half-hour later, over coffee at Walgreen's drugstore, she'd asked him to play the young man in the scene opposite her. They'd agreed to do the audition together.

Since the days of Whitmore's acting class in L.A., Jimmy's greatest dream had been to get into the Actors Studio to study with America's "Method" gurus, Elia Kazan and Lee Strasberg. At Whitmore's prompting, he'd contrived to get himself to New York. But, curiously, once in New York, he'd made no attempt to try for an audition at the Studio. When I'd asked him about this, he'd explained that he was afraid he wasn't ready, that he might blow his one and only chance. But, running into Chris like that was serendipity, and he'd grabbed at the opportunity, not giving it a second thought.

Chris and Jimmy worked on the scene over the next couple of weeks, shaping it, changing it, and then finally throwing it out altogether to start working on another short scene that Chris had also written. But as audition day approached, they got nervous and, lacking objectivity, asked me for whatever advice and guidance I could offer. I was flattered, frankly excited at the idea of playing director, being a party to an audition for the exalted Actors Studio, however anonymously. By doomsday, they were as ready as they would ever be—and unimaginably nervous.

Like two terrified children, they headed for the Studio to place their humble offering before the high priests of their craft. Suddenly, they were next in line. But, just as they were about to be called in to do the scene, Jimmy panicked. Chris later told me he'd suddenly exclaimed, "I'm not going out there! We're not ready yet!" And with that, he fled the building. But she caught up with him and nailed him. She was damned if he was going to fuck up her audition.

Out of the 150 who tried out that day, they were two of the fifteen who were accepted. Jimmy was reputedly the youngest member of the Studio. He was twenty-one, and he finally belonged.

That night, I helped him draft a letter home to his uncle and aunt, Marcus and "Mom," as he called Ortense. He rarely wrote letters and felt awkward at the task of composing just the right words. He didn't need much help that night, however. I kept a rough copy of that draft. It read:

I have made great strides in my craft. After months of auditioning, I am proud to announce that I am a member of the Actors Studio. The greatest school of the theater. It houses great people like Marlon Brando, Julie Harris, Arthur Kennedy, Elia Kazan, Mildred Dunnock, Kevin McCarthy, Monty Clift, June Havoc, and on and on and on. Very few get into it, and it is absolutely free. It is the best thing that can happen to an actor. I am one of the youngest to belong . . .

If I can keep this up and nothing interferes with my progress, one of these days I might be able to contribute something to the world . . .

Tell Mrs. Brookshire [Adeline Nall, as she was later to become, Jimmy's high-school drama teacher] *when you see her that I have never forgotten the Thespian creed: "Act well your part for there all honor lies."*

Jimmy also asked his aunt and uncle for financial help, one of the things he disliked doing more than anything else and therefore rarely did. In fact, the few letters I knew him to write during all our years of friendship were usually pleas for help and painful to write. The cost of living in New York was high, and the jobs he had been getting afforded him little more than enough for rent and meager meals. In two years, the only new clothes he had bought had been one very inexpensive suit, his first since high school. So, putting pen to paper, he forced his hand:

I would more than appreciate it if you could spare 10 dol-

lars or so. I need it rather desperately. I am sorry that when I write I always need something. Sometimes I feel that I have lost the right to ask; but because I don't write isn't an indication that I have forgotten. I shall never forget what you and Mom have done for me. I want to repay you.

It takes time and many disappointments. I'll try very hard not to take too long. If I have asked for help at the wrong time, please forgive me and I will understand.

I remember wondering why he didn't turn to his father, but perhaps instinctively, I knew, as he must have, that his father might let him down. I'm sure he didn't want to risk the disappointment. Of course, a few days later, a letter of encouragement arrived from Indiana. Enclosed was some money, more than he had requested. He was grateful, but clearly felt guilty about having had to ask for it. He would try to make it stretch, but we both knew it wouldn't go very far.

Money, however, was soon to be the least of Jimmy's worries. Shortly after he received the answering letter from home, another envelope arrived for him, one I recognized only too well from past experience. From a genial Uncle Sam, it began familiarly: *Greetings . . .*

Jimmy panicked. After all the sacrifice, after the struggles of the past two years, just when he had realized his dream of getting into the Actors Studio, just when he was finally getting to the point where they would at least let him read for leading roles in some of the better television dramas, just when he was beginning to feel the promise of success, Fate and Uncle Sam were conspiring to snatch it all away. How could he give it all up now and go off to Korea, waste a couple of his prime years, possibly get himself killed, or worse, maimed?

Hunched over the desk, he tortured the dilemma for hours while I sat on the bed beside him looking over his shoulder as he started one letter after another to his draft board, only to crumple each and toss it aside. Far into the night, we deliberated the various draft dodges we'd picked up from disillusioned World War II vets we knew at UCLA and other students who'd faced the same depressing prospect. Most of their ideas were impractical, involving ploys like letters from corruptible doctors or psychiatrists, rare to find at best and ruinously expensive where available. Unlike my situation, Jimmy had no previous medical condition that might get him an exemption; he had already learned that his nearsightedness wouldn't help. The only ruse guaranteed to work was the most repugnant and, for most, profoundly humiliating: declare yourself a practicing homosexual. Jimmy said he had no moral compunctions about making such a declaration. Practically, however, the potential consequences to his budding career, if it were to come out that he had taken that route, did give him pause. In fact, the prospect paralyzed him. Early the following morning, he finally decided to phone and wake the only other sympathetic confidants he felt he could trust, Rogers Brackett and Alec Wilder, to solicit their advice. Both Rogers and Alec agreed that he should take the risk. Then, with a concurring nod from me, he decided to go for broke.

He dictated various versions of the letter to me and finally settled on the one he felt read best, which he then copied in his own careful hand. While I caught some sleep, Jimmy agonized over the sealed and stamped envelope, neatly addressed to the draft board. In the end, however, feeling he had no other option, he mailed it.

Apparently the draft board never questioned it. His exemption came through much faster than mine had, and, as with me, the threat of the draft vanished. But the fear of repercussions from that letter haunted him for the rest of his professional life, a concern he confided to others, incautiously as it turned out.

15

Gay Old New York

DESPITE THE DIZZYING DOWNWARD SPIRAL THAT WAS MY JOB AT CBS, I was beginning to enjoy life. I even made new and unexpectedly liberating friends who would brighten my prospects for a future social life of my own. It started one day when I surprised myself by coming to the defense of a coworker in the CBS mail room. His name was Alex, and he wore his hair in bangs and walked a little "funny." He was, I was learning, also the favorite object of ridicule by the presumably straight, largely Ivy League mail-room boys. Not content merely to make fun of him behind his back, they started doing it to his face with the whole mail room looking on. With a kind of practiced resilience, Alex seemed to be rising above the taunts and holding his own, at least in front of the "guys." But apparently the daily onslaught took its toll.

One afternoon in the men's room, I heard him in tears in a cubicle. I coaxed him out and did my best to persuade him that his tormentors were juvenile sacks of shit and not worth paying attention to. Taking me for a fellow traveler (whatever gave him that idea?), he explained that he and his lover of several years had quarreled that morning, and his feelings were raw as a result.

Later the same afternoon, returning to the mail room from one of my hourly runs, I found the "guys" having another go at him. He was doing his best to brave it out, but I could see that he was shaken and again on the verge of tears. I have no idea what I said to stop the harassment, but stop it I did. There was, of course, no suggestion of a physical confrontation, certainly not from me, just a verbal lashing, a very loud and no-holds-barred threat to report to management the next person to target Alex. I left the room shocked at myself and certain that from now on I now would be regarded as "just another queer."

Alex, however, became a devoted friend on the spot, and soon after so did his lover, Billy Marchant, a playwright whose comedy *The Desk Set*, starring Shirley Booth was soon to be a hit on Broadway. In time, they would draw me into their theatrical circle. As for me, much to my surprise, I found I had acquired a small, but enjoyable aura of respect at work, probably as word spread through the corridors of CBS of a fierce queer on the loose.

What I did not know at the time was that I had also attracted the attention of two other mail-room boys, whom I shall call Jack and George, both about my age. Although they had hardly spoken to me prior to that, they approached me shortly after the incident and, explaining they had an extra ticket, invited me to join them witness the Republican Party's rally for its presidential candidate, Dwight Eisenhower, at Madison Square Garden the following night. As it happened, I was a Democrat, in fact, an avid Adlai Stevenson fan. (How could I not love a man who, when asked by the press what his response was to the Republicans' dismissal of him as an "egghead"—a derogatory epithet used to describe intellectuals at the time—was to quip spontaneously with the double entendre, "I'd say, 'Eggheads of the world unite! You have nothing to lose but your yokes.'") However, the chance of attending any presidential rally, even a Republican's, was impossible to resist.

It was one of the most spectacular experiences of my young life. The excitement, the hysteria of that crowd when Ike made his entrance, will go down as one of the most exhilarating moments I can recall. Despite my politics, I found myself, like everyone else around me, standing on my seat and cheering wildly for a man I did not particularly want to become president: my first, sobering experience of the contagion of mass hysteria.

As we parted that evening, Jack and George, who turned out to be roommates, invited me to a small dinner they were giving the following Saturday night. Aside from my visits with the Colgates, it was my first social invitation since coming to New York, so, of course, I accepted, pleased that they hadn't asked me to bring a date.

What an eyeopener that evening was! I found myself in an attractive, albeit small, East Side apartment, in the company of my two male hosts and their five other guests, all male, all about my age. Over drinks before dinner, I was treated to an openly homosexual conversation, not in the least campy, but comfortably frank and natural. Surprising only to me, I'm sure, they were all friends, all bright, educated, professional young men who were clearly accustomed, among fellow travelers, to making no bones about their homosexuality. Previously, in Hollywood, I'd been invited to a number of strictly gay gatherings mainly attended by younger men with older escorts. My God, I thought now, there's an entire underground society of my generation out here! They've been having a party, and I finally got an invitation, not as some older guy's trick, but as one among others! These young men were all very close in age, educated, and committed. And they were completely open about their homosexuality and their relationships. Nirvana!

How I would have liked to introduce Jimmy to my new friends. But I knew instinctively that it wouldn't work. His role had been defined, almost exclusively, as an older homosexual's toy-boy. He relished being unique in any setting, the center of attention, not just one among others. Maybe, I figured, in time that would change.

As for the role I'd been playing to keep a hostile world at bay and also to keep up the pretense with Jimmy, I finally realized that it was keeping me from having something I secretly wanted. Ironically, I had been criticizing Jimmy for playing the same game, donning a different role for each encounter, while my game was basically the same and had been all along, though I preferred to remain blind to that truth. In any case, he at least had exposed his true self to me, which was more than I had done for him. Still, having carefully structured my present life to protect myself from discovery, it would be some time before I would muster the courage to shrug off my protective armor, breathe the invigorating air of honesty, and dare the world to reject me. Meantime, at least I now knew what was out there and waiting for me: a real life within a society of like-minded friends . . . and some day, perhaps, even Jimmy.

After arriving in New York, Jimmy had taken up the recorder—a wooden flutelike instrument, dating back to sixteenth-century England—which he practiced relentlessly at all hours in our tiny hotel room. Under Alec Wilder's tutelage, he had become quite accomplished. Frequently, especially when he was in one of his sad or depressed states, he would reach for his recorder and play, as if to drive away the anger and anxiety and give expression to his feelings. More often than not, this would be on a sweltering summer evening when our only window had to be left wide open for the little air there was. The recorder has a mellow, haunting sound, and, surprisingly, we never had one complaint from the other tenants. As for me, I enjoyed his sad little concerts and would read or write or just daydream while he played. I still have an image of him, perched in the open window or sitting cross-legged on his bed wearing only his shorts, piping plaintive tunes for hours on end: Pan, lamenting a lost love.

Despite being released from the threat of the draft and gaining the respite of a couple of weekends in the country with the Ayres, Jimmy was growing despondent again over the lack of work, and his moods darkened. As in the past, he started to spend the late-night hours roaming the city, getting to know anybody who looked interesting to him: cabbies, waitresses, shine boys, newsstand vendors, winos, Greenwich Village cellar intellectuals, so-called Forty-second Street "degenerates" of all persuasions, and, in general, anyone willing to indulge his ravenous need to know what made people tick. From time to time, he would drag me along with him. I resisted at first, but then gave in, letting go of my fears, finding each nighttime adventure an introduction to a new and often fascinating world, one I had never dared explore on my own.

Out of the exotic army of night people encountered on those excursions, one stands out vividly in my memory. Moondog was to be found nightly in front of Carnegie Hall or on the corner of Sixth Avenue and Fifty-fourth Street. Dressed like a Nordic Viking in a handmade robe, cape, and horned helmet, he had become a New York institution, playing strange musical compositions on dried bones and other unique percussion instruments of his own design for whatever passersby might donate. Jimmy developed a genuine admiration for him, always stopping to shoot the breeze, making sure he had something to eat, and, when he could afford it, making contributions to his general welfare.

The out-of-the-ordinary and the talented drew Jimmy like magnets. Once drawn to them, he stuck to them. Professional photographer Roy Schatt, was a good example. I quickly discovered that Roy was not merely an exceptionally gifted photographer, but a philosopher as well. Together, we would spend hours over coffees in his studio or some all-night diner, exploring the human condition—and our own. Over the next couple of years, Roy took dozens of photographs of Jimmy and a few of me. Starkly contrasted to the old-style Hollywood "glamour" photos taken for our composites in L.A., Roy's work was natural, immediate, and dynamic, and it served Jimmy particularly well. Many of those shots of Roy's still define the James Dean millions came to idolize later: the loner in the indifferent city. Roy's photographs of me were among the few taken over the years that didn't embarrass me; in fact, they made me look pretty good. Clearly, the man was a genius.

The money Marcus and Mom had sent in response to Jimmy's letter was soon gone, and, once again our funds were running precariously low. To make matters worse, the television season was in hiatus and the theater in the doldrums, leaving most actors to sweat out the sizzling New York summer or take jobs in summer-stock companies out of town. Jimmy had decided not to do stock, but to remain in the city and take his chances picking up one or two of the few jobs available. In a way, this was fortunate for me because without his contribution, I couldn't have afforded the rent, which would have meant a return to the dreadful Y. All this left us pretty much dependant upon my meager salary from CBS, the kindness of waitress Marie at the next-door coffee shop, and a new and unexpected source of income right on our doorstep.

Just off the lobby of the Iroquois, where a little bar named "The James Dean Room" could be found until a few years ago, a commercial photographer's studio once flourished. Late one morning, the desk clerk phoned our room. Believing that Jimmy or I might be interested, he explained that the photographer's male model for the day had failed to turn up for an important rush job and the photographer was desperately looking for someone to replace him. It would pay all of ten dollars. Jimmy happened to be out, so I responded to the emergency. Half an hour later, after being subjected to a fast manicure, a glass of wine was placed in my hand, and both wine and hand were photographed for a magazine ad. The photographer was delighted, and Jimmy and I were ten bucks richer. From that day on, we took turns working for the photographer whenever he had something for us, which fortunately turned out to be fairly often.

About this time, Jimmy was preparing his first scene as a new member of the Actors Studio. As with anything he took seriously, he put everything he had into his preparation. When the day arrived, he was reasonably confident. What he hadn't prepared for was Lee Strasberg's criticism. Jimmy, as I had long ago learned, did not take criticism easily, not even Strasberg's.

Apparently Strasberg tore him apart in front of the other students, clawing at his psyche, digging deeply, too deeply for Jimmy. Instead of being devastated, Jimmy was enraged.

"That man has no right to tear me down like that!" he stormed to me on his return to the hotel. "I don't know what's inside of me! I don't know what happens when I act, inside! But if I let them dissect me like a rabbit in some sort of clinical research lab, I might not be able to produce again! You keep knocking a guy down like that and you'll cut off his balls! What good is an actor without balls?"

He swore he would never go back to the Studio. Strasberg's techniques might work for some, but never for him. He simply didn't have the stomach to survive the soul-searing, psychologically destructive criticism Strasberg seemed to take pleasure in dishing out.

True to his word, he didn't return to the Studio for some time. Unfortunately, I wasn't on hand when he did, so I missed the reconciliation, if that's what you can call it.

During the hiatus, however, having deprived himself of any sense of satisfaction he might have derived from the Studio and still unable to snare an acting job, he sank into one of his most surly depressions. The merciless heat of the city, his sense of rejection, his frustration at being broke again brought him to the point of despair. To make matters worse, the grating daily news of Senator McCarthy's relentless witch-hunt for purported Communists in the entertainment industry, an inescapable topic of discussion among our friends, became an almost impossible subject for him to confront as it sent him into a practically incoherent state of rage. How we all loathed that contemptible man!

Then, unexpectedly, whether out of compassion or by design—and I came to suspect the latter—Rogers Brackett phoned and invited him for another weekend at the Ayres's country home. For once, I was actually grateful to Rogers.

On Monday, much to my relief, Jimmy returned from the country refreshed, rejuvenated, and excited. With renewed enthusiasm, he reported that he had thoroughly enjoyed pottering in the Ayres's garden and, quite incidentally, listening to "Lem's" plans for his forthcoming Broadway production of N. Richard Nash's latest play, *See the Jaguar*. I had the feeling that somewhere in the back of that shrewd, calculating mind, there was a plot brewing, a plot concerning the not entirely vague hope that there just might happen to be a tiny part for him in that play.

Disaster, for me at any rate, struck late in August, when the Ayres invited Jimmy to join them on a ten-day cruise to Cape

Cod aboard their yacht, with the proviso that he "pitched in as a member of the crew." Fully aware that Lem was about to start casting *Jaguar*, in which Jimmy now knew for certain there was a meaty part for him, he snatched at the invitation. Just how much he suspected that Lem's interest in him went somewhat beyond the role in question and more to the couch on which it would be cast, I wasn't sure. But from his previous reports of weekends up the Hudson, I foresaw what eventually came to pass. Jimmy later conceded grudgingly that, while Shirley turned a blind eye, he put out for Lem. I never did find out if there was a fly on the ceiling aboard the yacht, or if this time, it was flapping sails in the moonlight. With Jimmy, there were few graphic details, except those provided with the intention of shocking. The whole adventure was a gamble, although by now, Jimmy knew the game pretty well, yet not well enough to be sure it would definitely pay off. There were never any promises, only the carrot.

My problem was that Jimmy couldn't come up with his share of the rent for the period during his absence, which meant that we'd have to give up our room at the Iroquois. I couldn't afford the rent on my own, not even for the two weeks he'd be gone. Totally unconcerned about our future living arrangements, Jimmy left the problem entirely in my hands, his eye focused only on his mission. Understandable, but nonetheless difficult to cope with. Fortunately, walking up Sixth Avenue, I ran into a former classmate from UCLA, a girl I shall call Tina, who, until then, had been sharing a five-room summer sublet just two blocks north of the Iroquois on Forty-sixth Street. However, Tina's roommate had just left *her* in the lurch by moving in with a lover and husband-to-be, so she offered to let me move in and stay until the sublet expired in September. I accepted, provided that Jimmy could join us upon his return from Cape Cod. Tina had also known Jimmy at UCLA, and as there was more than enough room in the spacious flat, she readily agreed; the more help with the rent, she figured, the better.

Jimmy returned two weeks later and moved in with us, and for another month all went relatively well. A "railroad" apartment, necessitating passage through other people's sleeping quarters to reach the bathroom or kitchen, the flat was large and accommodating. It even afforded us the landlord's modest library of recorded classical music, in which we could explore the universe of Mozart and the exquisite concertos of Vivaldi's *L'Estro Armonico*. It was also the scene of our first sampling of pot, a single joint provided by an acquaintance of Jimmy's. After waiting for the magic, which never seemed to materialize, we shrugged and laughed it off dismissively; and laughed and laughed and laughed.

With our combined resources and additional help from Dizzy's Plaza Theater salary—she was still living at the Rehearsal Club, but taking scant meals with us—we were just able to scrape by. But, as the expiration date of the summer sublet neared, we realized we had to face the inevitable. Where would we all go next? There were four of us now. Dizzy's earnings barely covered her rent at the Rehearsal Club, mine barely covered my own expenses, Jimmy had no foreseeable income at present. *Jaguar* was still up in the air. Only Tina, who had a job as a salesclerk at a midtown department store, seemed marginally solvent. Confident we would be successful, the four of us decided to combine our strained resources and look for an affordable apartment further uptown, whereupon we embarked on the traditional New York apartment hunt, armed with the Sunday *New York Times* as our guide this time.

16

Fairmount

THE BROWNSTONE WAS JUST OFF CENTRAL PARK WEST AT 13 West Eighty-ninth Street. Our apartment was on the first floor and consisted of one large bedroom with twin beds, a sitting room with two daybeds, and a couple of lounge chairs. This gave onto an open kitchen with a counter separating it from the living area, beyond which there was an adequate bathroom. After the summer sublet, it seemed a bit cramped for four, but better by far than anything else we had seen in our price range. Dizzy said that she didn't want to share a room with Tina, a total stranger, so she and Jimmy ended up sharing the larger bedroom-cum-dining room with twin beds, while Tina and I shared the smaller living room with its two daybeds. There was little privacy, but we now were used to that from our previous arrangement. I had long since discovered that privacy was a rare luxury in New York living.

We came provided with little practical gear, so we had to beg and borrow unwanted kitchen supplies and such from friends. What we were unable to borrow were bed linens, so we were forced to sleep in bare blankets initially. One night, shortly after moving in, Jimmy returned from dinner with one of his more financially solvent friends, possibly Rogers or Alec, carrying a large carton. Without a single word of explanation and ignoring our dumb stares, he silently, carefully set about taking out two clean, baby-blue sheets, one matching blue pillowslip, a downy pillow, and a cozy blue blanket. In a performance that would have done justice to Marcel Marceau, he proceeded to make up his bed, smoothing and tucking each corner neatly, every fold made with consummate care. Once satisfied, he stripped down to his shorts, slipped between the fresh clean sheets, and snuggled beneath the blanket, cooing and gurgling into his pillow like a contented babe in its crib. Without a word, without so much as a look between us, the three of us rose as one, seized one side of his mattress, and dumped him out of bed, leaving him to laugh uncontrollably in a tangle of bedding on the floor.

For a time, it seemed like being back in the penthouse. We would dine—if you could call our perfunctory meals that—by candlelight; we would read poetry or plays and, inevitably, wind up playing brownstone bullfight. Down from the wall would come the cape, the sword, and the practice horns. Dizzy and I were assigned the roles of first and second bulls. Tina was dismissed as too short and lacking the proper spirit. Jimmy would strike the pose of a true matador, stomp his heels on the floor, and summon, "*Aie, toro!*" Invariably, after a quarter-hour or so of bull slaughter, a knock would come at our door. The gentle, Hispanic building superintendent would appear in his bathrobe and beg that the *corrida* cease for the night so that he and his wife, who lived directly below, could get some sleep. We blessed that super for his reliability. We didn't even have to bribe him. Contritely, Jimmy would oblige and put away his toys.

Unfortunately, within only a matter of weeks, community living became less attractive. Jimmy and I had lived in cramped quarters and managed pretty well to tolerate one another. But living with two women was another matter. If we weren't complaining about the maze of bras, panties, and stockings adorning the bathroom, they were complaining about toilet seats left up, bathtub rings, and snoring. We haggled over unwashed dishes, open windows, closed windows, menus, radio programs, you name it. It resembled a double marriage gone sour. The only comic relief came the night I woke everyone by falling out of bed. I had dreamed that I was spiraling down the twenty-three flights of stairs at CBS and somehow wound up on the floor. It was good for a laugh, but only one, after which we each went back to our corners for the next round.

Jimmy was becoming more irritable by the day as he waited for word from Lem Ayres about the dream role in *Jaguar*; I was getting more and more fed up with the spin I was in at CBS; Dizzy was desperately trying to laugh her way through the encroaching gloom; and Tina wondered why everyone was so irritable. Poor Tina, she didn't really deserve to be ostracized, but her attitude begged improvement.

Late one night, leaving a dour Tina to pout herself to sleep in her daybed, Jimmy, Dizzy, and I went out for chili and beans.

Jimmy broke the glum silence.

"Let's split this hole," he suggested.

"Thought you liked their chili," I reacted.

"I meant New York. Let's go to Indiana to the farm."

"Sure." Dizzy was whimsical. "Why not? We can catch the next plane."

But Jimmy persisted. "I mean it. You'd love Marcus and Mom's place. It's clean and fresh, with lots of trees and open fields. Good food, chicken, steak, all that jazz. Cows and pigs."

"Horses?" Dizzy wondered. She loved horses with a passion and purportedly rode like a champion.

"Of course, horses," Jimmy assured.

"I'm ready," Dizzy volunteered.

I worried about losing my job.

"Tell them you're sick," Jimmy dismissed.

"Sure," Dizzy encouraged. "Tina can call in and say you've got the flu or something. We haven't got a phone, so they can't check on you."

The idea was beginning to have a certain appeal. "Yeah. I guess they'd probably have to pay me if I were sick."

Jimmy pursued the idea. "You're supposed to get paid tomorrow, right? Well, if you don't pick up your check tomorrow, and you don't come back for a week, you'll have two checks waiting for you when you get back. It's a paid vacation!"

"It won't work," I sighed. "Besides, we can't afford the fare."

"What fare?" Jimmy grinned. "We'll hitchhike!"

"Hitchhike?!" Dizzy and I exclaimed in unison.

Jimmy soothed our worries airily. "It's only eight hundred miles. And it won't cost us a single cent, once we get to the farm."

Early the next day, packing a single suitcase, we gathered our combined resources and slipped out of the apartment into a foggy morning, leaving a note for the sleeping Tina requesting that she phone CBS to inform them that I had the flu. We took a bus over to the New Jersey Turnpike and started hitching in the direction of Indiana. After what seemed an interminable wait, a ride finally picked us up and took us as far as the end of the Pennsylvania Turnpike.

After a few more rides, toward the end of the day, we were picked up by a strange, weasel-like man, who had made not-so-subtle suggestions that we stop at a motel, rent a room for the night, and all get better acquainted. Instead, we had him drop us at the next town, a remote and desolate spot as it turned out. It was now past 10 P.M. Not a restaurant or diner was in sight, only an ice cream parlor, and it was about to close. With three free thumbs up, we ate our ice cream cones at the roadside in an icy drizzle, praying for a ride.

Mercifully, within minutes, a Nash Rambler station wagon pulled up, and we hopped in. There were two men in the front, the driver, who was a big guy, too big to be the owner of such a small car, and a young sailor.

"This fellow's only going as far as Youngstown," the driver assured us in a gruff voice. "After that, one of you can move up here with me. That'll give you all more room to spread out and catch some sleep."

The three of us exchanged wary glances. However, this new driver seemed open and friendly, just a good Joe who liked company on a long drive. "Helps keep me awake at the wheel," he explained.

After we dropped off the sailor, I moved up front, and we all settled down for the long ride ahead. Our ride would pass

fairly close to our destination in Fairmont, but it would take
the whole night to get there.

"Guess we should introduce ourselves," the driver suggested. "My name's Clyde."

Introducing us, Jimmy asked, "What d'you do, Mr.
Clyde?"

"It's not *Mr.* Clyde. Clyde's my first name. I'm a catcher."

"What do you catch?" Dizzy wondered.

"Baseballs," he replied. "I'm a professional ballplayer."

Using the lead, Jimmy began to draw him out. His full
name was Clyde McCullough, and he was a catcher for the
Pittsburgh Pirates. He was headed for an exhibition game in
Des Moines, Iowa, a game he would have to play after another day and night without sleep.

Then he turned the conversation to the three of us, wanting to know who we were, what we did, and where we were
headed.

"You know, more than any other people," he offered after
hearing our responses, "I admire show people, especially actors. When I think of all the sacrifice and heartbreak that must
go into a career in the theater, I can't help but wonder how
you kids manage to stick to it.

"I think it's great, having a specific goal like that and sticking to it, regardless of the odds. I mean, I know people generally don't have much respect for artists. This country's like
that, I guess. We never seem to give enough credit to our
artists, especially theater people, for the cultural benefits they
provide us. Why, hell, this is still one of the few countries in
the world where the arts aren't subsidized by the government.
It's embarrassing. Here we are, the greatest, richest country in
the world, and we haven't got the sense to subsidize the arts."

Mr. McCullough had just made three lifelong friends.

As we drove through the long night, he told us of his life
and his dreams, of his wife and kids, of his farm in Maryland.
We told him of our individual aspirations and our frustrating
lack of progress, and he consoled us and encouraged us to
keep at it. When we stopped for coffee at a roadside café, he
saw our hungry looks at the sight of the plates of ham and

eggs being carried past by the waitress, and he bought us three full meals and refused to take any money.

Back in the car, he asked if we'd like to ride on all the way to Des Moines to see the game, then ride back the next day and be dropped off at our destination in Indiana. Grateful for everything he had done, we thanked him sincerely for the kind offer, but declined, explaining we had very little time for our visit, as it was. We talked and laughed and sang our way through the rest of the night, and when he dropped us at the highway intersection just north of Fairmount, he drew me aside and whispered, "I know you kids haven't got much money," and pressed some bills into my hand. Touched, I shook my head and passed them back to him. This was to be our adventure, our test of fortitude. For me, it was at least. He understood and put the money back in his pocket. As he drove off, he looked back and waved, calling, "Good luck! Good luck!"

We stood and watched his car disappear down the road.

Jimmy said quietly, "What is essential is invisible to the eye." Dizzy was blinking back tears.

We never saw McCullough again, but I never forgot him. Twenty years later, I had occasion to speak to him by telephone. He had no idea that one of his passengers had been James Dean. He remembered every moment of that night drive, as if it had happened the night before. So had I.

Fairmount was a peaceful little farm town near Marion, not unlike the small farm towns in Wisconsin where I grew up. Set in an expanse of grainfields, interspersed with occasional sycamore groves, green glades, and dense woods, it boasted a modest Main Street, lined with shops and stores and the inevitable ice cream parlor. It was neat, polished, and unremarkable enough to have been a movie set on a Hollywood studio back lot. The "extras" that populated the scene, however, bore the unmistakable mark of authenticity, especially when they spoke in their distinctive Indiana accents.

The Winslow farm was situated just outside town, not far from the local cemetery and a trim little country church. A three-story, white-clapboard house, it was as neat and friendly as the Quaker family who lived inside. A large red barn and several smaller outbuildings set further back from the road finished the Winslow Homer-like portrait: pastoral, pristine, definitively American. The farm itself was surprisingly large and boasted the latest in modern equipment and lots of live-stock, including chickens, cows, sheep, and pigs. It was sur-rounded by sweeping fields of freshly harvested corn and wheat and bordered by thick woodlands with running brooks, silent ponds, and a variety of wild game. In all, it seemed an ideal place to grow up.

From the moment we arrived, Marcus and Ortense Winslow opened their home and hearts to us. Mom, as Jimmy called Ortense, was a gray-haired, soft-spoken woman with a quiet dignity. With obvious pleasure, she saw to it that we had plenty of food, clean warm beds, and TLC. With quiet joy and obvious affection, she attended to the whims and needs of her older "son," as she considered Jimmy, and showed special af-fection to Dizzy and me. We were, after all, her Jimmy's dear-est friends. Nothing was too good for us. The more Jimmy praised her cooking, the more lavish the meals became.

Marcus and Mom's only child, Marcus Jr., "Markie," as they called him, was more like a little brother to Jimmy than a cousin, and Jimmy doted on the five-year-old all the time we were there. Evenings, after dinner, Jimmy could be found on the living-room floor with Markie, playing the boy's favorite games or reading to him from his favorite books. As for Mar-cus Sr., a gentle man with a dry, canny humor, he gave us the run of the farm, taking the time and patience to show Dizzy and me around and explain the mysteries of modern farming. After a brief lesson, he offered to let me drive the tractor. Af-ter some prodding from Jimmy, I managed it quite well.

Having known Jimmy as an unattached loner for so long, it was a revelation to watch him reach out and touch his early roots and relate without guile or reservation to people he gen-uinely loved. Clearly, he was back in his element and relishing it. At the first opportunity, as if drawn by a magnet, he led Dizzy and me out to the barn. Inside, he moved directly to a shrouded object in one dark corner. In a single movement, with the deftness of a matador, he whipped off a dust cover and revealed his prized motorcycle beneath, a CZ, I'm reminded. He dusted it off as tenderly as you'd powder a baby's bottom, then mounted it, kicked it to life with a roar, and took off out of the barn, leaving Dizzy and me to follow through a cloud of exhaust and swirling straw.

We watched from the front porch as he raced up and down the level road that passed in front of the house, putting on a spectacular show for us that ended with a heart-stopping piece of bravado. Lying prone, stomach on the seat of the bike, feet extended straight out behind him, he roared past us in a display of skill to match any professional stunt rider. I held my breath until he righted himself and came to a skidding stop in front of us. Dizzy squealed with glee and, her nickname being apt, instantly accepted his invitation to a ride. As they took off, rearing up on the back wheel, I prayed that I would be spared. Of course, I was not. Trying not to look the chicken I was, I reluctantly climbed on behind Jimmy, clung to him for dear life, and never once opened my eyes. It would be the first of two times I ever rode a bike with Jimmy, two times too many.

As he wheeled the bike back into the barn and covered it again with tender care, he patted it fondly.

"Guess I'll never sell it," he remarked to Marcus. "It's like a friend. Friends are hard to find in the theater." It was early in his career, and he was yet to learn how wrong he was about that.

Often after dinner at the farm, we would linger at the big dining-room table while Jimmy painted verbal pictures of his life in New York for Marcus and Ortense, explaining the progress he was making there. Little Markie would listen in wide-eyed wonder, the love for his big "brother" shining on his face. As he talked, Jimmy would sometimes hold Ortense's painfully arthritic hands in his, gently stroking them, as if to caress away the pain. There was more love in that gesture than all the loving words in the dictionary, and one could see in her eyes that Ortense knew it.

Jimmy and I shared a bedroom, and Dizzy had one to herself. When everyone was bedded down for the night, Jimmy spoke to me in hushed tones. "Someday, when I make it, I'm going to see that Marcus and Mom sell this place and move to a drier climate, like Arizona, where Mom's arthritis won't bother her so much. Someday, they're going to have the kind of life they deserve without all the hard work and worry."

This was a Jimmy who seemed a far cry from the knife-wielding hustler on a Santa Monica street corner at midnight or the kept boy who depicted his homosexual benefactor as a slimy lizard. This was the motherless child who referred to mine as his "second mother," the friend who kissed me so tenderly on the lips as he tried to bring me to acknowledge my true identity and gave me his most prized possession as a token of his love. How was I to put them all together? Never in a lifetime.

A few days before it was time to leave, Jimmy took us to his old high school where he strutted his stuff and shared the limelight with Dizzy and me. His former drama teacher, Adeline Nall, was delighted to turn over her classes to the three of us. Jimmy spoke inspiringly on the art of acting; Dizzy demonstrated some modern dance movements; and I related some of my experiences in television, explaining the roles of director and writer. None of us was really qualified to lecture on our subjects, except Jimmy to some extent, but what an ego trip it was to see those rapt young faces eating up our words, totally enthralled. It also helped remind each of us that, despite our failure to achieve true success as yet, we truly loved the professions to which we aspired.

After too short a time, a call from Jane Deacy, the call Jimmy had been waiting for so anxiously, brought our rural idyll to an end. Lem Ayres wanted Jimmy back in New York to read for the role in *See the Jaguar*. We had slept well, eaten well, and been embraced with tender loving care. What more could we ask? So, pausing at the cemetery in Marion, where Jimmy stopped for a moment alone at his mother's grave, Marcus drove us to the main highway and left us there to hitchhike the eight hundred miles back to the city and the continuing adventure of finding our ways.

17

Go West, Young Man

WHEN WE GOT BACK FROM FAIRMOUNT, JIMMY DISCOVERED THAT the chances of his getting the *See the Jaguar* role seemed slimmer than they had been when we left town, mainly because another young actor had been reading the part during all the backers' auditions and now seemed in contention for the job. But Jimmy clung to the hope that he could do a better reading and snare the part, despite the odds. The character suited him even better than the witch boy in *Dark of the Moon* would have, and he was determined not to let this one slip through his fingers. No matter what it took.

He was all nerves the night of the reading, rushing around the apartment, trying to get dressed, in a state of panic.

"Oh, no!" he suddenly bellowed. "No, no, no, no!"

"What?" Dizzy risked, alarmed.

"I haven't got a clean shirt to wear! I haven't got a goddam shirt! Oow, oow, oow!" he wailed. "What'm I going to do?"

Reluctantly, I went to my drawer and took out my only clean shirt, kissed it farewell, and handed it to him, recalling the overcoat aria in *La Boheme*. "You get the part, and it's yours."

"We'll wait for you at the Paris!" Dizzy shouted to him as he dashed down the stairs and out into the street.

Later, in the Paris Theater, I tried to concentrate on the movie, but it was impossible. Dizzy closed the box office and met me downstairs in the coffee bar where we sat in silence drinking cup after cup until our nerves were totally jangled. Unable to sit still any longer, we left the Paris Theater and started walking down Fifty-eighth Street in the direction of the address where Jimmy had gone to read. Halfway there, we spotted him walking slowly up the street toward us, his overcoat collar turned up, hands thrust deep into its pockets, chin on chest, and a cigarette dangling from his lips. We stopped short by the sight of him, braced for the worst. He walked right up to us, then raised his head and grinned. The shirt, not to mention the part, was his.

During the weeks that followed, Jimmy spent most of his conscious hours learning his lines, running them with Dizzy or me until he was letter perfect. He also turned his attention to a far more difficult task for him than learning lines. Alec Wilder had composed a haunting little song for Jimmy's character to sing. The problem was Jimmy couldn't carry a tune. Night after night, Dizzy and I drilled him, making him repeat the simple minor-key melody again and again. It seemed a hopeless task, but we persisted until at last he almost had it. But, having conquered it, he refused to leave it. In the middle of the night, I would wake to the sound of him singing that damn song mournfully in the dark and have to bury my head under my pillow to shut it out. I can still hear it:

> "Green briar, blue fire,
> Blaze up higher and higher,
>   Dog barkin' on the hill,
>   Be still, my child, be still.
> Green briar, blue fire,
> Fire, fire, fire . . . fire, fire . . ."

The production was affording Jimmy his first real opportunity to work closely with top professional talent on Broadway, and he meant to wring the experience dry. Through his past experiences, mainly in television, Jimmy knew he had garnered himself a reputation for being difficult although he didn't understand why. On more than one occasion, he admitted to me that he was aware of the problem, but insisted that it wasn't his intention to be difficult; he simply expected far more from the actors and television directors with whom he was working than they were giving. He felt passionately that a director or an actor should be an artist, above all consistently true to himself and the script, and dedicated to the importance of the work. He had witnessed how, all too often in the mad rush of live television, there was little or no time to devote to the fine points, technical problems usurping most of a director's time and focus, the limited rehearsal time and the physical jumble of a live television studio floor challenging even the most experienced performers. As a consequence, many actors and directors with whom he worked had, in his estimation, failed him. Yet, to tell the truth, instead of according them the same respect that he felt was due him, Jimmy all too often demonstrated outbursts of rudeness and unprofessional behavior, about which he only managed to feel bad afterward. Clearly he could not, would not, mend his ways. Art, not good behavior, was god in his bible.

Fortunately during the *Jaguar* rehearsals, Jimmy learned to respect and trust his director, Michael Gordon, and the lead, Arthur Kennedy. As rehearsals progressed, his excitement mounted. Some nights, he would return to the apartment with detailed descriptions for us of all that had happened during the day. Vividly he explained the progress he was making with his character, thanks to guidance from Gordon and help from Kennedy, for whom his admiration was growing daily.

The play opened mid-November, out of town in Connecticut. Jimmy got good notices, but the critics were troubled by the play itself. Of course, I reminded myself that this was the main purpose of out-of-town trials: to refine the script and polish the production. But I couldn't help worrying for Jimmy's sake. It was his first Broadway play, and he would want it to have a respectable run.

Since my arrival in New York, I'd had few opportunities to witness Jimmy's acting. We had no television set, either at the Iroquois or the West Side apartment, and as a consequence, I'd only been able to see him a few times on other people's sets, at Jerry's Bar, or a couple of times as an observer on the studio floor and then only in rehearsal, not the best vantage point, as anyone who ever worked in early live television will attest. As a result, I looked forward to Jimmy's opening night in New York, but with cautious expectations.

On that cold December night, when the curtain came down at the end of the play, I sat stunned by what I had seen. For three full acts, Jimmy had played his part so convincingly, creating such a perfect illusion as his character, "Wally Wilkins," that I actually forgot it was Jimmy up there. Of course, I had read the play over and over, run lines with Jimmy until I knew them as well as he did, yet I, nonetheless, found myself deeply moved by his character's tragic fate.

Backstage, after the play, Jimmy's dressing room was jammed with friends and well-wishers. Compliments and praise filled the air. Through the crush, Jimmy caught my eye and mouthed, "See you at Sardi's. Ask for my table."

At Sardi's, while Jimmy worked the room, Dizzy and I anxiously held his table. Finally, after an age of waiting, the reviews arrived, and a hundred hands were clawing for copies of the *Times* and *Tribune*, eager to know the critics' views of the play.

Walter Kerr of the *Herald Tribune* concluded his indulgent critique with "What started out as a surprisingly convincing evening ends as a disappointingly contrived one." The rest of the critics agreed unanimously that the play was burdened with overly insistent symbolism and contrived attitudes, making it just too pat. On the other hand, all the critics were in accord on the subject of James Dean. Mr. Kerr captured the general sentiments of the others when he wrote: "James Dean adds an extraordinary performance in an almost impossible role: that of a bewildered lad who has been completely shut off from a vicious world by an overzealous mother and who is coming upon both the beauty and the brutality of the mountain for the first time."

Jimmy was instantly besieged. Admiration and acceptance flowed from everyone he knew and some he didn't. As I looked on, my thoughts were perplexing. Mixed with the genuine happiness I felt for him were feelings of envy and fear. Perhaps this was the beginning of the end of the struggle for

Jimmy. For almost three years, we had striven together to attain our individual goals. Never once had it occurred to me that one of us might arrive before the other. Never once had I thought that one of us might be left behind. Now, as I watched him across the room, I somehow knew it would be me. Had the time come to stop sharing the dream and start functioning alone? I thought back to the day when I drove away from the penthouse in Santa Monica for the last time, to the night when I read the note from Jimmy telling me that he had left for New York, and I suddenly felt abandoned once more. The last thing I heard as I left the restaurant was the sound of Jimmy's laughter as he bathed in the praise.

See the Jaguar ran only six performances before it closed. Ironically, Jimmy's first Broadway show had been a flop, but had proved a personal triumph for him. Now able to afford a place of his own, he decided to move out of the brownstone, back into the Iroquois. Since the three of us couldn't carry the rent by ourselves, we also moved out and struck out on our own. For a while, I shared a place with an acquaintance, while Dizzy took a room somewhere in midtown. We lost track of Tina.

After *Jaguar*, Jimmy was pretty hot around town. His agent was besieged with requests for interviews and offers. MGM's New York office sent for him and said they wanted to do a screen test, but Jimmy balked at the idea of leaving New York and working in Hollywood. Television offers were coming along more frequently, and his financial position was improving rapidly.

I gather Jimmy didn't see much of Dizzy after we gave up the brownstone. He told me later that she left for a Caribbean island and took a job dancing in a nightclub. Their paths weren't to cross again for another year or so and then only briefly in passing. She had returned to New York from her island while Jimmy just happened to be in town from Hollywood. After that, I believe he never saw or heard from her again. Nor did he ever mention her again to me.

It was at his suggestion that I moved back to the Iroquois several weeks later, taking an available room directly across the areaway from his. As the windows of our rooms faced each other, we now found ourselves seeing a lot more of each other again, literally as well as socially. On warm spring days, we could sit on the sills and chat, almost as if we were living together again. Almost. There would also be days when the shades were drawn. We never pressed one another to know what went on behind them. Some nights, at loose ends, he would come tapping at my door, just wanting company. Sometimes we'd sit on my bed and talk ourselves out, then fall asleep together. Usually, he'd be gone when I woke in the morning.

Shortly after our return from Indiana, my gyroscopic chores at CBS ended. I was promoted to the press-relations department where I worked with a tough old pro named Ann Harding, who was nothing like her namesake, the glamorous movie star of the thirties and forties. My Ann Harding wasn't the least bit glamorous. In fact, she was quite intimidating at first. A tough and opinionated New Yorker, she was in her early fifties, I estimated. But, beneath the Iron Maiden act, I soon found a kind, understanding friend. Sympathetic to my ambition to write, she allowed me to stay after hours and use the office typewriter and paper. Sometimes she provided me with soup and sandwiches for my dinners, maintaining that they were actually meant to be her lunch, but insisting that she hadn't been hungry. If I tried to thank her, she'd snap at me. I grew very fond of her.

Her largesse and indulgence resulted in several magazine articles and a tale that Jimmy encouraged me to set down in short-story form titled *Show the Nice Lady Your Tail, Daniel.* A coworker and friend at CBS managed to get it to Lillian Hellman, whose reported approval of it did much for my ego, though little to get it published.

At about the same time, I was introduced to an attractive, though slightly older, advertising executive who took a shine to me. I had been slowly expanding my circle of gay friends and allowing myself to go with the swim of things for a change. Although an affair with a middle-aged guy didn't exactly fulfill my erotic or romantic dreams, if Jimmy had a Rogers, I reasoned, why shouldn't I have one, too?

It was thus that I first met Eleanor Roosevelt, at one of my new admirer's dinner parties. Seated next to her and being utterly in awe, I was immediately terrified that she might engage me in conversation. I needn't have worried. Principal among the other guests was a purportedly famous male supper-club singer, who did most of the talking initially. With a reputation in the biz as "the lyricists' singer," he was, I assumed, more or less a male counterpart to the exquisite Mabel Mercer.

Unfamiliar with the "in" cuisine of the East Coast at the time, I had never been introduced to *consommé madrilène*, a clear tomato-based soup, usually served chilled and jellified. So, when it was served as the first course, before tasting it I remarked on the interesting novelty, unabashedly confessing that I had never had "Jell-O" at the beginning of a meal. "Mabel" instantly pounced on my gaffe, pointing out, with a hauteur that would have put Rogers Brackett to shame, that "Jell-O" was a working-class dessert, whereas anyone who knew anything knew that "*consommé madrilène*" was an elegant French appetizer. I was duly put back in my box.

Bless her, Mrs. Roosevelt merely turned to me and patted my hand. "You know," she offered, "you're quite right. I've always thought of madrilène as a sort of savory Jell-O myself." And then addressing herself to the guest of honor: "And on the contrary, it's become quite a common fad lately, you know. Even available in cans, I gather." Grateful for her saving grace, I was also pleased to note that Mabel took her remark as something of a rebuke and assumed a low profile for the rest of the evening. From that moment on, I became a devoted fan of Mrs. R's.

On my way home from CBS one evening in April, I heard someone call my name as I was passing the RCA building on Sixth Avenue. To my surprise, I found myself confronted by a smiling Bobby Ellis, my actor friend from CBS in Los Angeles. Delighted to see him, I asked him how long he was going to be in town.

"Until we're cancelled," he replied with a pleased-pussycat grin and explained that he had just been cast as "Henry Aldrich" in the new NBC television sitcom "The Aldrich Family," based on the long-running radio show of the same name. But that wasn't all. He had married his girlfriend, and they'd moved to town for the run of the show. Assuring me that his wife would be delighted to see me, he promptly invited me to the show's dress rehearsal that night and dinner afterward.

Scrunched down in my seat next to Bobby's wife halfway back in the vast darkness of the Roxy Theater, I found myself cringing at what was coming from the stage. Aside from three unidentified men who were seated five or six rows in front of us, the auditorium was, fortunately, dark and empty. Finally, unable to stop myself from indulging in one of my more unfortunate habits, I turned to Bobby's wife and whispered, "I've got an eight-year-old brother who could write better material than this."

Somehow my whispered remark carried in the empty house, and, without turning, one of the three men seated in front of us announced in a rather stern voice, "I just paid for five new scripts today, and they were all crap. If you think you can do better, bring me a good script. Otherwise, shut up." It was the director, Alex Segal.

Later, over dinner in a West Side restaurant, I apologized profusely to Bobby for the embarrassing incident, but he laughed it off.

"So, take him at his word," he suggested with a shrug.

"Write a script?"

"Why not?" his wife wondered, clearly assuming that anyone, even I, could write a sitcom script.

"Sure," Bobby agreed. "You get the general idea, don't you?"

"Yeah, I guess," I admitted. "I used to listen to "The Aldrich Family" on the radio when I was a kid. The format hasn't changed."

"So?" Bobby challenged. "I can look it over for you. You know, make sure the dialogue suits the characters as they are now. Anyway, you heard him. The material that's coming in is crap. What've you got to lose?"

That was a Friday night. On Sunday night, Jimmy read my first draft, shook his head, handed it back to me without saying a word, and went off to see a movie. Hardly encouraged, I stayed up half the night rewriting. On Monday morning, Bobby read what I had written over the weekend, made a few line changes, and turned the script in to Segal. I waited in agony for his reaction. A career move from press-relations writer at CBS to scriptwriter at NBC could only be considered up. Segal's answer came the next day. He would pay me the exorbitant amount of one hundred seventy-five dollars for my script and seventy-five for fixing each of the five scripts he had previously bought, about which he had complained. I had no agent, of course, but I wasn't about to quibble. The agent could come later.

Living through my first show, the one I had written in one weekend, the one that would be broadcast live coast to coast on network television the following week, with me credited as the writer, was an excruciating experience.

Watching the rehearsals was painful enough, and they didn't bode well for the broadcast. I was to observe the on-air, live show from what was then called the Sponsor's Booth, a soundproofed room overlooking NBC's Studio 1A, which I was informed by a proud network executive, already ensconced in the best seat, was the studio from which Maestro Arturo Toscanini's NBC Symphony Orchestra broadcast each week. The Booth boasted rather grand upholstered chairs and a wall-to-wall window that overlooked the studio floor below, as well as a giant television monitor. I don't recall who sponsored the show, but a group of about seven suits, presumably including the sponsors and their ad men, filed in and took their seats for the broadcast, the ad men and the network executive confidently nodding and assuring the sponsors that the show was sure to be a huge ratings winner.

As the final seconds ticked down to airtime, I quietly slipped out of the Booth and spent the first five minutes of the show losing my lunch in the men's room. When I returned, the assemblage was craning to see the action below and mercifully ignored me. I sat as far in the back and as near the door as possible and listened in agony to each insipid line of dialogue piped in over the audio system.

It's still embarrassing for me even to mention that first inept script, but I feel somewhat mollified recalling that one small role was played by a relatively unknown young actor at the time named Paul Newman. Well, I suppose we've all got to start somewhere. Even Jimmy did that silly Pepsi-Cola ad.

When my stint as rewrite man on the "Aldrich" show ended, I approached Segal for his advice. Did he think I should pursue a writing career in television and, if so, how? "Go west, young man," was his reply. I wondered how far west, worried that he meant Hollywood. "That's where television's headed, kid," he predicted. "That's where we'll all wind up." True to his word, we did. At least, he and Jimmy and I did.

Quitting my job at CBS, I bought a one-way plane ticket back to L.A., packed my duds, and paid my final week's rent at the Iroquois.

It was a sunny May afternoon, and I was hurrying up Sixth Avenue toward Cromwell's, already late for a farewell lunch date with Jimmy, when I heard a familiar summons.

"Hey, Willie!"

I stopped and turned. He was leaning against the RCA building, one foot propped behind him on a polished brass fireplug sticking out of the wall. I had walked right past him without noticing. He gave me a smile, the one that always managed to get to me.

"I thought we were meeting at Cromwell's," I said. "Sorry I'm late. I've been packing."

"Got these for you," he said, handing me three books, which surprised me, as he wasn't much of a reader and rarely gave gifts. One book was a paperback of Carson McCuller's *The Heart is a Lonely Hunter*; another was a paperback of Virginia Woolf's *Orlando*.

"Ever read it?" I hadn't. "Let me know what you think."

When I did read it on the plane to L.A., I wondered if he meant Woolf's use of androgyny to apply to me, to himself, or to both of us. I never asked, but I suspect it was to himself.

The third book was a hardcover copy of *The Maurois Reader*, comprising three novels, *The Silence of Colonel Bramble*, *The Weigher of Souls*, *Bernard Quesnay*, and several short stories, one of which, *Harpies on the Shore*, revealed the source of one of his frequent admonitions to me. I opened it, highly curious now.

On the flyleaf he had written in his childlike printed handwriting:

> "To Bill—While in the aura of meta-
>   physical [*sic*]
> whoo-haaas, ebb away your displeasures on
>   this.
> May flights of harpies escort your win<u>ge</u>d
>   trip of vengeance."

It was signed, "James Dean." Not "Jimmy," or "Deaner," but "James Dean."

I grinned and teased, "At last! An autograph!"

"Guard that with your life," he advised mockingly. "It'll be worth a small fortune one day."

"Promise," I teased.

"Promise," he assured me.

Then remembering, I told him I'd left some of my books and clothes in his room. "Hope you don't mind. Too much luggage as it is."

"Don't worry, I'll look after them." He looked over the rim of his glasses with a knowing grin and added pointedly, "Until you get back."

Our parting handshake turned into a lingering hug. I could still feel his warmth as I walked back to the hotel. I could still feel it on the plane back to Los Angeles. Even as I recall the moment now, I can still feel it. Funny how a simple hug can stay with you so long.

18

A Winged Trip of Vengeance

IT WAS STRANGE BEING BACK IN L.A., STRANGE AND NOT A LITTLE depressing. In the first place, it wasn't New York; in the second, I was back living with my grandparents until I could get some work and find a place of my own. I signed with Frank Cooper, purported to be one of the best writers' agents, and went home to wait for the phone to ring. Frank's stellar reputation notwithstanding, I was still waiting a month later and getting anxious. With my savings running low and growing desperate, I started phoning Frank twice daily. Impatient with my calls, he had finally asked me a somewhat relevant question: "What did you come out here to do?"

That was an easy one. "To write, of course."

"So, go write something!"

Turning to my Olivetti, I turned in a half-hour pilot for a television sitcom. Within a couple of weeks, on the basis of my sample script, I was offered my first writing job in Hollywood. However, it wasn't in television, but radio, specifically a new show to star the currently popular comedian Stan Freberg. Stan would be playing a Wisconsin nerd, freshly transplanted to Los Angeles and living with relatives, whom, of course, he would soon drive nuts with his nerdiness. Having been told I was a former Wisconsinite—hopefully not a nerd—the producers felt I might have special insight into the character. Despite everyone's best efforts, the series wasn't picked up after the first order, and several months later, I was once more looking for work. Figuring two Olivettis were better than one, Frank decided to team me with another of his clients and submitted us for several jobs, using sample scripts from each of us. Fortunately, my new partner was a likable, easygoing young writer named Ted Hartman, who had a couple of youngsters and a tolerant wife, who fed us well and encouraged us at every opportunity. Ted also turned out to be second-generation show biz, his father being Paul Hartman, a well-known actor-comedian at the time who was the star of a new television sitcom, "Pride of the Family," also starring Fay Wray of *King Kong* fame. While visiting the set of the show with Ted one day, I was introduced to the young actress who was playing Hartman's and Wray's thirteen-year-old daughter, a charmer named Natalie Wood. How could I have imagined that, within two years, she'd be starring with Jimmy in *Rebel Without a Cause* and eventually become a friend? A small world indeed, Hollywood.

Over the next few months, Ted and I churned out a sitcom pilot for NBC, "Our Uncle Dudley." In the title role, it would star Rudy Vallee, former crooner of the thirties and forties, then playing comedic characters in features. The show was also adorned by the presence of the reigning queen of comic *grande dames*, the Marx Brothers' inimitable Margaret Dumont. Sadly, however, "Our Uncle Dudley" was a dud and never got picked up. Ted and I glumly went back to our Olivettis. But at least we'd been paid.

Meantime, Jimmy and I managed to keep in touch by phone sporadically. As he could now afford long-distance phone calls, whereas I could not, he would call from time to time to find out how I was doing and bring me up to speed on his own progress. Shortly after I'd left for L.A., he moved out of the Iroquois into an apartment of his own on West Sixty-eighth Street. He'd appeared in leads in almost a dozen television dramas, only a few of which I'd been able to catch. As for work in the theater, his friend, director Frank Corsaro, had cast him in a nonspeaking role in an off-Broadway production of *The Scarecrow* at the Theatre de Lys, which sadly closed in less than a week. He'd also been cast in an Actors Studio production, Calder Willingham's *End as a Man*, but had to bow out before the opening due to his television commitments. He was clearly on a roll, granted a small roll, but enjoying the ride. Then, sometime before Christmas, he phoned with the news that he'd been cast in a new play, *The Immoralist*, adapted from a story by André Gide. With Geraldine Page and Louis Jourdan in the lead, it was headed for Broadway in the spring. Jimmy would be playing the provocative role of a homosexually seductive, Arab houseboy. That begged a comment, but I prudently held my tongue. Jimmy did not take teasing well, and this was already a fraught subject. I didn't hear from him during the rehearsals, but tried to phone him after the opening. I'd read his good review in the *New York Times* and wanted to congratulate him, but was unable to reach him despite several tries. I finally gave up, confident he'd be in touch sooner or later.

Indeed, a week or so later, I was wakened one morning by the sound of banging on the door of the apartment. I couldn't imagine who would raise such a ruckus until I heard the voice out in the corridor, "Hey, Willie, open up!" Who else? When I opened the door, I found him leaning against the jamb, shaking his head.

"Man, I thought you died in there," he teased.

I expressed my astonished delight in seeing him.

"C'mon, grab some clothes," he said. "We're going to the desert. Gadge wants me to get a tan."

"Gadge?"

"Kazan. I'm doing a picture for him."

I grabbed some things and jumped into the passenger seat of his rented convertible. But it wasn't until we were bucking traffic on the newly completed Hollywood Freeway that he opened up and told me about his new role, a kid from a farming community near Salinas. The script was based on a book by John Steinbeck, *East of Eden*.

"So, where'd you say we're headed?" he asked, before I could pump him for anything more about the project.

I mentioned Borrego Springs in the Anza-Borrego Desert, a favorite retreat of mine, about an hour's drive south of Palm Springs between the Salton Sea and the mountains to the west.

"Sounds good," he nodded. "Palm Springs is too commercial, anyway. Wouldn't want to run into any Hollywood types, would we?" The question was punctuated by his familiar sardonic chuckle.

Impatient to know how he got a lead in a Kazan movie, I now pressed him for details. Recalling it all, he seemed mischievously amused.

During rehearsals of *The Immoralist* and the subsequent out-of-town run in Philadelphia, it seemed that Jimmy—typically, I couldn't help thinking—began to feel that producer Billy Rose was demanding changes that didn't make sense. He watched with mounting frustration while what he perceived as the beauty and power of the play were undermined until he could see only a hollow shell of what had promised to be a great piece of theater. He began to clash with Rose about the changes, something the boss wasn't about to tolerate. Hoping to avoid a showdown, Jimmy turned for support to Daniel Mann, who had replaced the original director. Mann, however, sided with his producer, possibly afraid of being replaced himself. Jimmy felt betrayed and lost all respect for Mann as well at that point. To make matters worse, just before the play opened, Mann turned on Jimmy when he was seeking direction, and in front of the entire cast shouted, "What makes you think you're so important here? You're the least of my worries! I've got other people to attend to!" That was the last straw. Jimmy took a walk and his understudy, Billy Gunn, had to step in. It was of course assumed that, according to Equity rules, Jimmy would be fired. But the incident was smoothed over by the Equity representative and, mollified by Jane Deacy, Jimmy went back to work. Temporarily.

It would have been a matter of normal procedure for any good agent to propose Jimmy for the role of Cal Trask in Elia Kazan's upcoming Warner Brothers production of *East of Eden*. But Jane Deacy wasn't merely any good agent; she was one of the best. Besides, to Jimmy, she was "Mom," and to

Jane, he was her prize duckling. She later confided to me that when she read the screenplay for *Eden*, she knew at once that the role of Cal Trask, a motherless lad with a boyish exuberance, a desperate need and infinite longing for love and acceptance, was ideal for Jimmy. Apparently, what she didn't know was that she and Kazan were already on the same wavelength about her client.

According to what Elia Kazan wrote later, James Dean had initially only been one more promising actor, a member of the Actors Studio, one to be watched and catalogued for future reference. He had seen Jimmy act on a number of occasions—doing his audition for the Studio, in television plays, in *See the Jaguar*, and in the out-of-town run of *The Immoralist*—and each time, he had observed something he now needed for his next picture. He knew in his gut that this kid with the strange, edgy quality would be perfect for his lead in *East of Eden*. As for Jimmy, he had always looked upon Kazan as a demigod, a great artist, a master of his craft, a champion of his school of acting, a man who had shaped the talents of his principal idol, Marlon Brando. Kazan personified everything Jimmy respected, but he was about to become something more, something that Jimmy couldn't know: the maker of his destiny.

As we sped through the desert, Jimmy chortled as he recalled the behind-the-scenes machinations that went on during the rehearsals for *The Immoralist*, machinations of which, he hastened to add, he had only gradually become aware. With Jimmy in mind for *East of Eden*, Kazan had him read for the part while *The Immoralist* was still in rehearsal and clearly made his mind up. Although the deal with Warner Brothers hadn't been set as yet, Kazan was planning a screen test of Jimmy and had assured him in confidence that he had the part, except for one problem: Jimmy had a run-of-the-play contract with *The Immoralist*. If the play opened to good reviews and had even a modest Broadway run, Warner Brothers wouldn't let Kazan delay the start of production on *East of Eden* for him. Jimmy got the hint.

On the opening night of *The Immoralist*, to the astonishment of the cast and fury of the production staff, and relying entirely on Kazan's word, Jimmy gave his two-weeks' notice; it was done quietly, but with a certain satisfaction in light of the bad treatment he felt he'd suffered at the hands of the producer and director. Making his revenge sweeter still, when the reviews came out, the critics had singled him out for special praise and predicted a great future for him in the theater. Subsequently, for those sixteen performances, he won the David Blum Award as the most promising actor of the year.

We were heading for the desert now with the rental top down so Jimmy could fully benefit from the sun. As we sped along, I realized I had never seen him in such high spirits. He was upbeat and confident, and clear in his thinking about the picture. It was only when the subject of Hollywood came up that he bristled.

"I took a lot of crap out here the last time," he ruminated, "but I'm not going to let them do that to me again. This time I'm going to make damn sure of it."

I recalled the many sessions we'd had before he left for New York and knew exactly how he was feeling. As a young hopeful in Hollywood, too many doors had been slammed in his face. Too many casting directors and agents had treated him like dirt. Too many arrogant people in positions of power had demanded too much bootlicking. Back then, he'd been a naïve, unaccomplished kid, fresh off an Indiana farm, who'd bought into the prescribed methods for getting ahead in Hollywood. He had danced to the tune of all the would-be "Caligulas," as he'd characterized them, and wound up with little to show for it. But that was then, and this was now.

"I don't need Hollywood," he vowed. "I just want to make this picture and get the hell back to New York. Maybe they don't need me, either, but now I've got the advantage. I've got something they want, and if they want me, they're going to have to pay for it."

"You sound like a hustler," I teased.

"Yeah," he grinned, privately pleased with where his thoughts were. "And I'm gonna fuck 'em like they've never been fucked before."

But this time, talent was *all* he had for sale, he asserted.

There would be no Tinseltown crap, no gross publicity campaigns for James Dean, no false laurel wreaths, no blind acceptance of movieland standards, no falling into the trap of believing that stardom brought with it fulfillment and completion. Initially, his aim had been higher, far higher than Hollywood, and he didn't mean to lose sight of his original goals. He still had a long way to go, a lot to learn before he could actually think of himself as having arrived. But along the way, he would not permit Hollywood to bury him in the permanent grave of stagnation as it had done to so many before him. Hollywood would have to accept him on his terms or not accept him at all. About this, he was absolutely adamant. I found myself wondering how long he could hold to such lofty principles and display such an arrogant attitude. Hollywood had a long history prior to the arrival of James Dean and had doubtless encountered a fair number of high-minded types in the past. But an uncountable number of actors had been left on the cutting-room floor and thrown out with the trash. I knew Jimmy had the tenacity of a Gila monster, but even a Gila monster has to roll over on its back to allow the poison in its jaws to flow.

While we stopped for lunch at a roadside diner, Jimmy recounted how he'd spent Christmas with Marcus, Mom, and Markie and taken his prized motorbike back with him to New York. This was a dream he'd long entertained. Of course, New York was hardly the place to bike free as a bird, but apparently any place will do when you're aching to roar. I had visions of him doing stunts like the one I'd witnessed him do in Fairmount, only down Fifth Avenue, instead. However, he satisfied his urge by buzzing around town from appointment to appointment, parking the machine in the entranceway of his apartment building when he wasn't on it, which, I assumed, hadn't been often. Apparently gossips around Gotham were now accusing him of copying Brando. He just shrugged it off. After all, he pointed out, he'd been biking long before anyone had even heard of Marlon Brando. Ironically, however, the week before he was to leave for Hollywood, he'd taken a spill, which prompted Kazan to instruct him to "stay off that fucking motorcycle!" So instead of biking across country as he'd originally intended, he stored the bike until he could get settled in L.A. Then, he'd have it shipped out.

As we resumed our drive south through the desert, we both fell silent for a time. I don't know what Jimmy was thinking, but in my mind, I was reviewing his path, his journey to this extraordinary moment in his life, suddenly on the brink of possible stardom. Above all, what stood out for me was not just his fierce determination to succeed, but his sincere and relentless dedication to his art. I realized that, at long last, it wasn't just bullshit.

An actor's duty is to interpret life had become his credo, one he pronounced repeatedly, echoing his god, Stanislavsky. *To do so he must be willing to accept every experience that life has to offer. In fact, he must seek out more of life than life puts at his feet. In the short span of his lifetime, an actor must learn all there is to know, experience all there is to experience—or approach that state of perfection as nearly as possible. He must be almost superhuman in his struggle to inform himself. He must be relentless in his efforts to store away in the warehouse of his memory everything he might be called upon to use in the expression of his art. He must be willing to dredge up from his subconscious every dark mystery hidden there. Nothing should be more important to the artist than life and the living of it, not even the ego. To grasp the fullness of life is the actor's duty; to interpret it, his problem; and to express it, his dedication.*

As a disciple of this concept of art and the artist, Jimmy had made it his goal to do his best to attain, at any expense, a state of perfection as an actor through life experience. He had refused to consider any limitation in his quest for that experience. Conventional barriers had to be sidestepped if they interfered; accepted patterns had to be avoided if they threatened to hamper. Even the ego, the all-important self, which most protect at all costs from the possibility of abuse, even the sacrosanct "I" had to be ignored in order to suffer whatever pain and accept whatever reward that came with the search. The dedication had to be complete.

I studied him as he focused on the road ahead and suddenly felt I saw him for the first time. At twenty-three, he was more gifted, more dedicated, more insightful than anyone I knew of our age. In obedience to Stanislavsky principles, he had opened his heart and mind, had consumed every course of life's sometimes bitter banquet that had been offered him without regard to personal or popular taste, storing its nourishment for future use. He had given and taken more than most, and, although I'd been slow to see it, he was, in his mindset, already far ahead of his century.

Deep in his own thoughts for a time, he finally glanced over to catch me studying him and embraced me with his smile.

The desert heat was now frying us, so we stopped for gas and bought cooling soft drinks. Jimmy sat on a bench in the shade of the station and stared off over the vast expanse of shimmering sands, his expression serious, his mind obviously churning. I joined him. We sat there in silence a few minutes, then finally he chuckled sardonically and said, "Gadge thinks I could win an Oscar for this role."

In our younger, more cynical days, we'd joked about the Academy of Motion Picture Arts and Sciences and their yearly Oscar competition, convinced it was a joke and probably manipulated. Back when the rules were less rigidly enforced, word around town had it that, among other ruses, executives of the major studios enrolled their assistants, secretaries, and even bit players and stand-ins, as Academy members to enlist their votes for the studios' contending nominees. We'd decided then, if ever the day came when we were up for an Academy Award, we'd naturally refuse a nomination, much less accept an Oscar. We were very young.

"Of course, if you won, you'd refuse it," I said with a straight face.

"Try me, and see," he grunted.

Back on the road, he ruminated for a few minutes, then shook his head and said conclusively, "They'll never vote me an Oscar . . ."

I was about to ask him how he could be so sure when something suddenly hit the windshield and bounced off. He

Jimmy with lariat, between shots on *Giant*, 1955.

Jimmy, right, as Malcolm in a UCLA production of *Macbeth*, 1950.

Bill Bast, poolside, 1950.

Jimmy with Bill's mother on the "penthouse" roof, 1950.

Jimmy's signed photo, "To my 2nd Mother" for Bill's mother, 1951.

Beverly Wills' birthday party. Clockwise, from top: Bill, Jimmy,
Debbie Reynolds, Beverly. June 1951.

ALL EXCITED. Beverly Wills (above) has told Louella Parsons of her engagement to wed William Bast. Beverly, a UCLA co-ed, is the daughter of Comedienne Joan Davis. Bast heads television for Columbia Broadcasting System. Beverly is 19 years old.

Beverly Wills, Joan Davis' Daughter, to Wed CBS Aide

By Louella O. Parsons
Motion Picture Editor International News Service

Beverly Wills, the 19-year-old daughter of famous Comedienne Joan Davis and Cy Wills, is engaged to marry William Bast, TV director for CBS.

The happy young lady telephoned to tell me that she had just announced her engagement to her sorority sisters at the Gamma Phi Beta house at University of California Los Angeles.

"I want you to know right away, too," the excited young lady said. "Of course, I'm going to finish school — I'm just a freshman.

"I've know Bill for a year and have been in love with him for months," she continued.

"Mother, who is in New York, telephoned and asked me not to marry until I had completed my education."

When I commented that Beverly, whom I have known since she was a very little girl, sounded exactly like her mother, she said:

"Yes, don't we? But my voice doesn't cost as much as mother's."

Beverly has been on the air with her famous Ma a number of times.

She's always had a sense of humor. When she was a little girl, she called herself Beverly Wills of Beverly Hills.

Louella Parsons announcement of Bill's and Beverly's engagement, *L.A. Times*, January 10, 1952.

J.A.'s Wonderful Awards

Junior Achievement National Convention, New Jersey, 1946. Bill Bast, front row, second from right; Bayard Colgate, crouching at left.

© Author's collection.

Yale Club rooftop restaurant, New York City, 1946. Back row, from left: Bill Bast, Beatrice and Bayard Colgate.

© Author's collection.

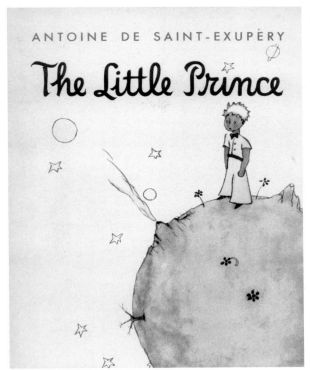

ANTOINE DE SAINT-EXUPÉRY

The Little Prince

Bill Bast, photo by Roy Schatt, 1956.

Jimmy, caged, in *See The Jaguar*, 1952.

To Bill

While in the area of metaphysical whooo-haaas, ebb away
your displeasures on this.
May flights of harpies
escort your winged Trip of
vengeance.

James Dean

Jimmy's inscription to Bill inside *The Maurois Reader*, 1953.

© AUTHOR'S COLLECTION.

Jimmy as Cal Trask in *East of Eden*, 1954.

Jimmy washing his new white Porsche Speedster, 1955.

1955. Jimmy tells his favorite Arnold Schoenberg joke; Beulah Roth in background, enjoying it. A violinist in rehearsal of a new Schoenberg concerto, daunted by the difficult score, complains to the composer: "A man would need six fingers to play your concerto . . . !"

Jimmy gives the tag line, Schoenberg's sardonic reply to the violinist: "I'll wait."

Jimmy with "Marcus," Elizabeth Taylor's gift kitten, at the Roth's apartment. 1955.

Jimmy entertains "Marcus" at his Sutton Street house, 1955.

Kendo match, Los Angeles, 1955. From the left, Bill, Jimmy and Beulah's niece and Beulah.

Kendo match, Los Angeles, 1955. Jimmy on the sidelines, alone and pensive. Note the "receding" hairline shaved back a couple of weeks before, to age his character, Jett Rink in the last scenes of *Giant*. He would still look much like this when he died.

Bill Bast portrait for softcover edition of his Dean biography, 1956.

For: Bill Bast

By hand.

HOTEL Algonquin
59 West 44th St., New York 36, N.Y.

What I tried to say was:

Don't jump on a cheap
bandwagon — especially
when it's an hearse.

Rogers Brackett

Rogers Brackett's
note to Bill, 1956.
© AUTHOR'S COLLECTION.

JAMES DEAN

A BIOGRAPHY BY WILLIAM BAST

Front of the
hardcover edition of
Bill's 1956
biography showing
Roy Schatt's photo
of Jimmy wearing
Bill's sports jacket.

Seita Ohnishi's memorial to James Dean at Cholame, California.

slammed on the brakes and skidded to a stop in the sand beside the highway, then jumped out and ran back a few yards, looking for whatever it was we'd hit. I got out and joined him. Spotting it, he crouched and gently scooped up a small bird that was lying, wounded, in the road near where we'd hit it. Tenderly, he stroked the dying creature, murmuring to it like a heartsick mother over an injured child. After a minute or so, the little thing stopped trembling and died in his hands. He scraped a hole in the sand beside the road and buried it.

The death of that bird was strangely affecting. That a creature so free, so independent, so beautiful, should die so suddenly and arbitrarily, seemed especially sad. The death of an earthbound creature, shackled by the laws of gravity, might have seemed less so in comparison since death might have brought a liberation from all that held it down. But the death of a living creature that soared so enviably high, to a place beyond our natural reach, an elusive thing of ineffable beauty and infinite mystery, seemed somehow sadder. We remained silent for the rest of the drive.

19

Borrego Springs

The only hotel in Borrego Springs at the time was situated somewhat above the road, nestled near the base of the hills, with the Anza-Borrego Desert sweeping away into the distance before it. It consisted of a group of unpretentious wooden structures, comprising a central building, flanked by smaller, individual cabins. The main building consisted of a reception area, a central dining room with kitchen beyond, and, unseen, offices in the back. Outside along the front, there was a veranda where guests could sit and have drinks while taking in the panoramic expanse of open desert and the distant mountains to the south. However, at the time, there didn't seem to be any other guests to enjoy it, only us. The surrounding area appeared to be quite isolated with no other buildings, hotels, homes, or stores as far as the eye could see. The silence was almost eerie, yet there was an exhilarating, expansive feeling about it all. We were to have Borrego Springs very much to ourselves.

After checking in, we were shown to our cabin, which consisted of one large room with twin beds and a bath. It was already late in the day, so, hot and sweaty from the long drive, we showered and went for a swim in the generous pool, then fell asleep in the sun on our chaises. That evening, we had dinner in the dining room, then sat on the veranda awhile, drinking margaritas, after which we took a long walk out into the desert along the road that ran in front of the hotel. The night was so clear that the stars seemed within reach and the silence so complete that we hardly spoke. Jimmy draped an affectionate arm around my shoulder as we walked back to the cabin.

A little later, lying in bed in the dark, my head was swimming from the margaritas. I was sure I'd have a bitch of a headache in the morning, but I didn't care. Jimmy was back, and everything felt right.

Words spoken in the dark that night and never forgotten:

"You okay?" he asked softly from his bed.

"Couldn't be better."

"Sure 'bout that?"

I hesitated for a moment, not sure if it had been a signal, then gathered my courage. "Guess there's always room for improvement."

I heard a deep, slow sigh, then, "Well, then, there now . . ." that old familiar non sequitur of his. "Why don't you c'mon over here?"

And so, there it was, *el momento de verdad*, as Jimmy might have put it, the moment of truth—in the bullring, the moment just before the kill.

In the heartbeat between his invitation and my response, thoughts and memories flashed through my mind with the speed of light: a midnight street in Santa Monica, Jimmy flashing a knife; midnight talks, intimacies, and confessions; his erection pressed against me in bed, his arm around my waist; endless giggling with giggle-some Dizzy, his insistence that he'd never really fucked her only "played around"; his tortured relationship with Rogers and admitted "opportunistic" submissions to at least one television director named Stevens, others only hinted at; the kiss before the absurd Astor Bar exercise. Surely this was wake-up time, if ever there would be one.

I slipped under the sheet beside him, my heart beating so hard I was sure he could hear it.

"What took you so long?" he wondered.

"Scared, I guess."

"Nothin' to be scared about."

And there wasn't.

• • •

The next morning, we rose early. The desert was glorious; life was glorious. Two horses were saddled for us, and we rode out into the hills above, where a chuck wagon breakfast was waiting with enough bacon and eggs, flapjacks and maple syrup, and hot coffee for a dozen guests, even though there were only the two of us. After eating our fill, we mounted up to ride back, pausing to scan the desert below bathed in the mellow light of the early-morning sun. It stretched from horizon to horizon before us and was framed by haze-blue mountains. After denying my true feelings so long, I was finally unburdened. I couldn't remember when I had felt so free, so expansive.

Suddenly, without thinking, I spread my arms, as if to embrace it all, and on an impulse shouted at the top of my lungs, "Hello, America! Hello, America! Deaner and Willie say, 'hello!'"

It was a spontaneous outburst from Jimmy's less-than-spontaneous friend, and it broke him up. He laughed and he laughed, until tears filled his eyes, and I was more pleased than I can say. My heart sang, and I renamed my horse Pegasus, declaring that I would ride him into the sun.

"I *am* the sun," came Jimmy's reply. And for me, he was.

During our remaining days in Borrego, I never saw Jimmy so relaxed, nor had I ever felt so relaxed with him. There were no brooding silences, no unpleasant mood swings, no tortured anxieties. Jimmy was happy, and that was the miracle. If only it would last. What would it be like, I wondered, when we left this safe haven and returned to the real world? I reassured myself by repeating over and over in my mind the one word I had never before been able to use in its newest sense: "We."

Immediately upon our return from the desert, Jimmy took me with him to the Famous Artists Agency in Beverly Hills where he was due to meet with his new agent, Dick Clayton. Dick, he explained, would be handling his affairs for Jane Deacy while he was in Hollywood. Still unshaven and shabbily dressed—a definite no-no at the time—we were led into Dick's classy office by a dubious secretary. Dick was a young

agent who had been selected to manage the problem child
from New York, and, judging from his warm reaction, he obviously had been prepared for his new client. Ignoring our un-
kempt appearances, he shook our hands with what appeared
to be genuine pleasure. Jimmy introduced me as his best friend
and "a damn good writer," which both pleased and embarrassed me. I had suddenly become particularly conscious of
my behavior, not wanting to arouse suspicions about Jimmy
and our new "relationship."

Jimmy had had almost a week to brood over his first confrontation with Hollywood. It was obvious that Dick, being
his first contact with the town that was a potential threat to
him, was due to be first in line to deal with the large chip on
Jimmy's shoulder. Almost immediately, however, it was clear
that Dick posed no threat at all. A mild-mannered, unpretentious guy with a gentle, nonjudgmental approach, he seemed
determined to put Jimmy at ease. As Dick invited us to sit
down, I could tell from Jimmy's attitude that he was out to
test this guy. Not knowing what to expect, I tried to appear
laid back, but was actually pretty tense.

Initially, they discussed plans for the picture: an advance
from the studio for Jimmy, the problem of an apartment for
him, and his need of a car. During all this, Jimmy squirmed in
his seat, scratched himself, put his feet on Dick's desk, grunted
monosyllabically in reply to questions, and picked his teeth.
But Dick played it easy, refusing to acknowledge the game. Finally, Jimmy got up and perched himself on the edge of Dick's
desk.

At that point, without warning, Dick's office door flew
open, and an older agent burst in from the outer office, bellowing, "Dick, where the fuck's that goddam secretary?" Ignoring Jimmy and me, the intruder blustered on for a moment
or two about the inefficiency of some girl in the office. He had
come to the wrong place at the wrong time.

Jimmy quietly cut the intruder off midtirade. "Excuse me.
Would you mind getting the hell out of here?"

Stopped short, the loudmouth eyed Jimmy as if he were
garbage, then turned to Dick. "Who's the punk?"

Dick laughed uncomfortably and introduced the intruder as a senior agent with the agency.

"I don't give a fuck who you are," Jimmy responded easily. "You know, you're pretty goddam rude. You come in here braying like an ass when we're in the middle of a conference. Haven't you any manners?"

I held my breath, waiting for the response. Taken aback only momentarily by the sudden and unexpected presence of his agency's hot new client, the intruder instantly cooled the attitude and began plying Jimmy with questions about the picture, his successes in the theater, his interest in motorcycles. Obviously he, too, had done his homework and read Warner's press releases. By the time Jimmy left the office, he had also simmered down, but only somewhat.

"Loudmouthed son of a bitch," he groused bitterly. "Three years ago, he gave me a hard time when I came in here for an interview."

Clearly, true to his promise, it was going to be get-even time, and I almost relished what lay ahead. However, whatever it might be, I knew that I, personally, had to tread even more softly now. I'd been there from the start; I knew what it had taken for Jimmy to get this far; I knew what it had cost and what was at stake. He had to do what he had to do, and that could mean jettisoning me. I knew that, and it scared me because I understood only too well that I would live with that as a very real, a very probable eventuality. To guard against it, the game had to be: hang loose, keep a low profile, have few expectations, be pliant, and never make demands. No chains would hold this tiger.

The next day, Jimmy took me along to the Warner Brothers studio for his wardrobe fittings. It felt just like old times. Still, I tried to be cool, unobtrusive. When he was finished, we dropped in to see Kazan in his office on the lot. Jimmy introduced us and told him about Borrego, that is, how great the place was. I wondered just how "great" Kazan, with his canny eye, might sense it really had been. This was the first true test. If Jimmy felt he'd been seen through because of my presence, it could be the beginning of the end. Much to my relief, Kazan was cool; if he suspected anything, he certainly didn't show it. In fact, he seemed casual and easy. He didn't even avoid looking me in the eye, usually a telltale sign. He was pleased with Jimmy's tan, but wanted him to put on more weight. "We gotta get this guy to eat more, beef up" was his message. No sign of courtly professionalism or role-playing for those two, they behaved like old friends. Only briefly, when it came time to discuss matters about the picture, did they get serious. As we were leaving, Jimmy invited Kazan to join us for lunch, but he declined because of a lunch date with the Warner brass.

We were leaving the main office building, headed across the street to the drugstore for a sandwich, when somebody behind us called out, "Hey, Dean!" We stopped and turned, as a classically handsome young guy caught up with us. Paul Newman's face was instantly familiar to me. I had seen him on Broadway playing a supporting role in William Inge's play *Picnic* before I left, and, of course, how could I forget his bit part appearance in my first, largely uncelebrated, television script for "The Aldrich Family"?

"What the hell are you doing here?" Jimmy asked after introducing us. Then, perhaps exulting just a little, he added, "Thought I left you in New York."

"You know, you're a lucky bastard," Newman conceded easily. "I wanted that part in *Eden* so bad I could taste it." Then, to me: "So help me, every time I went in to read for a part, this son of a bitch would be there. Got so's I couldn't turn around without running into him wherever I went. He even showed up for auditions for *Oklahoma* and got a test."

"*Oklahoma*?" I reacted in surprise. "You sang?" I marveled, recalling the ordeal of teaching him the song in *See the Jaguar*.

"Tested for the part of Curly," Jimmy admitted sheepishly. "Took singing lessons, too. Lotta good it did."

Newman joined us for lunch in a booth at the drugstore where Jimmy pumped him to tell us why he was in Hollywood, especially at Warner Brothers. Newman squirmed uncomfortably.

"I tested for the lead in *The Silver Chalice*," he admitted with what looked to me like a self-deprecating shrug.

"You get it?" Jimmy pressed.

Newman nodded. "Big mistake. A real dog." He slapped a fat script on the table as evidence. Big mistake.

Before Newman could grab it back, Jimmy had the script and was flipping through it, chuckling at the dialogue. "Hey, get a look at this," he invited me. I leaned in and looked over his shoulder. He stopped on a love scene, and we started to read it aloud, Jimmy playing Paul's role, I the girl's, breaking up over the lines. Unable to take any more, Newman finally snatched the script back.

"What're you going to do with crap like this?" he complained. "I didn't even want to come out here."

"So, why'd you take the job?" Jimmy asked.

"The fuck-you money," Newman shrugged. "You got to have it first to be able to pick and choose. I've got a wife and kids and an apartment in New York, but the fuck-you money's out here."

Jimmy gave him an earful on Hollywood. Newman wasn't encouraged.

"It's a rough business," he mused. "You figure out what you want, and you go after it. If you're lucky, you make it— like you, Jim. If you don't get the breaks—I mean, if somebody doesn't give you a push—you never make it. You can't get there on your own hook."

"That's bullshit!" Jimmy exclaimed. I turned to look at him, surprised by his sudden change of tone.

"Is it?" Newman challenged. "You know goddam well there isn't a single bastard in this lousy business who made it by himself. Anyone who's ever made more than ten bucks acting made it because somebody opened a door."

"That's total crap!" Jimmy insisted, still more defiant. I realized that Newman had, quite innocently, pressed the Indebtedness Button.

"Come off it, Dean," he challenged again. "You can't tell me no one ever helped you, ever made things a little easier for you."

"That's right!" Jimmy flared. "You goddam right!"

"Hey, take it easy," I tried to interject.

"I suppose you're gonna tell me you never got a boost, not even from someone who gave you introductions to the right people," Newman persisted, ignoring my effort to cool things. "Let's be honest, Dean. We all get help somewhere along the line. That's the way it's done."

"The hell it is!" Jimmy insisted hotly. "No one ever did anything for me! I did it myself. I don't owe anybody anything! Not one goddam thing!" And he beat his fist on the table to emphasize the point.

There was an uncomfortable silence. Jimmy sat there, his fist still clenched, the veins in his arm throbbing, and Newman tactfully changed gears, dropping the subject, while I stared into my empty coffee cup.

Although I was well aware of Jimmy's almost pathological aversion to indebtedness, I had never before seen him so tellingly defensive on the subject. He had to be aware that numerous people had extended him help and guidance over the past few years. Certainly I was and could name them. But I had long ago realized that, to him, there was a difference between unsolicited and solicited help. There had been gifts and favors offered without his requesting them for which he felt he owed nothing but thanks. Possibly he offered certain favors in exchange, as in Rogers Brackett's case, presumably volunteered not exacted, at least in Jimmy's mind. Except for his letters home to Marcus and Mom asking for money, letters clearly written with profound regret, I knew that he always accepted help, in whatever form it might have come, without assuming any sense of obligation. However, if his benefactors wanted something in return, he expected them to come to him as friends and ask, but not to thrust upon him obligations he hadn't sought. Among his friends, he was known to be generous and kind. But, whenever someone put him on the spot by expecting something in return for what he had considered a gift, he could suddenly turn cold and indifferent. Sadly, when applied to himself, his admonition to me, "For a gift one is always beholden," seemed freighted with a more negative interpretation.

We left Newman and joined Dick Clayton in search of a suitable apartment for us to share. Dick had done considerable groundwork, but, unfortunately, none of his finds satisfied Jimmy, although I would have been happy with a hovel at that point. Instead, after a few days of searching, Jimmy decided to heed Kazan's urging that he share an apartment above the drugstore across from Warner Brothers with Dick Davalos, the actor who was to play his brother in *Eden*. This, I later learned, was arranged by Kazan so that he could literally keep an eye on Jimmy from his Warner Brothers office, mainly because he distrusted his star's promise to stay off his bike, which had turned up in L.A. shortly after we returned from the desert and was considered an ominous sign.

I was only a bit disappointed, but not upset. Because it appeared that Jimmy would be on location in Mendocino and Salinas for much of the filming, Jimmy and I might have had to wait until the picture was in the can before we could find a place together. Besides, I wasn't holding out much hope about the future; I was sure he'd want to return to New York as soon as the picture wrapped, and New York wasn't on my agenda. I had a lot of catching up to do and needed to look to my own career.

One Sunday afternoon in May, while Ted Hartman and I were working on a new television project at my place, Jimmy turned up unexpectedly and asked if I wanted to take a drive to the beach. I jumped at the idea. I explained that Ted had to get home soon, so we'd be breaking shortly, if Jimmy didn't mind waiting. Jimmy nodded and said he'd listen to some of my records in the other room.

Ted and I went back to work, but after a few minutes, we became aware of some rather mournful music from the other room, and I remember wishing that Jimmy had selected something a bit more upbeat. We were writing a sitcom. About ten minutes later, Jimmy turned off the music, said he had somebody to see, and cut out, leaving as abruptly as he had arrived. It bothered me somehow because I had the feeling he wanted to talk to me. I dismissed it, however, and went back to work.

About fifteen minutes later, Ted and I decided to call it a day, and he left, as well. It was a special day, and he was eager to get home to his family. I stepped to the window to watch him go and was surprised to see Jimmy still sitting behind the wheel of his car in the street below. He was just sitting there, staring straight ahead at nothing in particular. Was he waiting for me, or what? Then it hit me, and my heart sank. Suddenly I understood everything, his mood, his need for company.

I hurried downstairs and outside. But by then his car was roaring off down the street. I called after him, but, of course, he couldn't hear.

I kicked myself for not realizing sooner. It was Mother's Day.

20

An Icon Prepares

DICK CLAYTON PROVED TO BE A GOOD FRIEND TO JIMMY, AS WELL as an excellent agent. To the best of his ability, he saw that most of Jimmy's needs and some of his whims were gratified. But always, of course, the career came first. So, in keeping with established Hollywood practice, Dick began introducing Jimmy to several female starlets—mainly his own clients, of course—and encouraged him to start dating for publicity purposes.

In point of fact, Jimmy didn't need much encouragement when it came to publicity or the cool high life of Movie Town USA. Soon he could be seen zipping around town in his new MG, frequently with the likes of Terry Moore, Ursula Andress, or any number of Dick's other promising young starlets. In fact, during prep for *Eden* Jimmy began to relax, let down his defenses, and enjoy life more and more in true Hollywood style, almost as if making up for past deprivations. Instead of having to rely on Rogers to pick up a restaurant or nightclub tab, he could now afford to splurge on his own, and he did so with a vengeance.

I realized that Jimmy was changing before my eyes. At times, I found myself in the company of my old friend; at others, it seemed more like the company of a stranger, a new Jimmy, a different Jimmy. Or, as I recall thinking to myself one night when we were out with some of his latest acquaintances, possibly this was one of many Jimmys. But which, I wondered, was the real one? Over a period of months, I witnessed what I can only call a gradual disintegration, a splintering of an already multifaceted personality, into a fragmented jigsaw puzzle. The trouble became, you never knew who or what you were dealing with at any specific time.

He seldom phoned while the picture was shooting up north in Salinas, and I began to feel cut off and insecure. I think Jimmy sensed this on his return for he became more attentive than usual for a while, as if to make up for the omission. One night over dinner, despite knowing my aversion to hanging around sound stages during shooting, he insisted I come out to the studio the following morning, catch a couple of scenes of *Eden*, and have lunch with him on the lot.

Normally, I feel uncomfortable visiting somebody else's set. Unless it's my script they're shooting, I feel I have no real business there. But that morning, Jimmy introduced me around and tried to make me feel at ease. When the company broke for lunch, explaining that he had to talk to Kazan briefly, he suggested I go on to the commissary and ask for the table reserved in his name. He would join me in a few minutes.

The minutes turned into a quarter hour, as I sat there alone at the table, being stared at by people waiting for tables. Finally, nearly a half-hour late, he appeared with Pier Angeli in tow. To my surprise, they were ushered to *her* table across the room where they began what appeared to be a head-to-head, very private, very intimate conversation. According to the gossip columnists, they were already a "hot item," so naturally every eye in the room was on them; I felt they were on me, as well. Jimmy, however, never cast a look in my direction. I had myself a quiet lunch and slipped out.

I waited a few days for him to explain, but got nothing. Maybe he was challenging me to bitch. That had to be it. Then one night at the Villa Capri in Hollywood, I decided to confront the issue. Over dinner, I finally risked asking Jimmy what was going on between him and Pier. Teasing, he accused me of reading too many gossip columns and shrugged my question off dismissively, insisting that nothing was "going on." I said he could have fooled me after the other day in the Warner commissary. I reminded him that he had invited me to watch the two of them carry on over lunch. He grinned, eyed me over the rim of his glasses, and said cannily, "You and half-a-dozen stringers for Hopper, Parsons, and Skolsky." He was, of course, referring to Hollywood's three top gossip columnists.

Noting my dubious, probably wounded look, he pointed out that Pier and he were just "fooling around." He enjoyed her company. There were no demands—well, none he couldn't cope with. It was all very innocent. Besides, it would be next to impossible for anyone to make time with Pier, even if he wanted to. Her Italian mother hovered over her like a hawk. Among all the girl's would-be suitors, he'd heard the old lady distrusted Mr. Dean in particular, which seemed to please him. He was clearly enjoying his role as provocateur, not to mention his press coverage. I relaxed to some degree, now sure that I, at least, wasn't somehow being used in this new game of his.

The lovely Pier had the lead opposite Paul Newman in the odious *Silver Chalice*, which was shooting on another Warner sound stage. Jimmy had wandered over during a break to see Newman one day and been introduced to her. They sparked to each other right away and started seeking out each other on the lot. Being carefully groomed for stardom, Pier was as avidly sought after by the press as Jimmy, so it was only natural for them to try to evade ever-prying eyes, not to mention Pier's ever-watchful mother. Unfortunately their furtiveness only served to tantalize the paparazzi, a source of considerable glee for the studio front office and some concern for Mamma Pierangeli. Much like Joan Davis before her, Mamma was a strong-willed woman with plans of her own for her daughter's future that definitely did not include the likes of James Dean.

From the beginning, Jimmy apparently enjoyed the game of circumventing Mamma's strictures on Pier's off-camera activities. But, as he had assured me, he was focusing less on Pier than he was on the press. Pier was nice, but the press was useful. So, despite and because of Mamma, the mischievous pair would sneak off and show up separately at parties, be seen together—and photographed—then sneak off somewhere and have dinner at the beach or some out-of-the-way hamburger joint where they wouldn't be recognized. Then they would go their separate ways.

In no time, as Jimmy intended, the press blew up his relationship with Pier and fashioned it into a Romeo and Juliet-like romance, two star-crossed lovers torn apart by a domineering mother and an interfering studio. But then the game backfired. After a while, I think Jimmy and Pier actually began to feel persecuted. At first, Pier had been using Jimmy, as he had been using her, not merely for the press coverage, but to bait her domineering mother. But I came to believe she began buying into the press' little fairy tale and actually started to fall for her bad boy. I also began to wonder if maybe Jimmy was also buying in, playing his real-life role with onstage conviction. But only up to a point, however. Or was that just wishful thinking on my part? I shall never know the answer to that particular question.

In any case, the game went on for about six weeks or so, from late June until *Eden* finished shooting the first week of August. Whether their act was ultimately played out for real, who can say for sure? One thing I had learned was never to ask Jimmy questions about his sex life. However, I have to say that although I enjoyed Pier's company the few times we were all together, I never got the feeling that there was anything serious going on, at least on Jimmy's part. Which, of course, is exactly what he had told me.

Some might wonder about Kazan's claim in his memoir (*A Life*, Knopf 1988) that he heard them "boffing" in Jimmy's dressing room from his office across the hall. Pardon my skepticism, but I figure he must have had remarkable ears capable of hearing "boffers" through the solid wall of his own office, across a wide carpeted corridor, then through Jimmy's own similarly solid dressing-room wall. Even more remarkable, passersby in the heavily trafficked corridor were apparently oblivious to what would have been even more audible to them, those thunderous "boffing" sounds coming from Jimmy's dressing room. If they had overheard, one would have expected them to rush to the nearest phone to dish the dirt to the highest-paying journalist. If the so-called lovers' passion had been that audible, half the studio would have known. Word would have flashed around the lot and gotten back to Mamma Pierangeli before the pair could climax and *Variety* print the details on the front page, which would have been the end of the trysts, not to mention Mamma's trust in Kazan.

As for the ludicrous notion entertained by one television biopic that the couple freely enjoyed a sexual romp in the nude on the beaches of Malibu for a couple of weeks, while Mamma Pierangeli was, what?—locked in a closet somewhere?—in reality, the woman rarely let the girl out of her sight for an hour, much less a week or two. And while on the subject of whimsical invention, the same film also portrayed Winton Dean informing Jimmy that he was not really his son, but the son of a man who had seduced Jimmy's mother prior to their marriage. Having known Winton and observed him and Jimmy together on a variety of occasions over the years, I can attest to their rather obvious genetic linkage. The kid had enough of Winton's physical and behavioral characteristics to make the father-son relationship apparent to anyone with even average perception.

As I had anticipated, as soon as *Eden* wrapped, Jimmy was off to New York to recharge his cultural batteries and fulfill some television commitments. As far as his "romance" with Pier was concerned, his departure turned out to be a fatal mistake. Though not soon enough to beat Mamma at her game, Jimmy suddenly phoned me to say he was returning to Hollywood in late September. He had a date with Natalie Wood to attend the premiere of Garland's *A Star is Born* and needed to renew his contract with Warner Brothers. Unknown to him, however, Mamma Pierangeli had used his absence to ace him. Less than a week after his return, Pier unexpectedly announced her engagement to singer Vic Damone. When I showed Jimmy the announcement, he was far from heartbroken. He was furious. True, he felt humiliated and deceived, but I got the sense that the chief source of his pain was not so much that Pier had jilted him publicly, but that Mamma Pierangeli had won the game. Never one to be outdone, certainly not by *la strega* (Italian for "witch," as Jimmy had dubbed the old lady), he started laying plans to have the last word.

The wedding of Pier Angeli and Vic Damone was scheduled for November 24 at Saint Timothy's Church on Pico and Beverly Glen. Jimmy briefly returned to New York, but was back in L.A. again in early November in time to appear with Natalie in a CBS television drama, "I'm a Fool," and also in time for the big occasion. Not that he had been invited.

The wedding was staged in full Hollywood style with half the movie industry in attendance. So was an army of press photographers, exactly as Jimmy had anticipated. After the ceremony, as the wedding party came out of the church to be showered with rice and confetti and photographed from every angle, the merriment was suddenly drowned by the thunder of a Harley-Davidson engine being gunned nearby. All eyes turned to the source. To their shock—and in some cases, delight—there was Jimmy, parked across the street astride his motorcycle. Wearing dark glasses, black leather jacket, and matching Brando-style cap, he had apparently been waiting for the wedding party to emerge. Once he had their full attention and the press had taken enough shots of him, he roared off down the street and out of Pier's life.

Hedda loved it. So did I, as I later told Jimmy. His face lit up in a wicked, satisfied little smile. "Do you really think I'd be dumb enough to show up *myself*?" he posed.

It took a second for his remark to sink in.

He'd hired someone else, a stand-in, a stunt man, an extra, someone who looked enough like him, but would never be recognized under all the heavy biker drag. Only the bike itself would be identifiable as his. When I put it to him, he just chuckled and said, "Shame on you, Willie. You have a devious mind." Come to think of it, he often said that to me. Pot calling kettle black.

In any case, that was the end of the Pier Angeli episode, except for the decades-long myth that she was the romance of Jimmy's life. I have to admit to perpetuating it in a 1975 television movie about Jimmy, but the two-hour format wouldn't allow for the necessary exposition. Besides, the movie was based on my first book about Jimmy, and that, it must be quite clear by now, was not the only omission. It was 1975, after all, and we were making a movie for network television.

On learning that I'd never read *East of Eden*, John Steinbeck's novel on which the picture was based, Jimmy had urged me not to do so. He felt the screen adaptation was so powerful that he wanted me to see the finished film first. He didn't want me to have any preconceived ideas about the story and characters, and was afraid that, by being familiar with the book, I might miss the material that had been cut in the screenplay adaptation. Respecting his wishes, I put the book aside and waited to see the finished picture. As the months of shooting, assembling, editing, and scoring went by, I started hearing rumors around town about Jimmy's impressive performance. My curiosity was more than piqued, but despite Jimmy's several invitations, I never attended one frame of it in dailies, waiting instead until it was edited and locked. If I was to come to the experience without preconceptions, so be it.

Finally, he announced that there would be an invitational screening the following night. I arrived early and found the lobby charged with excitement. Word around town had generated extraordinary interest in the picture and, particularly, one James Dean. Few had passed up the invitation.

Jimmy spotted me and asked me to sit with him. I could see he was extremely nervous. But I was nervous, too, and suggested that this might not be such a good idea, reminding him of my bad habit of reacting out loud. As he was sitting with Kazan and the producer, he relented and said he would see me afterward.

As I sat there waiting for the film to begin, a thousand emotions engulfed me. In all the years of struggling, of putting all our hopes into what we were trying to accomplish, sacrificing almost everything to succeed, I had come to identify with Jimmy's successes and suffer his failures. Jimmy had led me to believe, and I still do, that the feeling was mutual. Whenever things had been rough and our goals seemed unreachable, we had turned to each other for guidance, for reaffirmation, for courage to carry on. And, somehow, we had arrived at this moment. Now, as the lights dimmed, our cherished dreams of years past echoed anew in my mind and cried out to be realized on this night for Jimmy—my "teammate"—come what may.

With a blast of music that seemed to emanate from within my head and a splash of vibrant color that stretched across the full scope of my vision, the picture burst upon the screen. Suddenly there it was, his name, taller than a skyscraper—"JAMES DEAN." God, what a heartstopper that was!

When the lights came up at the end, I was shattered. I had just watched Jimmy relive the sad reality of his own emotional existence. As "Cal Trask," a young man driven by an overwhelming need to gain the love of a father incapable of demonstrating affection, much less love, a young man striving desperately to overcome his inbred belief that he was bad because his mother had abandoned him at an early age, Jimmy had played out much of his own story up there on that screen. His portrayal embodied so much of the young man I had known for so long and had grown to love, so much of the lost, tormented, searching, gentle, enthusiastic little boy, so much of the bitter, volatile, self-abusive, passionate, unpredictable monster who was my dearest friend, that the impact was almost impossible for me to bear.

Suddenly I was aware that my ears were filled with the thunder of applause, and I felt myself slipping, losing control of my emotions. I maneuvered my way up the aisle, doing all I could to keep it together long enough to get out of the theater and into my car. Then I saw Jimmy, straining to look for me above the admiring throng that surrounded him at the back of the theater. He spotted me and signaled for me to meet him outside, but I shook my head, turned and blindly hurried along a row of vacated seats and out a side door into the parking lot.

I don't remember driving back to my apartment, but I do remember stumbling inside and retreating to the furthermost corner of the furthermost room, in fact, the bathtub in the bathroom. Fully dressed, for reasons I still don't understand, I took refuge in the empty tub and let go of a torrent of pent-up tears.

I don't know how long I was there when I heard him knocking at my front door. I didn't answer, I couldn't. I didn't want him to see me in this state.

"C'mon, Willie, open the door," I heard him insist. "I know you're in there. Your car's out front."

I made no move to let him in, hoping that he'd go away. Instead, he found a front-room window partly open, pushed it up, and climbed in. He discovered me in the tub and sat down on the floor beside it.

"Why didn't you stick around? The picture that bad?" he teased gently.

"Bad? You should've warned me," I managed. I tried to explain that I didn't know what I thought he had been up to for the past few years, but I never imagined it would come to anything like what I'd seen on the screen that night.

"Watching you, every word, every look, every gesture, so real, so honest. All of a sudden, it hit me. It can happen! This is what it was all about! It wasn't just some dumb dream, some stupid kid game we were playing. It's for real! It happened to you. You made it happen. You finally made it happen."

I buried my head in my arms, deeply ashamed of the tears. He stroked my hair for a moment, then lifted my chin, dried the tears on my cheek with one finger, and kissed me on the nose and said, "Well, then, there, now—guess you got that off your chest."

He started to laugh, and after a moment, so did I.

"Look, they're waiting for me," he said, getting to his feet. He explained where he was expected. "C'mon, get your act together, and meet me over there."

I don't remember where "there" was, but I never went. I couldn't face a lot of people, not then. I knew he would understand.

From that night on, Hollywood was abuzz with the name of James Dean. As if anticipating the intrusions that would gradually come to distort his life, he fled once more to New York where Jane Deacy had set up several starring roles for him on top television shows. I was disappointed, but what was I to do? I knew it was inevitable. What I didn't have sufficient vision to see was that from then on he would belong to the world. He apologized before he left, explaining that in New York, at least he could maintain some objectivity about what was happening. There he could audit classes at the Studio, immerse himself in ballet classes and bongo lessons, and not be distracted by the Hollywood scene. But he knew that the one thing that he yearned to do most, another Broadway play, would be denied him: His contract with Warner Brothers stipulated that he keep himself free for another movie.

However, even as far away as New York, he couldn't escape the publicity he'd already generated on the West Coast. At first, it had focused only on the excited word of mouth about his performance in *Eden*, but soon the press found juicier fodder in his off-camera antics.

By the time he got to New York, his bad-boy reputation had preceded him, and Jane Deacy was apparently very worried, indeed. As Jimmy told me later, still feeling Jane's sting in the recounting, "Mom" collared him immediately and lit into him about "the Brando act." The comparisons in the press had to stop, she insisted, and he was the only one who could stop them. Allowing that Brando may have been an inspiration to him initially, she pointed out that even the suspicion of imitation was doing him damage. In the first place, he didn't need to borrow anybody else's act. He had talent of his own, a brilliant talent. Irritated, he insisted that he wasn't copying Brando, that the entire idea had been trumped up by the press to sell papers. But Jane didn't let up. Even if it wasn't intentional, she pointed out, even though he and Brando had similar backgrounds and came from the same school of acting, any semblance of a Brando act still had to stop.

Jimmy sheepishly admitted that he'd lashed back and actually sworn at Jane, something he instantly regretted. I knew he considered criticism, even constructive criticism, a form of hostility, but I was still surprised he'd offended someone he cared for so deeply. How deeply he'd hurt Jane neither he nor I ever knew, but she'd made her point, and that was probably sufficient comfort to her. She was an agent, after all, and had an agent's tough hide. But Jimmy wasn't like her other clients, he was like her son. As for Jimmy, I felt sorry for him; remorse was rare in him, and it must have been painful. But, he did make an effort to control his so-called "Brando act" for a while. Any similarities thereafter were purely instinctive. After all, it was true that Brando and he had too much in common not to share some behavioral characteristics. They were both boys from the Midwest with a passion for motorcycles, both products of the Method School, both artistic renegades.

As the day of the New York premiere of *Eden* approached, Jimmy started to panic. He phoned to tell me that he was thinking of skipping out on it. He'd had his share of movie premieres and knew what they were like: the floodlights, the confusion, the throngs of fans jostling at the curb and jamming the bleachers, the screaming as the stars got out of their limos, the radio and television interviews, the dumb questions from pushy interviewers. He knew that after the movie there would be gushing praise and fulsome compliments. All this he foresaw, and it made him nuts. After all, this was no party of innocent teenage girls from Immaculate Heart High School; this was a den of lions. They could tear you apart. Could he conduct himself as expected? Could he be sure he wouldn't slip up, say the wrong thing on camera during an interview, screw up publically? Could he risk making a fool of himself?

I told him he'd have to face it sooner or later to have a career in film. Hey, he was a movie star! What did he expect? Besides, he was always pretty good on his feet. But in the end, he still couldn't handle it. He skipped the premiere and came back to Los Angeles instead.

Despite his absence, the film was received as an unquestionable triumph for the new Kazan discovery. The reviews ranged from "just another Brando" to "completely unique." And almost at once, the process of mythmaking got under way.

21

The Night Watch

WHEN JIMMY STARTED PREPARATIONS FOR HIS NEXT PICTURE, *Rebel Without a Cause*, he was already being forced to adjust to his mushrooming popularity after the enormous success of *Eden*. True to his beliefs, he was determined not to let the notoriety interfere with his personal and artistic life.

At first, as is the case with many movie stars, his strategy became self-preservation, his tactic avoidance. This was an entirely new development for Jimmy, and his avoidance of studio publicity people and the press in general never appeared to me to be the act of defiance that they considered it. Nor was it an antisocial attitude that now kept him from participating in mainstream Hollywood life. I saw mainly fear, the fear that if he gave in to the star-making machine, he would lose focus, cease to work and live according to his own values and principles. I could see that he felt insecure in the face of such potentially overpowering pressures. But nobody gave him credit for that.

Ironically, his attempts to avoid the press and Hollywood scene garnered him even more unwelcome publicity. They were generally interpreted as expressions of contempt, irresponsibility, or, once again, a Brando-like affectation. Gadfly columnists would sneer, "James Dean bought himself a new suit the other day. Who does he think he is, Marlon Brando?" Of course, in those days, only stars like Marlon Brando bought new suits. If participation was a danger, avoidance became a stigma. When the relentless barrage of commentary turned abusive, Warner Brothers' publicity folk were ordered to step in to protect the studio's investment. Since they'd had their own problems with Jimmy because of his general lack of cooperation, they found themselves in the difficult position of having to defend someone who deeply distrusted them.

But Jimmy had the faculty of remaining a spectator at his own circus, so part of him now began to enjoy the farce as it grew. He knew his reputation was at stake, but, when we discussed the developing situation, I was surprised to see how ambivalent he was. He really didn't seem to mind too much. After all, he was getting more coverage than almost anyone else, including Brando. In the end, good or bad, that was all they cared about, wasn't it?

Upon signing for *Rebel*, he now felt flush enough to buy a new motorbike, one far superior to his first. As I had witnessed for myself, he was a good biker and took pride in demonstrating this around town, indifferent now to the fact that it was only enhancing his reputation as a Brando imitator. Now he often could be seen roaring down Sunset Strip on his bike in the direction of the all-night coffee shop located next to the primo legendary Hollywood hangout, Schwab's Drugstore where, as the world well knew, Lana Turner had been discovered. Googie's, as it was named, was the current favorite with the younger Hollywood wannabes, nonconformists, and night people.

It was to be expected that Kazan and Warner Brothers would warn him to stay off the bike until filming of *Eden* was over. An accident that might delay filming for weeks or months was a risk they couldn't tolerate, so they finally grounded him. Mothballing the bike temporarily, he bought a horse instead, a palomino, and boarded it in the San Fernando Valley for a time, then up in Santa Barbara. For a while, he'd drive up on weekends to ride in the hills.

"Y'know, Willie," he mused one night, "ever since you've known me, I've wanted a bike just like the one I've got now—the one sitting in the garage. Funny, isn't it? Now that I can afford it, they won't let me ride it. Screw 'em!'"

So, he sold the horse and went back to biking. When she heard about this, his new friend, singer Ella Logan, star of Broadway's *Finian's Rainbow*, grew concerned for his safety. She had mentioned her concern to me several times, but I told her I didn't think anyone could ever persuade him to give up biking. A canny woman, she said she suspected there was one person who could. A few weeks later, at one of the impromptu parties she used to throw at her home in Brentwood to entertain such friends of hers as Sammy Davis Jr. and Nat King Cole, she asked her friend Brando to have a word with Jimmy. As Jimmy and I were leaving the gathering, Brando took Jimmy aside and said this about biking: "It doesn't go. I found that out. You know, an actor with half a face is no actor at all. Forget it, why don't you?"

Jimmy listened, but had shrugged off the advice by the time he dropped me at my place. Ella feared she had lost the battle, yet a few days later, Jimmy informed her he'd gotten rid of the bike because he felt it too dangerous. Undoubtedly what he didn't tell her was that he'd found a replacement, a substitute recreation.

A while before he left New York to start filming *Eden*, Jimmy had befriended a young composer named Leonard Rosenman, whose talent he considered extraordinary. The two had developed an immediate bond, and Jimmy later prevailed upon Kazan to engage Rosenman to compose the background music for *Eden*. While working on the film, Rosenman made what turned out to be a fateful gesture on the set one day when he introduced Jimmy to a relative of his named Lew Bracker. As I understood it from Jimmy, Bracker, an insurance agent, was interested in selling him a life insurance policy. In the process of doing business, the two young men discovered that they had more in common than insurance, not least of which was a mutual love of sports cars. Ironically, as none but the gods could have predicted, just before *Rebel* started shooting, deprived of his bike and facilitated by Lew Bracker, Jimmy was prompted to buy his first Porsche and soon began talking about racing it professionally.

I was poking along Sunset Boulevard in my humble sedan one night several weeks after Ella's party when I had to stop for a red light. Someone pulled up next to me and started revving his motor deafeningly. I figured it was just some kid showing off and refused to give him the satisfaction of even a scowl. A second later, I heard the familiar call, "Hey, Willie!" I looked over and was amazed to see Jimmy, sitting behind the wheel of a stunning white Porsche. "What d'you think?" he beamed.

"Did you *buy* that?" I managed. It still hadn't sunk in that he could afford such extravagances now.

"Just picked it up," he replied. "Want a spin?"

I parked in a side street, and a few minutes later, he took off into the Hollywood hills with me in the passenger seat. The interior was immaculate and still smelled of new leather. I was impressed. I was also unprepared.

The Porsche, built low and sleek, took the hills as though they were freeways, hugging the road neatly with each treacherous curve. It seemed within less than a couple of minutes, we were snaking Appian Way along the crest of the Hollywood hills. It was 1955, and there were no seat belts, and I was hanging on for dear life. I was barely able to get a glimpse at the neon expanse of the Los Angeles basin below for fear of taking my eyes off the road. But Jimmy had things well under control, and he maneuvered the car expertly along the precipitous mountain drive, down through Laurel Canyon, and back to the spot where I'd left my car. I figured the ride had taken less than fifteen minutes to complete—and years off my life. We had probably covered ten mountainous miles. I had never, in all the time I'd known him, ridden in a car with Jimmy when he'd driven so fast. That night I swore I'd never ride with him again.

Shortly afterward, Jimmy entered his first sports-car road races in Palm Springs. On the first day, he took first place in the amateur class, driving his new Porsche. On the second day, he took third place in the professional class.

By coincidence, I was spending the same weekend at the Springs and ran into him by accident on the night of the first race. About one in the morning, I was on my way back to my hotel after a late dinner with some gay friends. Crossing Palm Canyon Drive, I heard someone laying on the horn and shouting my name. I spotted him across the street, driving a station wagon slowly along in heavy traffic. He was waving to me. Catching my eye and motioning me over, he swung into a gas station.

As I approached, I noticed two girls and another guy in the car with him, none of whom I recognized. Jimmy greeted me cheerily as usual, regarding me through bleary red eyes, which I took as the result of too much desert sun. But as he spoke, I realized he was pissed out of his gourd, a very unusual condition for him. I'd never seen him that drunk before. In fact, he rarely drank heavily. Chiding me for not telling him I'd be in Palm Springs, he wanted to know if I'd caught the race that afternoon. His speech was thick and slurred, his eyelids heavy. It upset me to see him in that condition, and I wanted to leave, yet didn't want to hurt him further. I explained that I hadn't known he was racing or I'd have been there for him. He made me promise to come to the track the next day for the main race and then introduced me to the other passengers in the car. I leaned in closer to acknowledge each, and as I did, I noticed that, up close, the muscles of Jimmy's face looked slack. For a fleeting moment, he searched my eyes as if he were trying to ask me something. Whatever it was, I didn't get it, but his gesture depressed me even more. He invited me to hop in, explaining that they were off to a party. I lied and said I was meeting a friend. He insisted, dismissing my "friend" with a wave of his hand, and said, "Fuck him." Then for some reason, I made a wisecrack that I've always regretted. "You know, I let a friend down once, Deaner. Never again."

He narrowed his eyes, as if trying to focus on me, nodded several times, letting it sink in, and slurred, "Sure, I unnersan . . . I unnersan." Then, still nodding, he shoved the station wagon into gear and took off, jumping the curb. I watched it weave away into traffic, realizing that I had done just what I'd said I wouldn't do. I'd let him down again, my best friend. I couldn't help wondering if he was simply disappointed be-

cause I hadn't joined him or because I was meeting another
friend, a "him" who was waiting for me. Considering his condition, it probably hadn't even registered.

After that first successful go at it, it was apparent that
sports-car racing was going to replace biking as Jimmy's main
recreational passion. Once again, Ella and some of his other
friends tried to dissuade him from it, but it became evident
that their entreaties were falling on ears now deafened by the
roar of the engines. His art was losing out to a greater passion: competition. Maybe he would mature out of it. Maybe.

Once *Rebel* was in prep, I watched Jimmy slip into a different way of life. It wasn't really unique since in a way it was
like our days back in New York when he had sought life
where it presented itself most intriguingly, in the wee small
hours, on the lonely streets of the big city. An actor was once
again preparing, or so I presumed. Only this time, the scene
seemed somehow inappropriate to the subject matter. *Rebel*
dealt sympathetically with innocent, troubled teenagers, not
offbeat night people.

At first, I reasoned that perhaps it was the role he was
playing in the film that was making him seek out the darker
side of Hollywood, focusing his late-night "research" on the
more offbeat aspects of life along Sunset Strip. I began wondering if it wasn't so much a matter of study or research, an
actor preparing, as a sense that this was where he felt he belonged—in the world of the displaced, the alienated. Once,
when we were with Ella, he had said, "I like you, Ella. You're
good. But, you know, I like bad people, too. I guess that's because I'm so damn curious to know what makes them bad."

By "bad," I don't think he meant "evil," although that
could have been a guilt-born allusion to the homosexual side
of his life. But, at the time, I got the impression that it was
meant more in the sense of "different" or "unconventional,"
that possibly his early Quaker upbringing had taught him to
associate "bad" with that which was considered unacceptable
to the Society of Friends, which would undoubtedly include
homosexual acts. I came to believe that it was his own pecu-
liarity, his drift from the straight and narrow, as it were, that

often led him to believe that he himself was basically "bad." And so, perhaps his quest was, after all, to seek out fallen brethren.

Shades of his early days with Rogers Brackett, Jimmy had moved into an apartment on Sunset Plaza Drive, above Sunset Strip. It was hard to imagine what might have drawn him back there except the satisfaction of thumbing his nose at Rogers, knowing that he could now afford the rent himself, though I never asked. Whether because it was nearby, or some other fascination that drew him there, throughout the shooting of *Rebel*, Googie's restaurant on Sunset Strip became his favorite hangout. Almost any night now, you could find him there until the early hours, working on endless cups of coffee, chatting to almost anyone he ran into, or consorting with his "spooks," as he referred to them.

Stopping off at Googie's on my way home after a party one night, I spotted him in a booth and joined him. He was with a blonde woman in her late twenties. He introduced us as I slid into the banquette beside him and explained that she was a motorcycle freak like him. Innocently, I asked if she had a bike of her own. She said she did have, but had to give it up after an accident. I assumed, then, that the accident had been serious. Without embarrassment, she shrugged and said that she had lost her leg. With that, she swung it out into the aisle to show me that it had been amputated at the knee. Only then did I notice the crutches tucked discreetly beside her against the wall.

Figuring Jimmy and I had things to discuss, she said she'd better be going. As she got up and collected her crutches, Jimmy asked if she was afraid of bikes since the accident. She admitted that she missed biking almost more than the leg. He offered her a ride home on his bike. I could see how much the offer meant to her. As they left, she turned and smiled at me. She was glowing. Jimmy said he'd be back in a few minutes. An hour later, he still wasn't back, so I went home.

A week or so later, I was having lunch at Googie's counter when she came in on her crutches, took the seat next to me, greeted me with a warm smile, and asked if I was there with Jimmy. I explained that he was shooting that afternoon.

"That's the greatest guy in this whole goddam town," she declared. "He's got real guts. Most of the creeps around here are afraid even to look at my leg. Not him. He wanted to know all about it. You know, how I lost it, when it happened, if I could still feel it like some amputees do, stuff like that."

I was getting a little uncomfortable, not sure where she was going with this, but too curious to stop her.

"When we got to my place, he looked at it real close, like he was examining it. You know? Then he asked me if he could touch it. Nobody ever asked to do that before. When he did, he wanted to know how it felt. Asked me all kinds of questions, like how it changed my life, you know, my sex life. I said not many guys get their kicks from fucking a one-legged girl. He laughed and laughed. Then he left. That's all—he just got up and left. I run into him here sometimes. We have a few laughs and talk a lot. But, nobody else around here is like Jimmy. He's, you know, a real human being."

Finally, somebody else had seen through the nonsense and found the real Jimmy, the Jimmy I had come to know and love. It may have been more of his actor-preparing routine, but I believe she sensed he was sincere, and I think she was right. It just sounded like Jimmy.

As for Googie's, I was beginning to find its late-night scene a bit seedy and oppressive, but that was when I'd usually find Jimmy hanging out there. One evening after a screening of avant-garde director's Kenneth Anger's latest film, *Inauguration of the Pleasure Dome*, I dropped by, anxious to talk to Jimmy about it. As usual, he was in a booth toward the back, but that night seated with a woman and a young man, neither of whom I recognized. For some reason, I was reluctant to intrude and was about to leave when he spotted me and motioned me over.

As I approached, I observed that Jimmy looked terrible. He looked sallow, a lit cigarette dangled from his lips, and he was sporting a two-day growth of beard. Languidly, he greeted me and invited me to join them. Then, letting his hand droop limply at the wrist, he indicated his friends and introduced me to them. I wondered if he was high.

"Maila, Jack . . . Willie."

The name "Maila" rang a bell. It was Maila Nurmi, "Vampira" herself, in the pallid flesh. Popular on local television at the time, she was a late-night horror-movie hostess. Her macabre makeup and camp act brought to mind Morticia, matriarch of the happy family of ghouls created by cartoonist Charles Addams for *The New Yorker* magazine and destined to become television's "Addams Family" sitcom.

Before I even sat down, Maila set the tone. Her heavy-lidded eyes glazed in intense detachment, and true to her television character, she lifted the rosary with which she had been toying, casually dipped it into the strawberry milkshake before her, and slowly drew the beads between her lips, lingering on the cross at the end. Then, in a bored, throaty contralto, she sighed, "Hi, Willie." Jack, whose full name was Jack Simmons, said nothing, just stared at me blankly. He looked to be about twenty years old, and I figured they were all high on pot. I wasn't, so I begged off joining them and left, not for the first time worried about Jimmy.

Thus began what came to be referred to around Googie's as "the Night Watch." Each night around midnight, the same group, with occasional variations, would convene to pass the time together. In those late, cool, misty hours, life in fifties Hollywood revealed its shadowed side. Absent its spotlights, the world became a place where the lonely and disenfranchised could find kindred souls. It was their time to escape the dull routine world of the dayworker and the slick, fast-talking Hollywood crowd.

I realized that Jimmy was again beginning to experiment with himself, maybe in an effort to explore darker corners, always using his craft, his art as his rationale. But once he explored each minuscule facet of his inner existence, per Strasberg's motivational probings, would he be able to put it all back into its box again when no longer useful for his work as an actor? Had he mastered the technique of tucking it all away when not in use, or would it one day run rampant? Would he cease to control it and it start to control him? It was from thoughts like these that the seed of an idea for a screenplay began to germinate in my mind, and I promised myself that I would one day write it.

Meanwhile, the press had not been idle. In no time at all, it seemed the tabloids were declaring that the Night Watch was into Satanism. They practiced the black arts, feasted on human flesh and excrement, so forth and so on. Though ludicrous, the notoriety fed the egos of some of the Night Watch coterie, transforming them overnight into quasi-celebrities and setting an official seal on their claim that Jimmy was one of their own. Hitherto anonymous in his night prowling, this nonsense also put the spotlight smack on Jimmy, giving the Warner Brothers' publicists yet another headache to deal with. For all intents and purposes, they somehow succeeded in killing the bad press at the time, but not before yet another thread was woven into the steadily evolving tapestry of the James Dean myth. The notion that Jimmy was somehow deeply involved with the occult has persisted to this day and is still promoted by some.

Aware of the gossip about Jimmy's association with the Watch, I finally broached the subject to him one day at the beach. What he said next more than surprised me, for suddenly I found him confiding very straightforwardly about matters pertaining to his sexuality instead of in his customary oblique manner. He said he was as aware of the gossip as I was, but surprisingly, it didn't seem to bother him as much as Maila's friend, Jack Simmons, was beginning to. Jack had apparently ingratiated himself with Jimmy as a "gofer," running routine errands for him. Jimmy told me he had indulged the kid at first, finding him in some ways not unlike the character "Plato" in the picture he was shooting, a kid who was constantly attentive, too eager to please, always anxious to be included. Typically, Jimmy had been studying their relationship as a sort of model for his own character's relationship to Plato.

After a while, he had begun to feel guilty about using Jack as research material, so he started paying him to run his errands. But apparently Jack wasn't the lost waif he appeared to be. Seems he had a will of his own; and he also had an agenda.

Finally giving in to Jack's persistent pleas, Jimmy wangled a bit part in *Rebel* for him. However, the more he indulged Jack, the more Jack became a pest, the bottom line being that Jack now wanted to have sex with him.

Troubled by this confession, if confession it was, I found the situation he described difficult to laugh off, although I was reassured by the obvious fact that he was deeply disturbed about it.

Insisting that he wasn't remotely attracted to the kid, Jimmy said he'd turned him down flatly. But Jack was persistent; if not sex, at least a kiss! Even that Jimmy had refused, making it abundantly clear that anything sexual between them was out. I gathered Jack was still hanging around Googie's, even though the paid gofering chores had stopped. What Jimmy didn't realize, but I subsequently learned, was that Jack remained undaunted and swore to friends that he would somehow, some day, have that kiss at least.

I saw less of Jimmy during the filming of *Rebel* mainly because he was so focused on the picture, but also because I was now busy writing for a television sitcom. I visited the *Rebel* set a couple of times, but made a point of avoiding those late-night sessions at Googie's, which alternately bored and disturbed me. I found it difficult to watch Jack fawn over him, despite Jimmy's obvious discomfort with the kid's public displays of adoration. It appeared as though, denied Jimmy's affection, Jack was determined to make the world believe he was, nonetheless, Jimmy's lover. Furthermore, and more disturbing to me, I also thought I perceived an underlying unease in Jimmy when I was around his new pals. Obviously my attitude toward them, toward Jack, was evident in my less-than-chummy attitude. Initially I figured Jimmy's discomfort was probably because he knew that I now knew, through his own recounting, what was going on subtextually. Or was it, I wondered, because I knew him so well, because he knew I was wise to his games and poses? Anyway, the last thing I wanted to do was to become a source of discomfort for him, so I decided to cool it for the time being. I'd immerse myself in work and the new delights of a recent introduction I'd had to the magical world of music, courtesy of a new friend, named Max Gershunoff.

After graduating from the Curtis Institute, Max had begun his career as first trumpet with Toscanini's NBC Symphony Orchestra some years before in New York. By the time I met him, he'd become the director of music for the Greek Theater in Los Angeles, an outdoor theater nestled at the foot of Griffith Park.

Early on, Max introduced me to his friend, Dimitri Mitropoulos, then principal conductor of the New York Philharmonic. Having invited the maestro the previous year to recuperate from a heart attack at his aerie high above Sunset Strip, Max was again playing host to Mitropoulos, who was by then quite fit and in Los Angeles to conduct a philharmonic concert in Pasadena. When Max introduced us, I found Dimitri not in the least intimidating, unlike other self-important maestros I'd met. To the contrary, this genuine musical genius, with his penetrating dark eyes and signature bald pate, was an addictive tonic of impish humor, erudition, kindness, and passion. He also turned out to be an inveterate movie buff with a keen desire to meet my friend Dean and promptly asked me to invite Jimmy to the Pasadena concert. Since Jimmy had recently started immersing himself in classical and contemporary music, he had, in fact, attended several of Mitropoulos's New York concerts and was equally eager to meet the maestro.

Unfortunately, fate and moviemaking would have none of it. At the last minute, Jimmy had to pass on the concert, because Nick Ray had suddenly decided to film the climactic denouement of *Rebel* the same night. Despite my subsequent attempts to get them together in Los Angeles or New York, their schedules always conflicted, and they never got to meet in person. However, I did manage to introduce them via long distance phone, putting through a call from Dimitri's New York apartment to Jimmy's place in Hollywood. Although I didn't exactly eavesdrop, I noted that they spoke for nearly twenty minutes, specifically about their mutual passions: movies and music. Even after his second heart attack, whenever I visited him in the hospital, Dimitri never tired of wanting to know "everything" about James Dean. In fact, at the mere mention of Jimmy's name, he would besiege me with questions: What is he doing now? Have you talked to him lately? When is this new picture coming out? Is he coming back to New York any time soon? Sadly, they never did meet.

Warner Brothers must have worked their magic, for by then the columnists weren't being as acerbic about Jimmy anymore. After an interview with the bad boy, during which Jimmy oozed charm, Hedda Hopper herself succumbed and climbed aboard his bandwagon. Immediately, all was forgiven and, if anything too scandalous did occur, almost all was overlooked. After all, Hedda herself had dubbed Dean "genius," and few in town dared contradict the iron lady with the big hats.

With a carefully calculated plan of attack, Jimmy next set himself the challenge of snaring the juiciest role in the hottest picture on Warners' slate for the summer. Even before *Rebel* was in the can, he told me he had started spending his spare time hanging around the George Stevens production offices on the Warners lot, fully aware that Stevens's next blockbuster was slated to be Edna Ferber's *Giant*. Having got hold of a script, he had zeroed in on the role of Jett Rink for himself.

Day after day, he would show up in Stevens's offices. A couple of times, I went along and watched him charm the receptionists and secretaries, much as he had learned to do when making the rounds of the casting offices in New York. Finally, gaining access to the great man himself, he started ingratiating himself to Stevens, joking and chatting and generally making himself at home.

Ironically, Stevens later admitted to me that he'd been keeping an eye on the sensation of *East of Eden* for quite some time and was already considering him for the role of Jett Rink. In fact, he'd been aware of Jimmy since catching him on a live television show out of New York a year prior to *Eden* and had entertained the idea even that far back. So, grinding his own ax, he indulged Jimmy willingly, discussing everything from photography to sports cars. He felt his only problem with Jimmy playing the role of Jett Rink was whether he could han-

dle aging from his twenties to his fifties. Jimmy swore he
would even shave his head if he had to, just to get the role.
(Those days, this wasn't something undertaken lightly; it
would be decades before a bald head would be considered
sexy.) In the end, of course, Jimmy got the part. However, he
didn't know then that Stevens would hold him to his offer to
shave his head.

First, Jimmy gave me the good news about snaring the
Rink role, then the bad news. The problem was the starting
date. *Rebel* was running over schedule and not due to wrap
until after *Giant* was scheduled to start. He would have to begin wardrobe and makeup tests for *Giant* while *Rebel* was still
shooting. To make matters worse, Stevens had set him up with
a "real Texan" in order to learn the lingo, and he was worried
about slipping into a Texas drawl on *Rebel*. Then, too,
Stevens was also starting him on riding and roping lessons. It
had been almost three years since Ted Avery taught him roping basics, and he'd need a serious refresher course to bring
himself up to Texas standards.

For me, the worst news was that a large portion of the picture would be shot somewhere down in Texas. In other words,
Jimmy's time was going to be cut out for him for the next few
months, and our long frustrated plans to find a place together
would have to go on hold once again. I couldn't help wondering if it would ever happen and, for that matter, if I still wanted
it to happen. Truthfully, I was torn. From where I stood in
Jimmy's life, as a half-involved, half-objective observer on the
sidelines, I felt comfortably safe. I didn't have to put up with
the excesses and the intrusions of his chaotic lifestyle and,
more disturbing to me, the mood swings. I needed relative
peace to work and was afraid any semblance of peace would
be sacrificed once I moved back in with my peripatetic, insom-
niac, and totally unpredictable "teammate." In truth, no matter how much I yearned to share life with him again, somewhere down deep, I was afraid for my stability, or more
specifically, my emotional equilibrium. The closer we might
get, the more complicated I feared things could, no, *would* become between us, and up went my defenses once more. Obvi-

ously, I, we were safer right where we were, each on his own turf. Yet, a part of me wanted to take the chance, wanted to risk it. Still, fate had stepped in, and I wasn't going to have to decide, not now. Not just yet.

Worried I'd be disappointed, Jimmy wanted me to promise I'd come down to Texas for a week or two while the company was on location in Marfa. It was very tempting, too rare an experience to miss, but having just taken on a television job that would keep me busy until he got back, I knew it was unlikely. I agreed, but would ultimately forgo Marfa, a decision I would always regret.

22

Dr. Jekyll and Mr. Hyde

SANFORD "SANDY" ROTH WAS AN INTERNATIONALLY CELEBRATED photographer who had done photographic essays on many of the Western world's artistic and intellectual elite, among them Albert Einstein, Colette, Jean Cocteau, Picasso, Chagall, Sartre, Simone de Beauvoir, and Moravia. Among his peers, he was considered not merely a brilliant photographer, but an exceptional artist. Over the eight years since he had switched his career to photography, and until he met Jimmy, he had traveled the globe with his wife, Beulah, living mainly in Europe, photographing more of the life and times of that era than probably any other American photographer.

The Roths had only recently moved back from France when Sandy was hired as the still photographer on *Giant*. He had been looking forward to working with the stellar cast, but James Dean, Hollywood's new *enfant terrible* was the prime object of his interest. Yet, frustratingly, Jimmy persisted in avoiding him. Only after we had become good friends did Sandy confide how he had finally gotten through to Jimmy.

His first day on the set of *Giant*, Sandy was discreetly slipping around, catching shots of the cast and director in action. Gradually he became aware that Jimmy was keeping the same wary eye on him that he usually reserved for publicity people. What Sandy didn't realize was that Jimmy, being avidly interested in photography, was also studying Sandy's stealthy technique. For several days, Sandy watched the young actor at work, observing the way he related to others on the set, yet avoided him. Sandy later told me how he finally made his approach to this quasi-feral creature:

"Look, Jim," he'd offered carefully, "I'd like to be your friend. That's all I want from you. Frankly, I don't need you for anything else. I'm an artist of some repute in my own right and a man of sufficient means. There's nothing you can do for me, nothing I can take away from you. I admire your talent and respect your way of thinking. I'd like to get to know you. I'd like to be your friend."

Sandy's directness appealed to Jimmy, and he immediately opened up. It wasn't long before Sandy and Beulah came to occupy a prominent role in his life. In the Roths, Jimmy discovered a source of intellectual stimulation and enlightenment, and, as was his custom, he affixed himself to them. When he tapped in them a source of unselfish caring, love, and comradeship, as well, they became "family."

Childless, the Roths needed him almost as much as he needed them. Though in their middle years, they possessed such an extraordinary zest for life that they seemed to enjoy perpetual youth. Their interest in virtually everything of cultural or intellectual value gave them an astounding degree of pleasure. They responded immediately to Jimmy's insatiable hunger for knowledge about the world of the arts and were eager to share the riches of their experience.

Soon he was dropping in on them unexpectedly, raiding their refrigerator, playing with their Siamese cat, Louis, and imposing his friend Bill on them, as well. Often the four of us would engage in long discussions that would go on half the night during which Sandy and Beulah would enlighten us about exciting new European artists and writers, most of whom were their personal friends. Sandy gave Jimmy pointers on photography, and together they listened to our personal and career problems, debated the directions we should take in the future, and, above all, encouraged us to get ourselves to Europe and learn what the rest of the world was like. Of course, aside from the tutorials, there were also great meals, plenty of laughter, and, for Jimmy, always the promise of Louis the cat to play with. In the Roths, Jimmy was finding the kind of family he needed: a close-knit unit of generous, stimulating minds, minds that were open and liberal, people who would not make any burdensome demands of him, yet give him their unqualified love. His obligation to them, if any, was fulfilled by his unsolicited love in return. As for me, I shared the sentiment and felt privileged to be a part of his new family.

Inspired by Sandy, Jimmy started experimenting with photography on the set of *Giant*. Studying Sandy at work as he caught the off-guard shots that had made him famous, Jimmy dubbed his crafty mentor "that sneaky eye." When he expressed a desire to try his luck, Sandy handed him the camera and told him to shoot away. And shoot he did, anything and everything. But his interest in photography didn't stop at still shots. Soon he was hovering over the cameramen on the picture, asking questions, and studying their techniques. Nor did his interest stop at cinematography. He had quietly been taking notes on the art of directing from the beginning. He already had three master filmmakers to learn from: Elia Kazan; Nick Ray; and now for *Giant*, George Stevens. However, of the three, Stevens was fast losing Jimmy's consideration as a "master."

"I get sick watching this crap, you know," he informed me one night. "They show up for a day's shoot without any real plan. Somehow, they sort of muddle through. Stevens has a method I call the 'around the clock system.' He's really no better than any other director, only he makes sure that he can't go wrong. Did you know he gets budgeted for more footage, more film, than any other director at Warner Brothers? He takes all the film he wants and shoots a scene from every possible angle—all around the scene, up, down, here, there. Used to be an editor himself, of course, so when the picture's in the can, he hires the best editor he can find who'll take orders and tells him what he wants. They spend a year, sometimes more, selecting the best shots and the best scenes from miles and miles of footage. And when they're through, surprise, another masterpiece! How the hell can you go wrong?"

The more Jimmy learned about the moviemaking techniques of directors generally, the more critical he became of them. He began condemning what he considered their lack of "true creativity." He was obviously itching to direct himself. Certainly the more he became aware of the mechanics of Stevens's approach in particular, the less respect he expressed for the man. By the time they left for Texas, I could foresee trouble ahead.

True to my intuition, once on location in Marfa, Jimmy began giving George Stevens a hard time. Later he would recount how, instead of retiring after a full day of filming, he'd take off with Bob Hinkle, the Texan who'd been hired to teach him how to be a true-blue Lone Star son. Together they would head for the country, spend the night shooting jack rabbits, and return in the morning, sleepless and exhausted. Although Jimmy knew Stevens was wise to his game, he was surprised that the director said nothing, unaware that Stevens was only bottling up his mounting irritation to unleash later.

In fact, as Stevens later confided to me, he was pleased that the notoriously unmanageable Dean, to whom he had entrusted the pivotal role in the picture, had appeared to be, at first, less of a handful than he had anticipated. His displeasure began in Marfa and intensified when the company returned to the Burbank studio. Back in L.A., he discovered that Jimmy, accustomed now to keeping late hours and oversleeping, had arranged with a member of the production staff to be wakened each morning by phone—several times, to make absolutely sure. For some reason, this lack of self-discipline further irritated Stevens. Worse, Dean would then show up late for his call anyway, keeping cast and crew waiting. Outraged by what he viewed as this total lack of professionalism on the part of an actor whose background was the legitimate theater, Stevens finally read Jimmy the riot act. Jimmy contritely promised to mend his ways.

Initially, he made an effort to turn up on time. But once in costume and makeup, he would find himself sitting around the set for hours, waiting for his scene. As any film actor will attest, this is what usually happens, and, although tedious and irritating, it goes with the territory. Jimmy didn't see it that way, complained to Stevens, and asked for what he thought fair consideration. But this was moviemaking, and nothing changed. So, Jimmy reverted to his former system of having a member of the production staff phone and wake him in ample time for him to be on the set when his scenes were ready to go before the camera.

This seemed to work until one Saturday when Jimmy was scheduled for an early call. He noticed that Mercedes McCambridge, another principal player in the film, was also on early call. Since her scene was to be shot first, he figured he wouldn't be needed until later in the day. So he decided to use the morning to move into the house he had just rented in Sherman Oaks. It was less than ten minutes from the studio and far more convenient than the apartment on Sunset Strip. Unfortunately, he chose the wrong day for the move. On that particular morning, Miss McCambridge slipped and fell in her shower, cutting her face, if not badly, badly enough. In a move to save time and money, Stevens immediately switched the schedule. He would shoot Jimmy's scene first and fill in with scenes involving other actors later. Only one problem: no Jimmy.

The production staff spent the entire morning unsuccessfully calling around town, trying to locate their missing star. With each hour, the cost of the delay grew greater and Stevens's temper shorter. Acting on a hunch, during the lunch break, Elizabeth Taylor jumped into her car and drove over to Jimmy's new house. Explaining what had happened, she quickly hustled Jimmy back to the studio. But unfortunately, the damage was irremediable. His temper finally shot to tatters, Stevens berated Jimmy for his unprofessional conduct before the entire cast and crew, declaring that it would be a welcome relief to Hollywood and the film industry if he would go back to New York and stay there. As he had done after his dressing-down by Daniel Mann, Jimmy now detached himself emotionally from the production and had little more to do with Stevens.

Nor did Elizabeth herself have an easy time with Jimmy at first, as she later told me. The day they met, just before the picture started shooting, Jimmy couldn't have been more charming. He even took her, as he had others, for a spin in the new Porsche. She returned convinced that everyone was quite wrong about him. The next time she met him was on the set after shooting had started. Approaching him in her friendliest manner, she expected the same kind of reception she'd received earlier. Instead, Jimmy glared at her over the rims of his glasses, got up, and strode off. Later, while on location in Marfa, at a company dinner in a local country club, she found herself seated at a table alone with him. After an uncomfortably long silence, she finally challenged him on his behavior. "You don't like me, do you?"

For a moment, Jimmy stared at her blankly then chuckled. "I like that," he replied, to her surprise. I believe what she failed to understand was that her accusation had revealed exactly what he wanted to know: that his indifference bothered her. From their first meeting, he had realized that she was accustomed to using her beauty to command the attention of every man she met. He had simply decided to see if he could break the pattern. Elizabeth apparently didn't hold it against him. For the rest of that evening, they talked freely and easily, and Jimmy allowed her to pass through the self-protective shield he had built around himself.

From then on, she resolved to stop taking offense when he became moody and uncommunicative. She understood that his moods were simply part of his complex nature, not meant to be taken personally by those close to him, a tough lesson to learn, as I had long before discovered. As nearly as I was able to interpret from our subsequent reminiscences, Elizabeth grew fond of the "boy" in Jimmy, and her motherly instincts took over. Sensing what she saw as his profound loneliness, she responded to his need with maternal affection. How often I'd seen that work for him. Yet, let it be clearly understood, I never once heard him address Elizabeth Taylor as "Mom"!

Jimmy was by that time smitten with the Roths' Siamese cat, Louis, the only cat I know reputed to have stalked across Pablo Picasso's loaded palette, then, encouraged by the artist, walk across a fresh canvas to create an *oeuvre*. (I still wonder

what became of Louis's masterpiece.) It was Jimmy's infatuation with Louis that inspired Elizabeth to arrange a surprise
for him, a surprise she hoped might help fill the gap of loneliness she sensed in him. One day on the set, she led Jimmy to
her dressing room and presented him with a furry ball of kitten all his own, Siamese by breed, male by gender.

"Marcus," he announced later, introducing me to the new
little friend snuggled in his arms. "That's what I've named
him—Marcus." The choice was a tribute to his substitute father, of course, his uncle, Marcus Winslow.

In the weeks that followed, he doted on little Marcus. He
hung a cord with a knot in it from the ceiling for the kitten to
pat around and rushed home from the studio in lunch breaks
to feed him and play with him. He even began getting in at
reasonable hours so his little friend wouldn't be left alone too
long. And thus, true to the rules set down by Antoine de Saint-
Exupéry, a few cockeyed ounces of fur began the amazing
process of taming the erratic James Dean and doing a better
job at it than I ever had.

Things were not going well for me, however, workwise. In
order to save money, I had moved in with a gay friend who
was willing to share the rent of his apartment in Beverly Hills.
Things went well at first, but after a while, the environment
became problematic as far as work was concerned. My roommate was friendly with a couple of lesbians, one of whom, Sallie Fiske, the brilliant, maddening, political journalist, now
late and much lamented, eventually became a dear friend of
mine. The two women spent a lot of time hanging out at the
apartment most evenings and sometimes during the day. For
some reason, the mixture of the four of us made for a neu-
rotic, nihilistic cocktail, and I soon found the atmosphere not
at all conducive to getting any work done. Unfortunately, my
finances at the time made it impossible for me to afford a
place on my own.

One night shortly after Jimmy got back from Texas, I was
telling Sandy, Beulah, and him about my latest discovery:
kendo. A brutally rugged, strangely graceful Japanese sport,
in which the exotically outfitted combatants use long wooden

batons to batter each other into submission, kendo had captured my fancy, at least aesthetically. In fact, I had recently taken to escaping the distractions of my roommate and his friends by attending the weekly kendo matches in Nisei Town, the Japanese district in downtown Los Angeles. Sandy found my description of the sport fascinating and said he'd like to photograph it. So Jimmy suggested that we all go downtown, catch a match, and go to a Japanese restaurant afterward.

A few nights later down in Nisei Town, Sandy was darting around the gymnasium snapping shots of the kendo matches while Beulah, her niece, Jimmy, and I watched from the bleachers. As the match heated up, Jimmy wanted a different perspective, so he moved to the bleachers along the adjacent wall. When Sandy rejoined us, he and I exchanged comments on how tired and worn out Jimmy was looking and concluded that the film must have taken a lot out of him. Beulah, however, pointed out that he only looked that way because they'd shaved some of his hair back, creating a receding hairline for the final scenes of the picture where his character Rink ages to his fifties. She was right, of course. Still, there was a fatigue in his face I'd never seen before. Sandy captured the moment on film: Jimmy hunched over, watching the match from the bleachers, looking like a worn-out old man. Sandy later gave me a fine print of the shot. A glimpse of Jimmy's future, I remember thinking at the time.

Jimmy drove me back to my apartment that night. With only slight trepidation, I invited him in to meet my roommate and his friends. The apartment was on the first floor and because it was a hot summer night, all the windows were wide open. We found my roommate and the two girls chatting quite civilly in the den. But before I could even introduce Jimmy, Sallie recognized him and, finding herself in the presence of such dazzling stardom, instantly freaked out, jumped up, and leaped out of the open window. Thanks to some shrubbery beneath the window, she was uninjured, a little flustered perhaps, but that's all. After I and the others retrieved her safely from the bushes and took her back inside, I walked Jimmy to his car.

"How do you get any work done in there?" he remarked, eying me over his glasses as he slipped behind the wheel.

"I don't," I laughed uneasily. "Not enough, anyway." I didn't tell him that my roommate was driving me crazy, that I was presently broke, and considering taking a job in public relations.

Shaking his head as if bemused, he drove off. However, I guess I underestimated his powers of perception. Apparently he saw much more of my true state of affairs than I thought I'd revealed. Furthermore, and maybe more importantly, that night he also witnessed me living an open and obvious "out" life for the first time in our relationship.

From the time Jimmy returned from Marfa, we'd begun seeing more of each other, starting many of our evenings at the Villa Capri, now Jimmy's favorite dining spot in Hollywood. Sometimes hanging out until closing time, we spent enjoyable hours with the friendly manager, Nicolas, known to friends as "Nicol," who also happened to be the landlord of the house Jimmy had decided to rent. Jimmy was being invited to a number of parties, to which he invariably offered to take me. I tended to decline much of the time, now highly sensitive to any speculation about the nature of our relationship. As I was leading a fairly "out" life now, the last thing I wanted to do was put him in any kind of compromising position.

A welcome calm seemed to have settled over his life since his return. It had gained more order, and he was also financially secure now. When he'd arrived to start work on *Eden*, he'd needed an advance from the studio just to get along until he went on salary. His contract had called for a mere ten thousand dollars, although by the time the picture was completed, he'd earned somewhat more. But with the incredible response to that first film, his price had soared. During the filming of *Giant*, Jane Deacy had already negotiated a twenty-thousand-dollar deal for him to play the lead in the first-ever color television "spectacular," "The Corn Is Green," scheduled to start rehearsing in October. At the time, it was an unprecedented price for television. And now, for his next feature film, *Some-*

body Up There Likes Me at MGM, his negotiating price had reached the hundred-thousand-dollar level, although the deal hadn't yet closed. Compared to the figures today's top stars get for a major feature that may seem like small change, but at the time it was most impressive. Ill equipped to handle his own financial affairs, he'd started to employ business managers, a sure indication in movieland that one has arrived.

As for me, despite the fact that it had never been my intention to be a comedy writer, I'd been writing situation comedy for the past two years. This had grated on me for some time. When Jimmy left for Marfa, I'd begun work on the idea for my screenplay, determined not to take another television assignment until I had at least an outline. But by the time he got back from Texas, I was broke, despondent, and looking for work in television again.

One afternoon shortly after our kendo evening, I stopped by Jimmy's rented house in Sherman Oaks. It was a two-story log-cabin affair, consisting of a large, vaulted studio with a bedroom balcony, a kitchen, and a small room at the back. I was hardly in the door when Jimmy suddenly sat me down and started asking me about my writing. Although I'd avoided the subject with him since he left for Texas, I suppose concerns about my current plight were written all over my face. If nothing else, Jimmy could read peoples' faces, and his remark to me when he dropped me off after the kendo should have been an indication that he was on to me. Patiently, he now insisted on knowing exactly what my trouble was, with no bullshitting. Somewhat reluctantly, I explained that while he was gone, I'd decided I couldn't go on writing television sitcoms. So I'd started working on an idea originally intended for television, but as I got into it, I realized it might work as a feature film. I went no further, waiting for his response.

"So, what's the problem?" he prompted. "Write it."

"I wish," I replied. On his questioning look, I explained with some embarrassment that I'd run out of money and was about to take a job with a public-relations outfit. It was either that or back to sitcoms. He asked what my idea was. Afraid he might not respond well, I hesitated, worried that the story wasn't worked out sufficiently to present. He insisted on hearing it anyway.

Reluctantly, I explained it was a sort of contemporary Jekyll-and-Hyde story, but the twist was that it dealt with a young character who'd been experimenting with drugs. Jimmy nodded thoughtfully, then asked if I'd worked out the story. I sketched out my approach while, distractingly, he played with little Marcus. He'd rigged that damn cord from the ceiling of the studio living room and now set it swinging so the kitten could bat at the huge knot he'd tied at its end. I wondered if he was even listening.

When I finished, he started to pace, as if mulling my presentation or at least trying to concoct a response that wasn't too hurtful. Finally, without even commenting on the idea, he turned to me and asked how long it would take to write the script. I figured that it might take ten weeks for a first draft, although I wasn't sure. I'd never written a full screenplay. He moved to the picture window overlooking the front lawn and gazed out without speaking for an interminable minute or two. Then he turned back with a frown.

"Look," he started. "I owe you some money from back in New York."

I cut him off, protesting that he didn't owe me anything, rather the converse.

"Will you shut up and let me finish!" he snapped impatiently. Then after a moment, he said, "Tell you what. I'm going to give you a thousand dollars. Think that'll last you through a first draft?"

"Deaner, I didn't come here to . . ." I trailed off, embarrassed.

But he would have none of my qualms and repeated, "I said, will that last until you finish the script?" He was speaking to me firmly now, like an older brother.

"Yeah, probably, but . . ."

"Good. And I want you out of that depressing dump you live in, too. You're going to move in here with me. When's your rent due?"

"On the first, but . . ."

"Okay. You can move in next week. I'm going back to New York for a while, and I want you in here at your typewriter when I get back. You can work in the back room where it's nice and quiet. We'll fix something up."

I started to equivocate, but he wasn't about to hear any excuses. In fact, he was more than insistent. It was like it was all planned, which I suppose it once was.

"On second thought, maybe I won't go to New York," he added. "Maybe I'll stay here and make sure you're not wasting my money."

"Why don't you write it with me?" I suggested.

"Dammit, this is *your* baby!" he exploded. "All yours! Understand? Sure, I'll be here if you want to kick around some ideas. But it's got to be *your* script. You've put it off long enough. Now you're going to do something that's all yours. You got that?"

Those words, or words very similar, still echo in my head, when I think of that moment. And they still move me, as they did that day.

"And don't get the idea that this is a handout. I think it's a fucking great idea. You can pay me back when you sell it." Then, looking over the rim of his glasses, he added, "Maybe there'll even be a part in it for me."

The sound of a car in the driveway alerted us. It was Lew Bracker. On a tip from Lew, Jimmy had just bought a new six-thousand-dollar Porsche Spyder, a high-powered sports model made of lightweight—make that, "eggshell"—aluminum and designed to reach speeds in excess of 150 miles per hour. Because he had completed his work on *Giant* and was once more free to race, Jimmy was planning to race the Spyder that coming weekend in Salinas, where some of *Eden* had been filmed on location. Lew had come to discuss some insurance business and tell him he could pick up the new Porsche on Saturday.

As Jimmy walked me out to my car, he suggested that I come along to the races that weekend, explaining that Sandy was going to follow him up in his station wagon. There'd be plenty of room for me. I reminded him that I had some packing to do, not to mention a script to write and a producer who was one mean son of a bitch hovering over my shoulder.

"Good luck, though," I said, extending my hand as we reached my car. "I'll keep my fingers crossed for you."

Instead of a handshake, he smiled and drew me into a warm hug. As I bathed in his warmth, my mind flashed back to our parting in New York only eighteen short months before—before he was a star, before we had reached the point where we were now, before I had given in to my long-denied love for this person I had known for five extraordinary years. Finally releasing me to get into the car, he leaned in close, one hand on the roof, the other holding the car door open.

"Make me a promise."

"Anything."

"You know what you want. You always have. Stop putting it off. Like I told you, there's nothing to be scared of." He patted my head gently. "Now, get out of here and start packing."

I started the car and put it in gear. It had rolled only a few feet, when he shouted after me.

"Hey, Willie!"

I hit the brakes and looked back out my window.

"Remember . . .! 'What is essential is invisible to the eye.'"

How could I ever forget? As I drove off, I glanced in the rearview mirror. But he was already gone, and all I could see was his white Porsche in the driveway.

By the time I got back to my place, my warm and wonderful feeling had slowly given way to doubt as I began to realize what I'd agreed to. I was going to give up my independence and once more move in with someone who had for years alternately courted me and scared the hell out of me. Which, I wondered, would I wind up with, Dr. Jekyll or Mr. Hyde?

We were leaving the Roths' after dinner the following night when Beulah asked Jimmy how little Marcus was doing. He paused, then, sheepishly confessed that he'd just given the kitten away. I stared at him, completely surprised. Beulah was actually shocked. He assured us that he'd entrusted Marcus to a friend who loved cats, a girl who should be able to take care of him better than he ever could.

"But why, Jimmy?" Beulah insisted, as if somehow betrayed. "Why? You loved him so."

Jimmy looked uncomfortable. "Well, you know, I worried too much about him." Then, as if in afterthought: "You know what a crazy life I lead. I figured, I might go out some night and just never come home. Then what would happen to Marcus?"

Jimmy had recently told me in confidence that, prompted by Lennie Rosenman, himself a devotee of the couch, he'd been seeing a psychiatrist. Apparently the experience had somehow backfired and left him rather depressed. It seemed, by pointing out that his conflicts were due to the insecurity brought on by his mother's death and his father's absence in his youth, the psychiatrist had only substantiated what Jimmy had long suspected. But by trying to apply the doctor's solution to his problem, he had wound up in a muddle. On the one hand, he was led to understand that the way to rid himself of his anger was to forgive his father and include him more in his daily life, demonstrating the kind of love he looked for in return. Yet at the same time, during each session, he was being reminded of all the reasons why he hadn't done these things and that, as far as he was concerned, he could never forgive his father.

However, he had taken the first step and finally placed a call to his father to invite him to Salinas for the races the coming weekend. His invitation was declined, although Winton did agree to have breakfast with him before he left.

Friday morning, Jimmy drove his station wagon into Hollywood to pick up the new racing Porsche Spyder, with its shiny, pastry-crust aluminum body and its mighty horsepower. Sandy, sports-car enthusiast and stunt driver Bill Hickman, and Rolf Wütherich, a young German who was to be Jimmy's pit mechanic at the races, would be joining them that day. Jimmy wanted to put some mileage on the Porsche, get used to the feel of it, instead of towing it behind the station wagon. So it was agreed that Rolf would ride with him, keeping his sharp mechanic's ears open for any engine eccentricities, while Sandy and Hickman would follow in the station wagon.

Jimmy called me from the Porsche dealer. There was still time for me to change my mind and join them. I stuck to my resolve, reminding him that I had a script to write.

"You don't know what you're missing," he said.

That evening, the last day of September, it was already getting dark early. Yet, I was still at my Olivetti when the phone rang.

"Bill?" the broken voice of a woman inquired at the other end of the line. "Have you heard?"

"Heard what?"

"Oh, God, I wish I hadn't called," came the whispered response.

I'd recognized the voice. "Beulah . . . ? What's wrong?"

"Jimmy's dead."

I froze for an instant. It was Beulah on the line, and Beulah would never joke about anything so serious.

"No," I said in instant denial.

"An accident, on their way to Salinas," she barely managed. "Sandy just phoned."

Involuntarily, I dropped the receiver on the floor. As I bent to retrieve it, I slipped off my chair. I think I blacked out for the first and only time in my life.

Moments later when I came to, I gathered my wits and dialed Beulah's number. Her line was busy. I tried again. Still busy. I gave up and dialed the Villa Capri. Nicol's heavy Russian voice came on the line.

"Is it true, Nicol?"

There was a pause, then simply, "Yes."

"Oh, God," I groaned and hung up.

I slumped in my chair and stared at my suddenly pointless movie outline, still poised in my suddenly pointless Olivetti, sitting on my suddenly pointless desk, in my suddenly pointless room, in my suddenly pointless life. And somewhere on a country road a 150 miles away, the mangled body of the one person in the world I was now sure I loved more than any other lay broken, dead.

So, it was over, I told myself finally. All over.

How wrong I was.

23

Will the Real James Dean
Please Stand Up?

JIMMY HAD LEFT NEW YORK, WHERE HE HAD BARELY EMBARKED upon a successful theatrical career, and returned to Hollywood in the spring of 1954. Over the amazingly short period of the next eighteen months, he had made three pictures and become the hottest young male star in Hollywood. Then abruptly, tragically, on September 30, 1955, his life had ended. I'd spent much of the five years, between the time we met and the time he died, in his thrall. I couldn't have guessed then that I would spend the next five decades in his shadow.

Not long after his death, I began to entertain the eerie suspicion that the strange odyssey I suddenly found myself embarked upon was being stage-managed from beyond by my perversely mischievous yet protective friend. It was an absurd notion, to be sure, but one hard to shake, considering the events that engulfed me and the persistent and powerful influence he was still exerting on my life.

After the initial shock of his death, I felt rage, selfish rage, directed at the Fates. How could he have been torn away from me, just like that, just when there was a promise of a foreseeable future—for us, together, as more than cryptically discreet "teammates"? It had been a future that I'd had time—such little time—to imagine and look forward to. But my rage is by nature short lived and soon turned to numb despair.

However, the gods were not entirely remorseless in their cruelty. They gave me the Roths, into whose care I entrusted my grief. Though their grief was based on a love more recently born, it was no less painful than mine, yet, sensing the depth of my loss, they took pity and shared the healing time with me. Beulah had truly been the surrogate mother Jimmy had so long sought and finally found, a mother figure who loved him without reservation, and Sandy, a substitute father figure who had unselfishly shared with him his thirst for life, his knowledge, his artistry. This childless, middle-aged couple had lost the only son they had or would ever have, and they put my grief to shame. Sandy and Beulah are both gone now, but I shall always be grateful for their unselfish solicitude during that profoundly painful period.

In her October 5 column in the *Los Angeles Times*, Hedda Hopper wrote, "I'm still reeling from the sudden death of Jimmy Dean, one of the greatest acting talents I've ever known. He was a tragic figure. So few understood him. He was reaching out for love and understanding, but got so little." One lunch with him and, of course, she among "few" understood him completely. There were others, even more egregiously unctuous, but you get the idea. Then, that same week, Dick Williams in his *Mirror-News* column, headlined, "DEAN'S TRAGIC DEATH CAUSES GIRLS TO FAINT," concluded, "Only the fact that funeral services will be held in Marion, Ind., Dean's birthplace, saves the occasion from probably turning into a maudlin spectacle here."

Little did he know!

Jimmy's remains (how cruel that word, how cold and insensitive!) were shipped back to Indiana, not unlike his mother's had been fifteen years earlier. However, unlike his mother, he was to be buried in the Park Cemetery in Fairmount.

From the first word of his death, the press latched onto the story with the tenaciousness of a pit bull, and by the end of the first week, it was still a front-page story of every major newspaper in the nation, indeed, one that resonated throughout the world. It was the first hint I would have of the enormity of Jimmy's hold on the public's imagination.

Hollywood columnist Sidney Skolsky had long been a habitué of Googie's restaurant and the adjacent Schwab's Drugstore, where he often picked up items for his column. As a result, he had been acquainted with Jimmy and the principals of the Night Watch, as well as many other denizens of the two haunts. Realizing there were a number of Jimmy's friends among them who wanted to attend the funeral, Sidney arranged a charter flight back to Indiana. One most eager to go along was Jack Simmons. However, unable to afford the plane fare, Jack was distraught and made his desperation quite public. As I understood it, having a good heart, Sidney took pity on the kid and took up a collection to cover his ticket.

After some serious deliberation, I had made the decision not to go back for the funeral. I thought of grieving Ortense, stoic, heartsick Marcus, bewildered little Markie; I imagined the hordes of hysterical fans, sensation-seekers, newsmen, radio, film, and television crews and, hovering over it all, the corps of studio publicists, on hand to make sure every lurid moment was milked for all it was worth, and I knew I could not be there, I could not be a witness to all that. Emotionally I was in no state to deal with it. Instead, along with the rest of the world, I watched the depressing coverage on television and followed the detailed reports in the newspapers and magazines.

As the days went by, there was no letup in the barrage of news coverage of the funeral itself and related sensational stories. In fact, the clamor intensified. I finally realized that the explanation might lie in the fact that *Rebel* was scheduled to premiere in New York on October 26, and it was likely that the hucksters were feeding the frenzy in order to hype their picture. I was appalled by the idea of such exploitation of Jimmy's death, his funeral, his grieving family. Worse, sickening incidents were being played up in the press, bizarre tales appearing daily about the outrageous behavior of some of his more passionate fans around the country. But, hey, what did I expect? That's Hollywood, baby. I prayed it would stop after the picture opened.

Instead, it only intensified. A macabre rumor floated back from Fairmount, a whispered tale from some of Skolsky's party that someone had broken into the mortuary the night before the funeral and pried open Jimmy's casket. Purportedly the body had not been "disturbed," whatever that might mean, but word spread that Jack Simmons had been the perpetrator. If true, it occurred to me that Jack might finally have found a way to steal his long-denied kiss.

If this was how it started, I could only wonder where it was all going to end. It didn't occur to me that it would never end, certainly not in my lifetime.

The initial flood of sensational stories appearing about Jimmy in the newspapers and tabloids persisted for several months, and they were eating away at me. One evening, while having dinner with my friend, Rupert Allen, a much-respected doyen of the Hollywood public-relations community, I finally unburdened myself. Only that day, a story had appeared in one of the tabloids about a pregnant Southern teenager's claim that James Dean had returned from the grave to father her child. Another made him out to be the ringleader of a satanic cult, and, more alarming, another, obviously born of the rumor about Jack Simmons's presumed mischief, concerned the "necrophilic desecration" of the corpse the night before the funeral. It was finally too much, and, to appropriate one of Jimmy's by now well-worn lines from *Rebel*, it was tearing me apart.

Compared to the outrageous tales published weekly in today's tabloids, I might appear to have been overreacting, but it was 1956, and the tabloids, the relatively few that were in print at the time, were still in their kindergarten stage. The impact of lurid journalism was far greater then than it is now. Still, weird tales from the crypt and the delusions of teenage fans were one thing. Less easy to shrug off was a stupefying story that appeared in the *Hollywood Reporter* that read:

Ranking the late James Dean among the immortals of art, Princeton University has placed in its Lawrence Hutton Hall of Fame the life mask of the young Warners star whose career was cut short by his traffic death last year. It will share space with similar memorials of Edwin Booth, David Garrick, Beethoven, Thackeray and Keats. Dean is the youngest artist ever so honored.

Jimmy in the company of Booth, Beethoven, and Keats? Certainly a fantastic tribute and one that would have tickled Jimmy immensely. Immortality had been what he'd once craved, but where was all this madness leading? Only two of his three pictures had been released at that point, and already he was being portrayed as everything from a necrophiliac's love object to a major god in the pantheon of the arts. Based on the only two roles they had seen him play until then, his fans were already turning him into a messianic sex symbol. The real James Dean, the Jimmy I knew, was getting lost in all the hype and hysteria. I wanted to remember him as he was, not as some hyped media freak. This was someone I loved and missed desperately, and I could hardly recognize him anymore.

"You're a writer. Write about it," Rupert suggested matter-of-factly over dinner. "Your relationship. The real James Dean, as you knew him. Record it, before it all gets distorted. Before you forget."

It made sense, but I was shy of the idea. Certainly it was inevitable that the floodgates of opportunism would open wide almost immediately upon word of hot young movie star James Dean's tragic death. Perhaps an early portrait of the James Dean I had known might serve to put him in proper perspective and stem the hemorrhage of distortions. But, write a book, a biography? Wouldn't it look like I was climbing on the bandwagon, too, indeed that I might be the drum major himself, out there in the lead? And what about our "relationship"? Just how candid could I be about the intimacies? How would I handle that?

But Rupert was adamant. It was a writer's obligation to record the truth, he insisted. With a wave of the hand, he dismissed my concerns, rather in the way Jimmy might have done. "You must write this book."

Within a week, he had contacted Ian Ballantine, the editor-in-chief of Ballantine Books. They would fly me to New York to discuss a proposal.

Before I left on my noble mission to record the "truth" as I knew it, I attended the Academy of Motion Picture Arts and

Sciences' Twenty-eighth Annual Awards presentations. It was being celebrated at the Pantages Theater in Hollywood, on the night of March 21 that year. Jimmy had been nominated in the category of Best Actor for his role in *East of Eden*. I'm sure for most of those attending the ceremonies that night, it was the usual evening of glamour and excitement. For me, it was profoundly painful. This would have been Jimmy's night. We would have come together—with dates, of course—nervous and anxious, to be sure, but on an incredible high, born of the realization that a night such as this was actually possible, at least for one of us. Instead, he was dead, and I was alone, and my sole focus was on the hollow prospect of his winning posthumously.

What a grim realization: If he did win, it would be posthumously, after death. What wouldn't I have done to have been able to reel back the past, like a strip of film, and re-edit it, cutting that one unacceptable moment, the one that ended everything for him, to give him at least this one night of triumph, this one last bid for his idealized immortality. As hot as he had been on the subject of immortality, he probably would have laughed at the sentiment and put me down for crediting with such importance anything so "crassly commercial," so "bogus," as he had once characterized the Oscar awards. But I would have seen through his act because I knew what it would have meant to him, how keenly he would have wanted to win, how secretly proud he would have been, despite the façade of studied intellectual indifference. I knew him too well, or flattered myself that I did.

His competition for the Oscar that year was formidable: Spencer Tracy for *Bad Day at Black Rock*, Ernest Borgnine for *Marty*, Frank Sinatra for *The Man with the Golden Arm*, and James Cagney for *Love Me or Leave Me*. How could a newcomer, an upstart, stand a chance in such illustrious company? The odds were favoring Ernest Borgnine. But the buzz around town was for Dean. As far as I was concerned, there was no contest. Undeniably, Borgnine's performance was good, but, to my mind, Dean's was more dynamic, more demanding, and had far greater range. Above all, his characterization of Cal Trask was, as Steinbeck surely intended, mythic if not biblical in scope and passion. *Rebel*, his second picture, having been released shortly prior to the voting, had put paid to the idea that his performance in *Eden* was a flash in the pan, purely the result of Elia Kazan's magic. *Rebel* was a pot-boiler, granted, but one elevated to the level of art by Nick Ray's direction and Dean's visceral performance. There had been nothing like Dean since Brando had burst onto the scene in *Streetcar*, and now he was the talk of the town. Forget what they felt about his off-screen behavior, almost everyone in Hollywood seemed to agree: James Dean had a golden career ahead of him, provided he didn't blow it with his craziness. And then, as suddenly as he had appeared to dazzle them, he was gone, a vibrant young actor cut down in his prime on the eve of his greatest triumph. It was a plot for a B-picture, a Hollywood publicity man's dream-scheme for a guaranteed Oscar win. How could the Academy not vote for him?

Easily, as it turned out. Ernest Borgnine won. Obviously, the members of the Academy had deemed his the better performance. On the other hand, maybe they just figured Dean didn't have any use for an Oscar anymore. Or, maybe they just hated the little bastard's guts, and this was their way of saying so. One studio executive, Jack Warner, to be specific, had dubbed him "that little bastard," and it had gotten around. (On learning this, Jimmy had impishly named his silver Porsche Spyder, "Little Bastard.") Well, Mr. Warner, nearly fifty years later, the little bastard's pictures are still running on television, at least one or the other of them, every month on the average, and Jimmy himself is a legend. Chew on that, wherever you are.

For me, the Academy's choice was a major letdown. But there was one saving grace, if you can call it that: At least Jimmy hadn't had to face the disappointment, too. He'd been extremely competitive and, above all, hated to lose. Anyway, I consoled myself, next year there would be *Giant*. Maybe he'd have another shot at an Oscar. On that score, the following week over lunch at Warners, I asked George Stevens what he thought Jimmy's chances were of winning. He poured cold

water on my hopes, however, confident that the strong sentiment surrounding Jimmy's death would have dissipated by
then. I was surprised, as well as slightly offended on Jimmy's
behalf, by his apparent indifference to garnering at least one
Oscar for his own picture, not to mention for one of his stars.

"I gather you don't credit his performance very highly," I
remarked in what I suppose was a somewhat accusatory tone.

"Don't get me wrong," he responded promptly. "Your
friend was very talented, but totally undisciplined. I'll say this
for him though, he was a shrewd little bastard. Only actor I've
ever known who could walk into a roomful of a hundred
people and pick out the only three who were journalists."

On the eve of my departure for New York, Elizabeth Taylor invited me to dine with her and her husband, English actor
Michael Wilding, at their Benedict Canyon home. She hinted
she had something "special" to show me. She'd grown deeply
fond of Jimmy, and his death had been particularly devastating
for her, as well. We'd been seeing more of each other since he
died, drawn together by our shared sense of loss.

I found Elizabeth curled up on the sofa adjacent to the fireplace, going through a pile of magazines. Joe Hyams, a journalist from *Redbook* magazine, had been up to the house that
day to interview her about her experiences with Jimmy while
shooting *Giant*, and she'd been searching for other articles the
man might have written. Unable to find any, she was in the
middle of telling me about the interview when, remembering,
she slipped from the room to fetch that "very special" something the journalist had given her as a memento. Moments
later, she returned clasping a slim book. Her eyes blinking back
tears, she passed it to me. It was a copy of *The Little Prince*.

"It was Jimmy's own copy," she explained, obviously very
pleased with her prize. "Look, you can even see where he underlined the passages he liked best."

I flipped through the well-worn pages, growing numbed by
what I saw. I recognized every marking, every passage she indicated. There, so familiar to me, were all the quotations that
meant so much to him, to us, underscored in pencil, some by
him, some by me. Almost afraid to look, I closed the book and

checked the dust jacket. Sure enough, above the title and about two inches from the upper left corner was the indentation caused by a paper clip. I knew then, with absolute certainty, it had to be the copy Jimmy gave me that night in New York. He'd left it on my pillow, his own prized copy of the book. Firmly attached to the upper left-hand corner of the jacket with a paper clip had been his handwritten note, the admonition, "For a gift one is always beholden." Though the note was missing now, the telltale impression of its paper clip remained.

Like a cruel reminder, there they were, the passages he had underlined in pencil, sentences and phrases I had carefully memorized three years earlier: *It is only with the heart that one can see rightly; what is essential is invisible to the eye. You become responsible, forever, for what you have tamed . . . if you tame me, then we shall need each other. To me, you will be unique in all the world. To you, I shall be unique in all the world . . . if you tame me, it will be as if the sun came to shine on my life.* And a passage that now resonated in my heart, that night more than ever, as I held that precious reminder of him in my hands: *. . . The wheat fields have nothing to say to me. And that is sad. But you have hair that is the color of gold. Think how wonderful that will be when you have tamed me! The grain, which is also golden, will bring me back the thought of you. And I shall love to listen to the wind in the wheat . . . Please—tame me."*

"Isn't it just the most wonderful gift?" Elizabeth asked in a voice quavering with emotion, jolting me back to the moment. I agreed, tempted to remind her, as Jimmy had me, "For a gift one is always beholden," but adding my own caution, "particularly to journalists."

Instead, I simply said I recognized it and acknowledged that it was very special to Jimmy. Then, handing the book back to her, with the painful realization that I was surely parting with it for the last time, I asked her if she knew where this journalist got it.

She shrugged thoughtfully. "You know, I never thought to ask him. I suppose from Jimmy's father or somebody."

For the rest of the evening, I disguised my mood as best I

could, yet left feeling somehow violated, although I never let on to Elizabeth. How could I tell her? When I'd left New York two years earlier, I'd entrusted the book to Jimmy along with my other things. How could either of us have anticipated then what would eventually happen? After his death, and especially after that night with Elizabeth, I berated myself for not having asked him to bring it back to L.A. on any of his several trips to New York. It must have still been in his apartment when he died. Presumably his effects all went to Jimmy's father, Winton Dean, so it seemed reasonable that Elizabeth was correct in assuming that Hyams had gotten the book from him.

I'd only been in touch with Winton Dean a couple of times since Jimmy was killed and then only to pay my respects. When I managed to reach him later, he didn't recall ever seeing the book, much less giving it to a journalist, which left me wondering just how it came into the journalist's possession.

It would remain a mystery until I got back to New York.

24

Unintended Consequences

IAN BALLANTINE RAISED HIS BUSHY CELTIC BROWS WHEN I TOLD him I'd only write the story of my friendship with Jimmy as I'd experienced it, and I'd no intention of treading softly. He grinned and advised me to write the book first, then we could worry about the content. Phyllis Jackson, my literary agent, concurred. "Don't worry about getting it right, get it written."

Luckily, upon my arrival in New York, I'd been able to sublet an apartment for the summer in midtown Manhattan, happily in the same building where my musical friend Max Gershunoff had an apartment. Other than Max, I'd see only a handful of people in New York over the following months. Most of that time, I'd be alone with my memories and my Olivetti.

Shortly before I began writing the book, I experienced probably the most awful nightmare I've ever had.

I was walking among bare trees in the landscaped grounds of a place like a sanitarium. It seemed to be a misty afternoon in late fall. Curious about the barrackslike buildings, I approached the side door to one of them, which opened slowly for me as I got near. The otherwise bare room within contained a single bed upon which a solitary man wearing a T-shirt and pants was sitting, cross-legged, slumped, his back to me. As if suddenly aware of my entrance, he turned and looked at me. It was Jimmy. "Willie!" he called out, scram-

bling off the bed to embrace me. I asked him what he was doing in this place. What was wrong with him? Still grasping me
by the elbows, he began babbling in broken phrases, repeating them over and over again, something to the effect that I
was the only one who could save him. His eyes were filled
with panic, terror even. Confused and frightened myself now,
I tried to calm him, to make sense of his words. Save him from
what, I pressed?

At that point, we both heard a sound from outside, a car
door slamming. He rushed to the window, and I followed.
Outside an ambulance had pulled up, and a nurse in white
was hurrying up the walk while two male orderlies slid something large out of the rear of the vehicle. They opened the coffin's lid, for this is what the object was, then turned to look at
us. In utter horror, I realized then that they were coming to
take him back to his grave. As the nurse and orderlies entered
the room, Jimmy threw his arms around me once more, fran-
tically imploring me not to let them take him. He was in tears
now as they wrestled with him, trying to pull him away. In a
final effort, he clutched at my shirt, clinging to me fiercely
now, pleading with me to hold on tight. But my shirt ripped
in his hands as he was torn from my grasp and dragged out
the door, shrieking now, "Save me, Willie, save me!" Frozen,
unable to move a muscle, I watched from the window as they
hauled him to the ambulance. As the coffin lid slammed shut
on him, he flung at me once more those accusing words of his:
"I trusted you! I trusted you!"

I was wakened by the phone, drenched in sweat, sobbing
uncontrollably.

Later that morning, I had a morose brunch with a friend,
Bill Theiss, a costume designer for films. Finally unable to
stand my silence any longer, he made the big mistake of asking
me about my dream. Halfway through describing it, my com-
posure crumbled, and I was reduced again to a shambles of
tears. Picking up the tab, Bill saw me back to my apartment.

It went on for days like that. I simply could not stop crying. But I knew what I had to do. I had to start writing that
book. It was the only way I knew to save him.

During the three-month writing process, I allowed myself few distractions except to see close friends. Being back in New York gave me the opportunity to visit the Colgates again. I'd stayed in touch with them, of course, but it had been too long since we'd spent any time together, and I'd missed them. While Jimmy and I were living together in New York, they'd heard me talk about him and his burgeoning career so much that they'd made a point of seeing all his pictures and had become fans. We'd talked on the phone after Jimmy's death, and they appreciated what a blow it had been for me. As a result, they were both very enthusiastic about the book, especially Beatrice, who gave me constant encouragement throughout the months of writing. I was equally touched by Ella Logan's enthusiasm for the project. She'd moved to a New York apartment near the one I was subletting, so was once again accessible. One of Jimmy's many surrogate mothers, she had adored him and now took me under her wing, as she might have an abandoned chick. Wonderfully supportive, she was there for me during the hard part of reliving the past so soon after Jimmy's death.

That summer and fall, I made two trips to Fairmount, Jimmy's hometown. The first was at the invitation of Vivian Gouche, a public-relations expert who had been approached with the idea of establishing a James Dean Memorial Foundation. While in Fairmount to lay the groundwork, we were invited by Marcus and Ortense to stay with them at the farm. The place didn't seem to have changed at all since Dizzy and I were there, but they had. Although still the same kind, gentle people I remembered, an aura of sadness and resignation now enveloped them, despite their efforts to disguise it. It was also sad for me to see what had happened to Jimmy's gravestone. Fans and souvenir hunters had managed to chisel chips out of it, lending it the look of something used for target practice.

Later in the year, I returned to Fairmount with Jane Deacy, Jimmy's agent, who had been persuaded to head up the newly established memorial foundation. This time I encountered a personable young man, possibly in his mid- to late-twenties, whom the Winslows were treating like one of the family. According to Ortense, he had introduced himself as a friend of Jimmy's, and, as such, the family had embraced him with open arms. Not only was he living with them, he was occupying Jimmy's old bedroom. He even seemed to have taken Jimmy's place as a surrogate older brother to young Markie. In fact, as far as I could determine, he seemed to have befriended almost the entire population of Fairmount. Everywhere we went in town, whether to the high school, the ice cream parlor, or the church, everyone knew him and greeted him warmly. If someone needed a friendly ear or help with the chores, apparently he was always there with a smile. It was no wonder they all seemed to adore him. Fairmount was that kind of town, and he was apparently that kind of guy. Even Jane found him adorable.

Yet I was puzzled. I knew, or knew about, most of Jimmy's friends, especially his close friends, but I had never met this young man nor had Jimmy ever mentioned his name. As I observed him interacting with the family and the townsfolk, I marveled at his determination to endear himself to one and all. Being something of a skeptic, it began to occur to me that he was, consciously or subconsciously, trying to take Jimmy's place. Or was he trying to *become* Jimmy, perhaps?

Ortense was out with Jane one afternoon, and Marcus was working in the fields. I returned from a visit with Jimmy's high-school drama teacher to find the new man in town home alone. He poured me a cup of coffee and started asking questions about Jimmy, general stuff at first. I obliged his curiosity, but gradually the questions turned to the nature of our relationship. I had the uneasy sense that I knew where he was going, so remained vague and evasive. He then asked if Jimmy had ever shown me his boyhood mementos, the ones he'd kept in a trunk in the attic. I didn't recall ever being in the attic, so he volunteered to show me.

Still uneasy, yet now intrigued by the prospect of seeing tokens of my friend's early life, I followed this stranger upstairs to the Winslows' attic where he opened an old trunk. Indeed, it contained items that dated back to Jimmy's teen years and earlier, including sketches, paintings, poetry, a high-school yearbook, letters, photos, and the like. As Mr. Wonderful went through them, I noted how he treated each with a care that bordered on reverence. I was growing more uncomfortable by the minute as this stranger pried into Jimmy's private life with a delight that seemed to me to border on obsession. Yes, the items in the trunk were interesting, even touching, but they were all quite definitely private property.

What happened next shouldn't have surprised me, but I couldn't imagine anybody being quite so insensitive or audacious. Suddenly, and without any qualms, this man, this stranger, this cuckoo in the nest, proposed that we have sex together, right then and there. I was totally flabbergasted, astonished that anyone could even consider doing anything so gross, so disrespectful of Jimmy's memory, right there, under the Winslows' own roof, in Jimmy's own home. Furthermore, the idea of having sex among Jimmy's youthful mementos went beyond being painful. But then, maybe he wasn't to know that. So, quite reasonably, I think, I said that I didn't think it was a good idea. I reminded him, in case he'd forgotten, that we were guests in the Winslows' home. Duly chastened, he backed off apologetically.

Of course, he was safe in thinking I'd never betray him to the Winslows. At that point, Marcus and Ortense were still in the earliest stage of their gradual loss of innocence. They were not yet equipped to understand, much less deal with, the unconventional agendas of some of Jimmy's worshipers. The truth would have been far beyond their ken and quite alien to their way of thinking, to say the least. Had I confronted them with reality at that point, they would probably have called me a liar and sent *me* packing. Aside from that, I hadn't been completely forthright with them myself, had I?

Back in New York, with the end of my sublet approaching, I found an apartment on East Sixty-third, just off Third. On the top floor of a brownstone in a quiet, tree-lined street, it suited me well. Except for the stairs, that is. My book would be coming out soon, and I was feeling expansive, so I took the plunge and signed a two-year lease. Unfortunately, the apartment was in the process of being refurbished and wouldn't be ready for a couple of weeks, so I decided to treat myself to a temporary stay in the Algonquin Hotel.

There was something very special about staying at the fabled Algonk, not merely because of its romantic history, but also because of its proximity to the more modest Iroquois, where Jimmy and I lived together earlier. However, I had only been in residence a day or two, when, one evening as I was returning from an early dinner, my old nemesis appeared beside me at the front desk, the reptilian Rogers Brackett (Jimmy's metaphor, not mine). On his way out, Rogers was turning in his room key to the desk clerk, and I realized to my chagrin that he was also a guest in the hotel. But before I could escape, he'd noticed me. Peering down his long nose, he greeted me with his usual cool condescension.

"Oh, it's you, Bill," he sniffed. Then, obviously referring to my soon-to-be-published book, "I see you've managed to jump on the bandwagon, too."

I said nothing, asked the desk clerk for my room key, and stepped onto the elevator. Rogers was definitely a spoiler, and I wasn't about to give him the satisfaction of any acknowledgment. However, even as the doors closed, I realized the damage had been done and decided to move out as soon as possible. As if to bolster my decision, the next morning, the desk clerk handed me a note from my box. Addressed to me, it read, "What I had to say was: Don't jump on a cheap bandwagon—especially when it's a hearse," signed "Rogers Brackett." Yes, I resolved, I would definitely have to find someplace else to stay.

Fortunately, Rusty Slocum came to my rescue. A young actor I had recently met, Rusty was renting a large apartment on Third Avenue conveniently near my new place, and he invited me to stay with him until it was ready. It was during this brief stay that he innocently provided an answer to the mystery that had periodically nagged me over the past months. According to Rusty, he had recently learned from Billy Gunn, Jimmy's understudy in *The Immoralist*, that Gunn and several other unnamed friends of Jimmy's had broken into his New York apartment the morning after his death. The rationale for the break-in was to find a copy, if there was one, of his incriminating letter to the draft board, about which Jimmy had told them. Apparently, they were afraid it might fall into the hands of the press and be used to tarnish Jimmy's image. This rationale made absolutely no sense to me, however, as I had helped Jimmy write that letter and if it still existed at all, was probably buried in the depths of some governmental vault somewhere. Furthermore, that may have been their declared pretext for the break-in, but it certainly wasn't the only item that disappeared from Jimmy's apartment that day. There was, for instance, the unexplained peregrination of my treasured copy of *The Little Prince* to Elizabeth Taylor's house in Beverly Hills via the *Redbook* journalist. Which raised the obvious question in my mind: How did *he* get hold of it? Until Rusty's revelation, I'd had no idea about any of this. Now I could only speculate as to which of Jimmy's noble-minded friends might have liberated it, possibly along with other treasured relics.

Still, I only had Rusty's word about the break-in. He could have gotten it wrong. However, over subsequent years, I heard the same story several times from different sources, but none that I could count as reliable. Ultimately solid details did emerge in an interesting source that appeared to be well researched, a book titled *James Dean – little boy lost, an intimate biography*. Published by Warner Books in 1992 and penned by one Joe Hyams, the break-in is described in some detail, and Billy Gunn is specifically nailed as one of the participants, along with "some other friends." After reading the details, it occurred to me that Mr. Hyams, a one-time contributor to *Redbook* magazine, may have been the unwitting recipient of stolen goods, which, quite innocently he passed along to Elizabeth as a gesture of kindness. However, to this day, I still wonder who copped my tan corduroy jacket, which also disappeared in the break-in. I had developed a sentimental attachment to it, as well. Not that it would fit me anymore, but Jimmy had borrowed it to wear for Roy Schatt's photograph, the one that ended up fronting the paperback edition of my book. Ah well, as Jimmy used to warn me, "There are harpies on the shore."

My book was rushed into print later that fall in hardcover and paperback to generally good reviews. With some donations from Ella's store of unused furnishings and unwanted paintings, and a tip from Truman Capote about good buys to be had from an antiques store downtown, my apartment was also furnished in short order, and I became the new kid on the block.

A week or so after moving in, while waiting for a red light to change on the corner of Sixty-third and Third, I became aware of a tall, elderly woman standing on the curb nearby. She was trying in vain to hail a taxi. I recognized immediately the unmistakable voice of Eleanor Roosevelt. After a couple of empty cabs passed her by, I offered my help. She thanked me, then took a closer look, "Mr. Bast, isn't it?"

I expressed amazement that she remembered.

"How could I forget? The *madrilène*, wasn't it?" she mused. "What a disagreeable man he was." And then: "By the way, congratulations on your book."

I was even more astonished that she'd even heard of it.

"Oh, I was a great admirer of your Mr. Dean," she smiled. "You must tell me more about him. Now that you're my neighbor, we shall have tea."

It turned out that she owned the brick house next to the brownstone I now lived in. I wondered how she knew I was a neighbor.

"Oh, they keep me apprised of all the new people on the street, you know," she confided.

I finally managed to snare her a taxi and held the door for her. Thanking me, she got in and instructed the cabbie, "The United Nations, please, driver."

That made my day. But as she rode away, I couldn't help wondering who, exactly, "they" were and how much they had "apprised" her about me. Whatever it was, it didn't seem to trouble her.

Sometime in the first week of October, Elizabeth phoned. In town for the charity premiere of *Giant* on the eleventh, she was staying at the Carlyle Hotel. Having divorced Michael Wilding in the interim, she announced somewhat giddily that she had a new man in her life. He turned out to be Michael Todd, producer of *Around the World in Eighty Days*, which, coincidentally, was opening in town the week after the *Giant* premiere. She confessed that, after only a brief period of dating, she was beginning to think Todd might be the right man at last. Yet, she seemed afraid to trust her own judgment; after all, she'd been wrong twice before. Explaining that Todd was escorting her to the *Giant* premiere, she invited me to join them. I got the sense that she was interested in my assessment of her new man. I accepted the invitation, not exactly confident I could be objective. I'd heard stories about the cocky, macho Mr. Todd and figured he probably wouldn't be my kinda guy. Although Elizabeth's call was an opportunity to do so, it didn't seem an appropriate time to go into the subject of my copy of *The Little Prince*. I felt uneasy about telling her the tale of the break-in, about which I had no corroboration at that point, nor indeed have I ever got up the nerve to do so.

The night of the premiere, Mike Todd turned out to be a diamond in the rough, as charming and intelligent as Elizabeth had portrayed him. Piling into Mike's limo, we were driven to Rockefeller Center's Roxy Theater. As we pulled up, I found it painful to realize that Jimmy couldn't be there to share with us this night, a night that promised to be *his*; word of mouth had it that, once again, he'd stolen the picture. I consoled myself with the thought that he probably would have skipped out again, as he had on the premiere of *Eden*. As for me, it wouldn't be my first premiere, but it would definitely be the biggest and the most spotlighted, if only as an appendage to the hottest celebrity twosome of the moment. I was usually ill at ease at such affairs, but within the comforting glow of Elizabeth's regal company, the evening promised a perfectly orchestrated, relatively relaxed experience, or so I assumed prematurely.

The aggressive press, the in-your-face film and television cameras, and the hysterical crowd outside the theater were nothing compared to the shocking crush of the exclusive, invited audience inside the lobby. As we entered, someone shouted, "It's Elizabeth Taylor!" With that, it seemed that everyone, even some of the more distinguished-looking guests, converged on Elizabeth, pushing and shoving to get an up-close glimpse. Before we knew what was happening, they were clawing at her, grabbing at her clothes, clutching at her arms. I could see the fear in her eyes turn to panic as she tried to tear away, desperately looking for a way out. Mike tried to shield her, but we were now completely surrounded, and suddenly, Elizabeth was pushed to the floor. Bellowing, Mike forced the mob back and gathered her up in his arms. Shoving his way through, he carried her to a lobby banquette. Meanwhile, I did my rattled best to keep lookie-loos and photographers away. Ten minutes later, Elizabeth was still trembling as we made our way inside and took our seats. After Madison Square Garden, it had been my second experience of the power of mass hysteria.

When Jimmy appeared on the gigantic Roxy screen, bigger and more lifelike than ever before, dear, sweet Elizabeth reached for my hand and held it throughout the remainder of the picture. Scene by scene, for most of the three hours and seventeen minutes, he was alive and with us again. So much of what he did onscreen seemed that familiar. Only in the final sequence, as the character of the middle-aged Jett Rink, did he become a different person. Seeing him like that brought to mind Sandy Roth's photograph of him watching the kendo match forlornly only a year before.

For those who are remembering the dead, there is a vast difference between photographs and motion pictures. In photos, the dead are still and somehow safely distant; in movies, they come alive again and can be far too real to bear. For me, even the festive mood of the party after the premiere was eclipsed by the visceral impact of having just seen Jimmy "alive" once more. Thanks to Elizabeth's and Mike's sensitivity, I managed to put a good face on it for the rest of the evening.

Ballantine had published the sanitized biographical account of my five-year friendship with Jimmy almost exactly one year after his death. I don't know what I expected, but I certainly wasn't prepared for the response. Within a month of its publication, a small army of devoted Dean fans and, somewhat more worrisome, seriously troubled folk were finding their way to my door.

One might dismiss them as proto-groupies, but that would be too glib, for there was often much pain, much genuine need. As a writer, I tried to maintain some sense of perspective, but with time, that became harder rather than easier. Most of them, especially the younger ones, came looking for some contact, any contact, even once removed, with the one kindred soul with whom they had come to identify—rightly or wrongly—based entirely on the three characters they had seen Jimmy play in his only three movies. Unfortunately, because of what they had read in fan magazines and, for my sins, in my biography, they believed he was the One who would surely have understood their anguish, their yearning, their unfulfilled dreams, their loneliness, their sense of alienation, whatever. Now, looking into their earnest faces and listening to their stories, though, I felt painfully inadequate. It was all but impossible to turn them away at first.

Gradually, however, I was to learn that overindulgence in the dispensation of solace can also become a self-gratifying and, eventually, emotionally taxing, full-time occupation. Miss Lonelyhearts, redux.

On the other hand, I also discovered that some of my correspondents were just looking for the thrill, the high, of knowing, touching, or with any luck, bedding "the man who knew him best," as the cover blurb on the paperback edition of my book identified me. Still others were simply opportunists, knocking at the door of someone they mistakenly assumed could gain them entry to the impenetrable worlds of film, television, or theater. Forwarded to me by Ballantine Books, mail from my readers had now begun to arrive daily from every corner of the country and, eventually, every corner of the globe. As the stream turned to torrent, the letters were piled into file boxes for weekly delivery. Patiently, I would work my way through the letters each day, intrigued by how folk were reacting to the book and what lay behind their individual obsessions with Jimmy.

One morning, after confronting about a month's worth of dizzying stacks of mail, I opened a letter that started, "Dear son . . ." This grabbed my attention. From the handwriting and postmark, I knew that it wasn't my mother. The return address given was somewhere near Milwaukee, where my father had been born. Could it possibly be? Somewhat like Jimmy, I, too, had been deprived of one parent, in my case my dad, after my mother divorced him when I was but three. Having neither set eyes on him, nor heard from him, in more than twenty years, I read on with interest:

"Well, you're not really my son, but I did hold you on my lap and you did put your arms around my neck and call me Mommy."

Evidently not from my dad, the letter turned out to have been written by a woman named Elenore, my long-lost father's second wife and therefore my stepmother. Being but three at the time of our embrace, I had no recollection of that moment, so special to her. But I did know my father had remarried shortly after divorcing Bee, although my mother had never let the name Elenore sully her lips. As far as Bee was concerned, Elenore didn't exist, although she had often fondly spoken of Margie, my father's sister.

Explaining how she had located me, Elenore's letter convolutedly related how Margie now had a teenage daughter, who was a Dean fan and had bought my book. Could the author of the book be Margie's nephew and her uncle's "long lost son," whose name also happened to be William, the girl had wondered? Whereupon, Margie took one look at my photograph on the book jacket and, convinced that she saw a family resemblance, promptly picked up the phone to call Elenore.

Elenore's letter went on to explain that she and my father had seven children, ranging in age from one to seventeen, pointing out that I, therefore, had five half-brothers and two half-sisters. I was duly staggered by this revelation. Suddenly I had seven more siblings. One or two would have been appreciable, but seven? I'd hit the jackpot. There was one sour note, however. As I scanned Elenore's list of their names, I was taken aback, indeed profoundly shocked, to find another son named

William, thus creating two William Basts sired by the same father. Granted, I'd been named after *his* father, my paternal grandfather. Having been deprived of his namesake, it was reasonable to imagine that the old man might have been pleased to have an accessible grandson who bore his name. Still, that my father would even have considered such a slight to his firstborn disturbed me and remains a canker that gnaws even today.

As if she hadn't done enough to disturb my equilibrium, Elenore concluded her letter by proposing a scheme that she and Margie had cooked up behind my father's back. I was to come "home" to Milwaukee for Christmas and "surprise" him.

In a way, I felt this proposed reunion with my father could be attributable either to my book about Jimmy, or—was it possible?—his intervention. Had Jimmy somehow "arranged" this strange turn of events from the beyond? After all, he'd never really been able to connect with his own father, so perhaps this was his "gift" to me? And if Jimmy had offered this gift, who was I to refuse it?

Sad to report, unlike family reunions to be found in Dickens or Harlequin romances, this one was not entirely heartwarming. Too many years, too much buried resentment on my part, and probably too much guilt on my father's kept it from being the unifying experience I had hoped for. Still, it was full of surprises.

I arrived in Milwaukee the day after a snowstorm. While in town, I had been invited to stay with Mary Leibrock, a former high-school chum, and her family. I'd asked Mary to accompany me to the reunion for moral support. Ideally, it should have been Jimmy, but maybe in some way he was present, too. Arriving at the Bast residence, a two-story house in the suburbs, we were greeted at the front door by Elenore, who turned out to be a slender woman wearing pedal pushers and a lot of lipstick. Having anticipated this occasion eagerly, she swung the storm door open to admit us and accidentally knocked poor Mary backward off the front porch into the snowbank. We were off to a good start.

Elenore helped me retrieve Mary, brushed off her clothes,

then led us inside, where my father was waiting alone in the living room. He got up when we entered, and Elenore introduced us, rather formally I thought. He shook Mary's hand, then turned to me. Neither of us made a move, but only stared at one another for an uneasy moment. Then he shook my hand as formally as he had Mary's and said it was good to see me after so long. I couldn't help feeling his greeting a bit cool considering the length of time since last we met. The sting of his inability to embrace me, or at least evince some genuine warmth, seemed to speak volumes, and like it or not, I was still vulnerable.

We were invited to sit down. My father and I took seats opposite each other and avoided eye contact as much as possible during what followed, although I did catch him studying me whenever I was engaged with someone else. Still a handsome man in his middle years, I could see how Bee might have fallen for him at the tender age of fifteen. But in his own fashion, he was as dour and uncommunicative with me as Winton had been with Jimmy.

Elenore now set about summoning my seven new siblings, rather theatrically insisting on introducing them to me one at a time. As they were led in, each demonstrated a different attitude toward me, some shy, some outgoing, some even affectionate. One of the younger boys and one of the girls refused to leave my side. It was only William #2, possibly aged nine or ten, who, though polite, proved taciturn and seemed to harbor some resentment at my presence. I certainly understood his feelings.

We spent an hour or so uncomfortably getting acquainted. For me, the strangest aspect of the experience lay in discovering how each child bore some physical likeness familiar to me, traits I saw whenever I looked in the mirror. When Elenore had run out of surprises, it seemed time to depart and allow everyone to relax and digest the events of the day. As I was leaving, my father finally made a move to communicate. He took me aside and told me that he thought it best to leave matters as they were, that, in his words, "These things never seem to work out." So, politely declining Elenore's invitation to share Christmas dinner with them the following day, I returned to New York.

That was more than forty years ago. My father is dead now, and I never spoke to or heard from him again. To me, the greatest irony was that, in the end, my effort to reach out and connect with him had worked out no better than Jimmy's had with his father. In that respect, maybe this was his gift to me. Now I understood how he must have felt.

I returned to New York and my mountain of mail and yet another round of Dean-seekers. Most were still in their teens or early twenties. Often they would be waiting on my doorstep, and inexplicably, they would sometimes manage to get me on the phone, which was and still remains a mystery to me as I had an unlisted number. On occasion, I'd be wakened in the middle of the night by a call from some desperate youngster, phoning from thousands of miles away.

More surprising to me was the number of mature Dean fans who started to materialize in my social life. Though most were simply admirers of his work, as curious about the continuing adulation surrounding my friend as I was, there were a surprising number whose interest was unabashedly prurient. They would buttonhole me at gatherings and try to pry out of me the "real dirt" about Jimmy. I vaguely recall one Betty Bettis King, purportedly an heiress of Texas' King Ranch lineage. I had barely been introduced to her over drinks at the Sherry Netherlands when she leaned in, grabbed my upper thigh, and focusing two intimidating, booze-glazed eyes squarely on my brow, shot her first and only question: "Let's skip the bullshit, honey. How big was his cock?" I didn't stick around for my drink.

But more surprises were in store for me.

Having been invited to join Jane Deacy for dinner at Downey's one evening, I arrived a few minutes late and was surprised to find that she had also invited Billy Gunn. When I got settled, Jane announced with uncharacteristic sentimentality that, as of that very day, Billy was now her client. Billy beamed bashfully in the warmth of her appreciation. Then, with great pride and enthusiasm, she declared that, aside from being a wonderful actor, Billy was also a gifted poet. In fact, she had just persuaded him to publish some of his poems. With that, she suggested that Billy read me one or two. Shyly, Billy riffled through his briefcase and selected "one of Jane's favorites."

As he read the poem, my heart sank. Almost at once, I recognized it as one of Jimmy's, one he'd written long before he met Billy. I could only imagine that the poems disappeared from his apartment during the break-in—along with the purported copy of Jimmy's letter to the draft board, my tan corduroy jacket, and my copy of *The Little Prince*. Once again, I held my tongue. Billy is dead now, so the truth can't hurt him, only perhaps his reputation, although he later became a poet and playwright renowned in his own right. Nor did I say anything to Jane, then or ever. Once again, I was caught in a bind. As with Elizabeth, I cared too much for Jane to disillusion her about her newfound treasure. To this day, I don't know if the poems ever got published.

One weekend with the Colgates, Beatrice observed over dinner that I seemed a bit tired and down. I explained that writing the book and now the seemingly endless parade of James Dean fans showing up on my doorstep was beginning to take its toll. Bayard suggested that I get out of New York, come up to Contentment Island for a month or so, do some sailing with him, relax, read and write, and forget about James Dean and his admirers. Beatrice agreed and urged me to come up for as long as I wanted. Then, knowing how long and how much I'd yearned to do so, she suggested I continue on to Europe for a while. It would be a complete break, a whole new world of experience, where I wouldn't be in James Dean's constant shadow. Bayard concurred and suggested I go by sea and use the time to relax and clear my head. He even offered to pay my fare. "Of course," Beatrice agreed, "you shall go to Europe! It's all settled." There they were, once again the *dei ex machinae* of my life, beloved guardian angels. I could not have loved them more, although I should have loved them better.

About this time, Marvin Paige, a good friend of mine and at that point in his career, talent coordinator for "Luncheon at Sardi's," invited me to guest on his show. A popular national noontime radio talk show, it broadcast celebrity interviews live from Broadway's famous theatrical restaurant. Aside from promotion for my book and a great lunch, the gig also included a complimentary new set of luggage, which I could certainly use for my first voyage abroad. Marvin's assistant at the time, a young lady named Rona Barrett, also worked for *Photoplay Magazine*. When Rona learned that I was off to Europe soon, she brought it to the attention of her editor. As a result, *Photoplay* approached me to write a couple of articles on movies shooting in Europe that summer. Otto Preminger's adaptation of a best-selling, six-handkerchief French novel by Françoise Sagan, *Bonjour Tristesse*, was already in production on the French Riviera starring David Niven, Deborah Kerr, and Preminger's ill-fated protégée, Jean Seberg. The other picture was filming on location in Norway: Richard Fleischer's *The Vikings*, starring Kirk Douglas, Tony Curtis, Janet Leigh, and Jimmy's and my old friend Ernest Borgnine. How could I resist?

My feelings were decidedly mixed as I embarked on my first European adventure. Yes, I was excited to be taking my first trip abroad, but still, as I sailed out of New York Harbor and I looked back at the towers of Manhattan receding in the distance, a certain sadness crept over me. I was leaving the place I had come to love, the one place where I had at last found my identity, the only place I had ever been truly happy. Perhaps I was leaving my new life behind too soon after having so recently claimed it. Still, I reasoned, at least for a time, I'd be leaving behind the army of Dean fans and all the memories connected with him. Besides, I would only be away a couple of months. It was bound to be an interesting adventure even though I was traveling alone with no one along to share it. I hated traveling alone.

Standing at the ship's rail as Miss Liberty was swallowed up in the sea mist, I tried to banish my nagging doubts and think about how Jimmy and I had listened to Sandy and Beulah talk of their magical lives in Europe, how we had dreamed of taking our first trip together. Yet my sadness persisted.

Now on my way alone, how profoundly I wished he were still alive and at my side. Then, as we reached open sea, the mist was swept away, and night spread her stars from horizon to horizon. I thought of the Little Prince on his asteroid, somewhere far up there, among them. It was then that an echo from the past arose from the sea to remind me of my previous venture into the unknown and to reassure me.

"You know, Willie," it whispered above the churning wake, "you and I would make good teammates." And I realized for the first time that I wasn't traveling alone.

25

When You Dine With the Devil

"AH YES, WILLIAM BAST, THE YOUNG MAN WHO KNEW JAMES Dean—intimately. Tell me, my dear, were you lovers?" This was John Gielgud's opening gambit, declaimed for all to hear, as I was introduced to him at an all-male gathering in a friend's apartment on Paris's Left Bank.

Although fairly redolent of mischief, of course, it wasn't the first time, nor would it be the last, that his baldly expressed question would be directed at me, but never would I hear it more elegantly and eloquently expressed than by England's second-greatest Shakespearean actor, Olivier having claimed first place. Nor would it be the last time I declined to answer explicitly, sensitive now to the ever-present threat of press exposure and possible damage to Jimmy's name. However, I could sense that the canny Sir John, as he had recently been dubbed, saw through my elliptical reply, yet decided to respect the evasion enough to change the subject with his usual grace.

This was my first visit to Paris and, after several days of sightseeing, I'd been invited to what our host, an American acquaintance, had euphemistically referred to as one of his Sunday afternoon "teas," the exact meaning of which I wasn't to learn until I arrived at his top-floor apartment on the rue Notre-Dame-des-Champs. There, a cosmopolitan mix of a dozen or so young and middle-aged men had gathered for drinks and a buffet lunch, and, I was quickly to learn, to adjourn to the master bedroom, should one be of a mind, where there was a nonstop orgy going on all afternoon. However, per the orgy, the house rules were strict: Participants only! Voyeurs prohibited!

Not being disposed to group sex, I abstained and remained in the salon, as had half of the other guests, including the decorous Gielgud. As he was familiar with the house rules, I was prompted to guess that he'd been to these affairs before. He admitted to having "dropped by" on occasion "whenever in Paris of a Sunday. The ambiance," he confided with a naughty smile, "suits me."

Leaving Paris, I arrived a few days later in the, then, tiny resort village of Le Lavandou near St. Tropez, there to cover the filming of *Bonjour Tristesse*. The company was shooting at an ideal location, a pink villa overlooking the Mediterranean. During a break in shooting, the unit manager dutifully introduced me to Preminger, then to Deborah Kerr, David Niven, and finally to waiflike Jean Seberg, who appeared to me to be under something of a strain.

Preminger had discovered her during one of those clichéd Hollywood "exhaustive talent searches." She'd been acting in a high-school play somewhere in Idaho, and he promptly signed her to an exclusive contract to star in his next film, an adaptation of Shaw's *Saint Joan*. Upon its release, however, the picture had been trashed by the critics, and, based mainly on his choice of Seberg for the lead role, the director had been excoriated by a merciless press. Presumably, Preminger believed the girl's performance in *Bonjour Tristesse* would vindicate his faith in her. On the set the next day, I sensed a desperate air of, come hell or high water, this time she would deliver!

While the crew set up for a shot, Seberg approached me timidly, explaining that she'd read my book and, rather endearingly, confessing that Jimmy was her personal idol. She was eager to know whatever I could tell her about his approach to acting. But, before we could get into it, the camera was ready to roll again, and she was summoned back for her scene. I watched with mounting sympathy as she tried to get

it right, but failed repeatedly to satisfy her overbearing director. After the fifth take, Preminger completely lost his temper
and started bullying her in shrill outbursts worthy of one of
his own over-the-top Nazi impersonations as an actor in B-
pictures years earlier. With cast and crew looking on aghast,
he screamed in her face, "You call dat actink?! A chimpanzee
could do better!" After two oppressive days of this sort of
thing, I figured I'd got my story and arranged my early departure. Need I say that the magazine later refused to print what
I wrote? I've often thought it a pity, though, that Otto never
got to make a picture with Jimmy. Now, that would have been
something to write about.

I flew to Norway next where I was met by a driver and
chauffeured north from Bergen into magnificent, enchanted
fjord country, arriving by nightfall at the Herdangerfjord,
where *The Vikings* unit was on location. I found myself bil-
leted with most of the stars, the director, and the production
crew on a palatial yacht that had been rented from million-
airess Barbara Hutton. Janet Leigh, Curtis's wife and the picture's female lead, was not on hand as yet, but due to arrive a
day or two later. As for the picture's principal star, Kirk Douglas, he was quartered at a hotel a few miles further up the
fjord, where, I was informed, he had been ill for a few days.
After I got settled in my stateroom, director Richard Fleischer
introduced me to cast members Tony Curtis and Ernest Borgnine. As I shook Borgnine's hand, I found myself thinking
rather unfairly that this was the hand that had accepted the
Oscar that should have been Jimmy's.

Anchored immediately alongside the yacht was the
"Viking warship." A wooden craft constructed especially for
the picture, it was hewn from Norwegian pine, modeled after
an authentic tenth-century version, and accommodated a crew
of perhaps thirty stalwart Norwegian lads, mostly students
from the University of Oslo, out to earn some *kroner* as
Viking oarsmen. During filming over the next couple of days,
I noticed a buzz among some of these kids, who seemed to
have developed an interest in my interviewing activity. This
puzzled me. A stringer from an American magazine was surely

nothing special. Then, during a lunch break, one of them approached me and politely introduced himself. Bjorn asked rather awkwardly, and in surprisingly good English, if I was the author of the book he had just read about James Dean.

So there it was. I couldn't get away from it, even in this distant northern Scandinavian wilderness, thousands of miles from the States, here was a kid who'd actually bought and read my book, and more surprisingly, recognized me from the jacket photo. He brought the book to my stateroom that evening, and I signed it for him. He stayed awhile to ask the usual questions about Jimmy and what it was like to know him. I told him it was like having an extraordinary friend who was forever surprising me. Before leaving, he informed me that the following night would be Midsummer's Night, a sight not to be missed in Norway.

Midsummer's Night, I found myself atop a towering cliff, facing an awesome glacier directly across the fjord. Down below, for miles in either direction along the banks of the fjord, traditional midsummer bonfires blazed. I spent the night in a pup tent with Bjorn and one of his mates, beneath the awesome spectacle of the midnight sun. Indeed, the sun never did set, and I, at least, never slept.

My *Photoplay* assignment now complete, I left the location and returned to Bergen where I phoned the airline to make my reservation back to Paris. The operator asked if I wanted to fly directly to Paris or go via London. I hadn't realized I'd had the option. I decided instantly to fly via London, one European city from Sandy and Beulah's past that had not been on my itinerary.

It turned out to be a wise choice, one of the wisest I've ever made.

England was enjoying a particularly warm and sunny summer that year, and London was responding joyfully. One evening at the theater, to my complete astonishment, I ran into my two old friends from the CBS days back in Hollywood, Alan and Ginny Young. So much in my life appears to be coincidence, although frequently I have been tempted to believe that another, unseen influence has been at work behind the scenes, pulling the strings, so to speak: Jimmy, for instance.

Over drinks, I learned that Alan had come to England initially to star in a movie version of *Tom Thumb* for puppeteer George Pal. Upon completion of the film, he'd been invited to stay on and star in a summer comedy series for Granada Television, "Saturday Night at the Chelsea." He and Ginny had brought over their two children and taken a mews house off the Bayswater Road for the duration. When they heard I was only planning to spend a few days in London, they insisted I stay at least a couple of weeks with them to do the place justice. Having no other plans or writing assignments, I took them up on their offer. Ginny, the kids, and I would explore London during the day while Alan was in rehearsals, and he would join us in the evenings for more English theater, of which there was, happily, an abundant supply. As the time approached for me to leave, Alan proposed that I consider staying on and help him rewrite some of his comedy sketches for the television show. Of course, I couldn't refuse.

With Ginny's help, I found an acceptable flat on the ground floor of a house on Derby Street. Located just off Park Lane near Shepherds Market, it was quite centrally located in the West End. My landlady, a sweet elderly woman, lived in the basement flat below and kindly saw to my needs. When I moved in, I had no idea how greatly the location would determine ensuing events.

I found walking in London a delight, so rarely took taxis as my flat was easily within walking distance of Granada's offices in Golden Square. However, returning along Park Lane in the evening, I quickly discovered I had to run the gauntlet of a bevy of hookers routinely stationed along the way. The girls could be rather aggressive, though most would back off when I politely declined their solicitations. Only one persisted, a Yorkshire lass named Sheila, who said she rather fancied Americans. I would pause to chat with her, hoping to draw her out about how and why she and the others had got on the game. This made her uneasy at first, worried that her pimp might be watching. She wasn't supposed to "chat up" potential clients, she confided. I suggested that perhaps we could meet in the little espresso bar nearby on the corner of Curzon Street after she was off duty. Embarrassed, she demurred, sure that the coffee-shop management wouldn't allow "her sort" inside. I boldly assured her that they'd better if she were with me. She rather liked the sound of that and finally agreed to meet me outside the place at midnight the following evening.

In truth, I was a bit nervous myself about our rendezvous. I had just learned that England was still burdened by savage and archaic laws concerning sexual behavior that punished prostitution, as well as homosexual acts, resulting in an ongoing hypocritical and ruthless witch hunt that had been responsible for considerable misery and ruination of reputations over the years. One of its more recent and publicized homosexual victims had been John Gielgud himself, one of England's national treasures. No wonder he found that the ambiance of Paris "suited him."

Overcoming her trepidations when we met later, Sheila entered the espresso bar on my arm, proud as a princess. Over coffee, she told me rather nervously how she'd come to London to learn nursing, but soon got hooked on drugs by a handsome Maltese lad who turned out to be a professional pimp. It was his job to procure girls for the so-called Maltese Syndicate, which had cornered the prostitution market at the time. It was the usual story: hook the girls on drugs, then force them to turn tricks or face the trauma of withdrawal. Once hooked, Sheila had given up her dream of a career in nursing and taken to the streets. I got pretty much the whole story that night, probably more than she should have told me.

After we left the shop, she walked me to my door around the corner and offered me her services, on the house, as it were. Of course, I declined, but I made sure to pay her for the sex we didn't have, just in case her pimp had seen us together. She could always tell him that I was the type that "just wanted to talk," which was true. After that, every time I ran into her, she tried to coax me with the same offer, but I continued to decline, using my watchdog landlady or incipient cold or general fatigue as an excuse. This apparently got her to thinking.

In keeping with my desire to prevent the same intrusion into my private life that had happened in New York, I was determined, perhaps foolishly, to avoid any publicity in connection with James Dean while in London. Here, I assured myself, I would just be an anonymous television writer, allowed to enjoy my life without the taxing intrusion of well-meaning, but emotionally draining Dean fans like those that had besieged me in New York. However, thanks to studio gossip, after only a couple of weeks of work on Alan's show, everyone at Granada Television seemed to be aware of my dirty little secret, including an aspiring young producer named Terry.

Unfortunately, as an American working in the U.K., I'd had a problem banking and cashing my paychecks, which Terry had kindly helped me resolve, and I owed him one. So when he asked me to break my rule just once and do him a favor by granting an interview about James Dean to his friend, Herbert Kretzmer, then a young reporter for London's *Daily Sketch*, I naturally relented. Obviously it wouldn't amount to more than a squib in Kretzmer's column. The following Monday morning, the floodgates opened, and the cat was out of the bag, big time.

The *Daily Sketch* headline blared: "DEAN—THE TRUTH THEY CAN'T TELL!" The article took up a full page and featured a photograph of me taken by Roy Schatt several years earlier that Kretzmer had somehow gotten hold of. The header declared, "DEANAGE MILLIONS AT JAMES DEAN'S TOMB: BUT NOW DEAN'S CLOSEST FRIEND RIPS THE LEGEND TO PIECES IN THE BOOK THAT WAS TOO FRANK!" Not only was I exposed and identified by photo, the article even gave my address as "a stone's throw from Shepherds Market" and described me, to my profound embarrassment, as "a slim, baby-faced American writer, who is wise beyond his 26 years." And there I was, held up for all of London to ogle at, on a Monday morning. I hated to think what Tuesday might bring. Sweet anonymity had flown the coop, and I was the dead pigeon it left behind.

Of course, my Park Lane friend Sheila saw my baby face in the paper and was beside herself with excitement to learn about the Dean connection. She waylaid me the following evening, gushing like a giddy teenager and begged me to meet her outside the espresso bar at midnight. She wouldn't take "no" for an answer, explaining that, as I'd been so good to her, she had a "special surprise" for me. How could I refuse her?

I turned up at the appointed hour to find that she had two, not unattractive young men in tow, both of whom appeared to be in their late teens. One was blond, the other dark, because, as she whispered into my ear, she didn't know which I preferred. Obviously, as I had declined her offer of a freebee, she had quite correctly deduced my sexual orientation. Before discreetly withdrawing to leave me with her two adorable boys, she took me aside and informed me that I wasn't to pay them as she'd already taken care of that. Considering the source, it was one of the dearest gestures anyone had ever made me. I was genuinely touched and tried hard not to show my embarrassment.

When she'd safely returned to her Park Lane post, I led the boys around the corner to the entrance of my building where she wouldn't be able to observe us. There on the doorstep, I explained to them that I didn't want to hurt Sheila's feelings, nor theirs for that matter, but, "tempted" as I was, I wasn't able to accept her more-than-kind offer. I pointed out that my flat was directly over my landlady's bedroom, and, because she was a light sleeper, I couldn't possibly risk taking them inside. Enlisting their help in my conspiracy not to disappoint Sheila by telling her the deal had not been consummated, I gave them each an additional fiver for their trouble and sent them on their way. The next time I ran into my friend, I thanked her profusely for her generous "treats" and was able to discern from her pleased response that the boys had kept my confidence. But she did ask me shyly which of the two I'd preferred. I told her it was a tossup, which was, I suppose, the truth. She was delighted, assuming that I'd had them both.

While in London, Alan had hired a public-relations man, a tall, shy, ginger-haired chap named Ken Pitt. Ken heard about my dismay over having been "exposed" in the press and suggested that I might want him to run interference for me. I appreciated the offer, but explained that I just wanted to keep a low profile. He pointed out that it was a bit late for that and suggested that, with his help, this could be an opportunity to publicize my book without having the situation get out of hand and turn into a circus.

A week or so later, he picked me up to take me out to a "special" restaurant for dinner to discuss strategy. As we drove out of the West End and entered a maze of dark streets on the south side of the Thames, which back then was definitely not "in" as it is now, I began to wonder where we could possibly be headed. Smiling like the Cheshire cat, Ken pulled up outside what looked like a warehouse. The street was narrow, grim, and dimly lit, but he assured perfectly safe. Thoroughly enjoying his little game now, he led me inside what turned out to be an empty warehouse. There, to my surprise and consternation, I found myself confronted by possibly as many as two hundred highly charged young people, all avid members of James Dean fan clubs from every corner of the U.K. At Ken's invitation, they had traveled to London to meet their idol's closest friend face to face and have him autograph their cherished copies of his book.

Trapped, I briefly considered various painful methods of murdering Ken for sandbagging me, but scanning those young, eager faces, my mind went back to the night, only a few years before, when Jimmy and I had confronted that roomful of awed high-school girls, the very first James Dean Fan Club. I also recalled my own youthful awe when the Colgates had turned up at the Junior Achievement convention in New York. Gathering my rattled wits, I thanked them all for coming, then spoke to them briefly, and took their questions. After about a half-hour of being grilled, I announced that I'd be happy to autograph their copies of my book. Of course, almost all of them had brought their copies, and the line stretched twice around the room.

When autographing the book, it had become my custom to ask each person his or her name and address the inscription familiarly. On that night, after signing perhaps fifty books or so, I heard a muted murmur ripple through the crowd. Looking up, I found myself confronted by a strange, middle-aged apparition. His hair was dyed an orangeish-blond and tousled in an unsuccessful imitation of what I guess he took to be the Dean look. He was wearing ill-fitting English jeans—a sad imitation of genuine Levis at the time—and a red zippered jacket, obviously in imitation of the one Jimmy wore in *Rebel*. However, that was where the similarity ended. As he stood before me, grinning at the look of stupefaction on my face, he proffered his book for me to autograph, an expectant hush fell across the room. I suppose he thought my reaction was one of amazement, whereas, in fact, it was dismay, dismay that Jimmy's image had become part of a grotesque game of charades in which I was now being expected to participate.

Clearly enjoying my reaction, he now pushed the book into my hands. I took it reluctantly, pausing before signing to scan the roomful of young faces behind him, all avidly waiting to see what I would do. Somehow, without making an issue of it, I had to let them know how I felt about this. So, as I had done with all the others, I asked his name.

He grinned and challenged me. "Can't you guess?"

Aware of my audience, I tried to smile easily. I wasn't a mind reader, I observed.

"Well, who do I remind you of?" he persisted.

I took a beat to study his features, pretending to be baffled, then, determined to make my point, replied so all could hear, "Nobody I can think of."

I could hear murmurs and sniggers of laughter in the crowd behind him. Had I been less emotionally involved with Jimmy, I suppose I wouldn't have reacted so unkindly, but I was on the spot, with a roomful of impressionable young people waiting to see how I would handle this. Reminding this stubbornly aggressive man that there were others waiting, I asked his name again.

"I'll tell you after you sign" was his irritated response.

I explained with forced patience that I always addressed my autograph to the person requesting it, so I would need his name first.

"Just autograph the bloody book!" he snapped.

"I'm sorry," I said loudly enough for all to hear. I closed his book and offered it back to him, unsigned. "If you're ashamed of your name, I don't think I want to sign your book." An excited murmur rippled through the crowd as I signaled to the next youngster in line. The impersonator glared at me, called me a shit, snatched back his book, and headed for the exit. Someone toward the back began to applaud, then more joined in, and finally, they were all applauding. Apparently, they'd gotten my message. Harsh or priggish as it may seem now, I found no joy in encouraging folk to impersonate someone I cared for and missed so much.

The following week, I was invited to appear on a popular live television talk show to discuss my book. As I'd done prior to other interviews, I asked the producer and host of the show to agree not to sensationalize the subject, but treat it with respect. However, on the air and in the middle of an interview that had been going along rather nicely I thought, I was taken off guard when the female interviewer suddenly announced that there was someone in the studio she'd like me to meet. With that, another guest appeared from off camera to join us. It was the same middle-aged Dean impersonator from the fan club meeting, once more outfitted in his Dean drag.

"William Bast," my host announced in a tone reminiscent of "This Is Your Life" and obviously relishing my surprise, "I'd like you to meet James Dean."

Swallowing my anger at what I saw as a blatant setup and betrayal of trust, I said, as I thought then, quite reasonably, "He may be trying to look like James Dean, but he's definitely not James Dean."

"Oh, but he is," she asserted smugly, apparently well prepared for my response. "*This* gentleman has changed his name by deed poll [i.e. legally, in England] to James Byron Dean."

I got up then, and in as dignified a way as I could, made my exit, replying as I did so, something like: "Well, if that's how you honor your word to keep this interview serious, *this* gentleman is out of here."

A week or so later, Gore Vidal and his companion, Howard Austen, invited me around for drinks to the house

Gore had rented in Belgravia. Christopher Isherwood and his new young partner, Don Bachardy, were also on hand, having, I believe, just returned from India. Both looked wonderfully tanned. After hearing some of Chris and Don's exploits, Gore turned to me and remarked, "Well, Bill, you certainly came off well in the *New Statesman.*"

I had no idea what he was talking about, not having read the latest issue and quite surprised to learn that I'd even been mentioned in the esteemed English literary journal. So, Gore produced the relevant issue in which the James Dean Fan Clubs of England book-signing event had been covered, including my confrontation with the would-be Dean look-alike. Apparently, to spare me any anxiety, Ken had kindly decided not to inform me that he had tipped off the *New Statesman* about the event. Reading the article, I was relieved that I had, indeed, come off well, including my handling of "James Byron Dean, II." However it made me realize just how narrowly I'd escaped disaster. The press, which, as Jimmy had discovered to his cost, like the spirit, *bloweth where it listeth* and is generally something best kept at more than arm's length by anyone wishing to preserve his privacy or peace of mind. To mix one's metaphors, when one dines with the devil, one must use a very long spoon.

26

Apostolic Succession

WHILE WORKING AT GRANADA ON ALAN YOUNG'S SHOW, I WAS introduced to Silvio Narizzano, at the time Granada's Television's top director of dramas and often referred to as the "John Frankenheimer of England." On a par with the BBC, Granada was considered the most prestigious television network in the United Kingdom, certainly when it came to dramatic fare. Over drinks one evening, I told Silvio about "The Myth Makers," an original drama I was working on. Basically I'd conceived it as an attack on the exploitation of Dean's death by the American and international press. Focusing on the grotesque funeral of a charismatic young movie star who is killed at a tragically early age, not unlike Jimmy, it dealt with the effect of the invasion of his rural Midwestern hometown by thousands of his bereft fans and the voracious media, and dramatizes the tragic toll this takes on his innocent, grieving family and the ill-prepared, small rural town. Silvio persuaded Granada to commission me to write a television version for him to direct, and it aired during the spring of that year. NBC later bought the teleplay for the American market, and it was broadcast live in New York on the "DuPont Show of the Month" under the innocuous title, "The Movie Star." Though it was well produced and starred Dane Clark and Kathleen Widdoes, I understood from those who had seen both versions that Silvio's was by far the better. Faber & Faber subsequently published the play in 1960 under its original title, *The Myth Makers*, in a collection entitled *Six Granada Plays*.

By now it was becoming abundantly clear to me that the Dean mystique was increasingly going to be part of my social appeal and, collaterally, of my sexual appeal, as well. In gay circles, I found that I was frequently introduced as more than just Dean's friend, but in fact as his longtime lover. Since my experiences after the publicity in Europe, I was becoming used to being sought out socially because of the book, but was growing ever more sensitive to the idea that I was probably also being approached sexually because of the Dean connection. Imagine how off-putting it is to have a sexual partner on the point of orgasm gasp in your ear "Oh, Jimmy!" when in fact your name is Bill. Personally, I found it deflating.

I think this also had less to do with ego on my part than a reluctance to be perceived as capitalizing on my relationship with Jimmy; socially the stigma was bad enough, sexually, a downer. Not surprisingly, I wanted to be sexually desirable in my own right. I now found myself besieged by would-be sex partners, both male and female, not knowing which new faces were genuinely interested in me for myself and which were primarily interested in bedding James Dean's presumed lover. Gradually it would become easier to distinguish one from the other. However, it was inevitable that some Dean worshippers were clever enough, or sufficiently desirable enough, to slip through my guard and into my bed. It's not the worst thing in the world, I suppose, but it left me with a troubled conscience. Worse still, whenever I gave in to the temptation and willingly indulged in sex with a partner I knew instinctively was there mainly because of the Dean connection, it made me feel that I'd turned Jimmy into my pimp.

The year was now 1958. Back in New York, Broadway director Morton "Tec" Da Costa, of *Auntie Mame* and *Music Man* fame, had hired me to work with him on a projected Broadway musical, *Saratoga,* which was being adapted from Edna Ferber's novel, *Saratoga Trunk*, for producer Robert

Fryer. Through Tec, I met master illustrator, Jon Whitcomb, of *Colliers* magazine fame, and his lover, Bob Young. Young, it turned out, had excellent television, publishing, and magazine connections, and subsequently persuaded me to take him on as my manager.

During that rather confusing year in New York, my one refuge was, as it had always been, Contentment Island. Every possible weekend I would spend my time in the comfortable presence of the Colgates. In Sandy and Beulah's absence, they had become my solace in times of confusion, my major source of pure, unadulterated affection. Always taking a keen interest in my life and career, they continued to wrap me in a cocoon of caring and security. No matter that I was no longer a lost kid, I was by that time confident that I would always have their love. How could I anticipate the unexpected schism that lay ahead?

Mercifully, it was not caused by some cataclysmic exposure of my sex life. To the contrary, it came about because of my close bond with Dimitri Mitropoulos. Dimitri had a penthouse apartment in the Great Northern Hotel on Fifty-seventh Street, just a block from where I had been living when I wrote the book, and I had spent a good deal of time with him. His interest in Dean had never abated, and, based on that tie, our initial relationship had evolved into a genuine friendship.

What an inspiration and delight he was! When he was still the principal conductor of the New York Philharmonic, before a concert he would sometimes treat me to an excellent Italian lunch or dinner at La Scala, his favorite midtown restaurant. He was partial to their *piccione e spinaci*, roast pigeon and spinach, and tried to induce me to try it. But I had convinced myself that the birds were caught daily by a bird snatcher in the New York Public Library park. An inveterate pigeon feeder, I had developed a fondness for the winged pests of Manhattan and felt eating them would be like cannibalizing friends. Nevertheless, he finally persuaded me to try his beloved *piccione* one night. I had to admit that it was delicious, but I never quite overcame my aversion to the idea.

For me, to be Dimitri's guest at one of his New York Philharmonic concerts or, later, a rehearsal or performance he was
conducting at the Metropolitan Opera was always an exhilarating occasion. At the time, however, I was unaware of the
strain he was under due to the savagery of the critics over his
effort to introduce his audiences to more progressive music
and the resultant subterfuge on the part of the Philharmonic
management to replace him with a brilliant young upstart
named Leonard Bernstein. Dimitri never spoke of it, but I'm
convinced that the damage it did him must have contributed
greatly to his second heart attack. That, and his financial trou-
bles, caused by a combination of a disregard for money and a
commendable, but costly habit of giving it away to those in
need, especially promising young artists, which would eventually ruin him.

Innocent of his mounting difficulties, I became greedy for
his company. Apart from being a brilliant musician and
scholar of both ancient and early Christian history, when
young, he'd studied as a monk at the famous Monastery of Si-
mon Peter at Mount Athos in Greece, under the aegis of his
uncle, its bishop. Despite his erudition, he was a delightful ec-
centric and an insatiable movie buff. Sometimes, after what
must have been for him an extremely taxing rehearsal or performance, we would sneak off to a late movie on Forty-second
Street. Often after a concert, he would rush off with Max Gershunoff and me to his neighborhood delicatessen and pick up
some "comestibles," which usually consisted of corned beef,
pastrami, bagels, and potato salad for a "midnight snack."
His dietary choices caused me understandable concern about
his heart condition. Returning to his penthouse with the food,
he would sniff the air disapprovingly, then scurry about
searching through the clutter of symphonic scores, opera li-
brettos, and stacks of multilingual, ancient, and contemporary
books, in search of the large bottle of shamefully expensive
French perfume—possibly Diaghilev's famed Mitsouko. The
contents of this would be emptied into an insect spray gun,
and the maestro would then proceed to mist the entire apartment with the costly scent. Having rid the place of its "mosty"

funk, we would then dig into his delicatessen goodies, which would be followed by talk and laughter until the small hours. Like an innocent child, he seemed neither to understand, nor care, that health problems and financial difficulties lay ahead, preferring to live in the moment.

Once the writing chores for Tec Da Costa on *Saratoga* were out of the way, there wasn't much keeping me in New York, and I found myself itching to get back to England, which I'd found intellectually and professionally so rewarding on my first stay.

I'd had an idea for a feature about Hitler's last days that I thought might interest movie writer/producer Carl Foreman. One among many American fugitives from McCarthyism in the early fifties, Carl had fled to England to become an alien resident, writing and producing features at Columbia Pictures. I'd met him during my previous stay in London, admired his work greatly, and was eager to collaborate with him. So, I wrote and proposed my idea to him.

I was still awaiting his answer, when *Colliers* magazine, having learned that I was returning to Europe, contracted me to write three articles. The first was to feature the three currently hot literary "Wilsons" of England: Colin, Sandy, and Angus; the second to be an interview with Italian novelist and short-story writer, Alberto Moravia. As for the third, Paulle Clark, a glamorous model pal from London, had recently introduced me to the Honorable Patricia Cavendish, who had hooked up with an aristocratic Spanish gentleman named Enrique, who was very amusing and, I understood, somehow related to Juan Carlos, the exiled king of Spain. Enrique had assured me that he could secure me an interview with Juan Carlos, who was presently marking time awaiting the departure or, preferably, demise of Spain's Fascist dictator, Generalissimo Franco, in hopes of reclaiming his throne.

Still hoping to work with Carl Foreman, and now armed with my three assignments, plus invitations to the next Venice Film Festival and a week or two at Pat Cavendish's titled mother's fabled Villa Fiorentina on the French Riviera, I was eagerly anticipating my departure for Europe.

I spent my last weekend on Contentment Island with the Colgates. Over dinner on our last evening together, the subject of their annual subscription to the New York Philharmonic came up. Unaware of my friendship with Dimitri Mitropoulos and admiration for him as an artist, they announced that they had decided to withdraw their support of the orchestra, specifically because of Mitropoulos. Their reason: the maestro's insistence on programming too much "modern" music, such as Bartok and Stravinsky. It wasn't that they merely disliked his programs, they loathed them.

"That music literally makes me physically sick," Beatrice declared rather passionately. "I had to leave in the middle of his last concert."

I suggested that she might be overreacting, but she would have none of it.

"No, no, I won't go back until they get rid of Mitropoulos. I can't stand the man!"

I had never seen her so adamant, and I knew there was no point in trying to reason with her. To make matters worse, Bayard concurred in her opinion. Obviously, it was not the moment to announce my devotion to their nemesis. But suddenly I found myself confronted by a yawning gulf in my allegiances, torn between three people I cared for deeply: Beatrice more than my own mother; Bayard, who had taken the place of a long-lost father; and Dimitri, whom I loved as a friend and mentor and admired as a giant among artists. I could see no hope of reconciling the one camp with the other nor could I imagine disavowing my allegiance to any of the three, so I held my peace.

As I left for England a few days later, I carried away with me the depressing burden of choosing between what seemed to me two painfully irreconcilable poles of my life. I would not have to remain torn between them for long. Dimitri Mitropoulos was replaced the following year as principal conductor of the New York Philharmonic by Leonard Bernstein and died in 1960.

Aside from the fact that it had become no secret that Dimitri had once had a crush on my friend Dean, I always felt they would have got along extremely well had they ever met, both being dedicated to their art. Though, to some extent their sexual orientations may have made them brothers under the skin, ultimately it would have been art that bound them. I like to feel that somewhere they are involved in an eternal discussion about the artist's obligation to his craft.

27

Harpies on the Seashore

IF I THOUGHT I OWED JIMMY A MAJOR DEBT OF GRATITUDE FOR my first, unexpected experience in Europe, I was in for even more surprises the second time around. On this visit, Jimmy would introduce me to a host of even more extraordinary characters and unexpected adventures than on the first. I have already touched on my suspicion that Jimmy was in charge of my destiny somehow. So it was, and so it would be for some time to come. How else to explain to myself the amazing twists my life was taking?

I arrived at Heathrow Airport on a Friday. Still bent on acting as my public relations man in the U.K., Ken Pitt met me and drove me to his house in an outlying London suburb where I was invited to be his houseguest until I could find a centrally located flat in the West End.

My first impression of famed English novelist Angus Wilson gave me the sense that interviewing him in his Sussex cottage was going to be more like having tea with a dear old auntie rather than a dynamic, internationally acclaimed author with an acerbic wit. After reading his books, *Hemlock and After* and the stinging *Anglo-Saxon Attitudes*, I'd expected a fierce literary lion. Instead he turned out to be a pussycat, though one, I quickly realized, possessed of a wicked eye for the mouse and sharp, though in my case sheathed, claws. Furthermore, having read my book, *he* insisted on interviewing *me*, diverting the conversation to James Dean at every turn. I was probably naïve in thinking he'd had no ulterior motive in agreeing to the interview. Still, it was impossible to be reticent with so canny an inquisitor, so I indulged him to some extent in hopes of getting enough out of him for a brief article. In the end, the encounter left me with the feeling that he'd got more out of me than I from him. Moreover, I also found myself marveling at the extent to which the knowledge of my association with Jimmy had spread in the world since the publication of my book. Teen fans and movie buffs were one thing, but internationally acclaimed scholars and authors were quite another.

Meantime, having stirred the cauldron once more, Ken had leaked word to the press that I was back in London and arranged for me to meet the second subject of my *Colliers* article. Colin Wilson was the English literary world's current answer to James Dean, a working-class lad who had just written an iconoclastic book titled *The Outsider* that had been received with great critical and popular acclaim. I was introduced to Colin at a Fleet Street bookstore where his book signing was in progress amid a heavy crush of media representatives, which Ken had obviously anticipated. Aside from his controversial book, Colin was also the darling of the English tabloids at the moment, having apparently gotten his young girlfriend pregnant. OUTSIDER GETS INSIDE! one tabloid had jibed. That alone would not normally have made the headlines, but the girl's outraged father had collared the scoundrel, and in true Edwardian style, threatened to administer an old-fashioned horsewhipping unless the villain marry the girl.

Having read about all this, I had figured Colin for a precocious young working-class lout who had somehow managed to scribble a book that posited the idea that anarchy lurks nearer the surface of order and reason than civilization is willing to admit. Instead, I was introduced to an affable twenty-four-year-old with a formidable intellect and guileless charm who, looking back, was a harbinger of the "angry young men" soon to emerge in class-weary England. Immediately ingratiating himself, Colin generously insisted on sharing the spotlight with me at his own book signing that evening.

Afterward, we went out for a pint of beer and got better acquainted. Inevitably, the subject turned to James Dean. Colin pumped me endlessly on the subject, but unlike Angus's questions, Colin's didn't probe into delicate areas.

From that night onward, Colin and his literary cohorts, among them fellow iconoclasts Frank Norman and John Braine, dragged me along on their ritual pub crawls, like it or not, during which they would down endless pints and argue the finer points of literature, filmmaking, and football. Of course, I was totally out of it, usually content with a pint or two at most, although I was always very generously and warmly included in their unintelligible conversations, regarded, I suspect, as an unfortunate, uninformed, and rather obtuse American. Although I found them astonishingly bright and highly entertaining, their scene was hardly my scene, and eventually I started hiding out just to get some work done.

On the other hand, *Boyfriend* composer-lyricist Sandy Wilson turned out to be more my speed: congenial, amusing, and mercifully less robust. His most recent musical, *Valmouth*, had not opened to good reviews, and he was hard at work, revising and rehearsing, but he indulged me graciously, making time for me to interview him. We hit it off from the first and became friends during what turned out to be my unexpectedly long stay in London that year. Sandy also turned out to be the exception; he never once pumped me for any details about my relationship with Dean, though I assumed he believed what I was coming to see was the common assumption among gays.

Finally I heard from Carl Foreman. It turned out he wasn't so hot on the Hitler idea after all, but suggested instead that I work with him on his next project for Columbia, *Return to Navarone,* a planned sequel to *The Guns of Navarone.* Eager to learn from the master scenarist, I jumped at the opportunity. But as we worked together over the first few weeks, I found my role becoming more of a stenographer than a collaborator. I stuck it out as long as I could, but finally bowed out gracefully, using the magazine commitments as my excuse.

• • •

En route to Rome, I made a detour to attend the Venice Film Festival where I found myself quartered in the Hotel des Bains on Venice's Lido. Stopping at the Excelsior bar for a drink my first night, I was introduced to a sturdy little man with a handsome crop of gray hair, who turned out to be the legendary director of the thirties and forties, Josef von Sternberg. Noted also as the man who "created" Marlene Dietrich, von Sternberg was being honored by the festival that year. Given my credentials, von Sternberg immediately wanted to know all about James Dean. Relieved that he was only interested in Jimmy's acting, we talked until the bar closed. Before parting, he asked me to join him the next evening for the festival's tribute to him and the screening of his 1935 film, *The Devil Is a Woman*, starring Dietrich and Cesar Romero.

Throughout the screening, von Sternberg, who turned out to be as garrulous as he was opinionated, reminisced continuously about the making of the film, so much so that I found the movie itself difficult to follow at times. Confiding to me in a running commentary of whispered asides, he pointed out all his personal touches. Faulting the limitations of the art director, for instance, he indicated the surreal sets he'd had to redesign using makeshift things like cutout tree trunks and wisps of toile for foliage. The lighting director didn't know his job, he complained, so of course he'd had to come up with his own special lighting effects. The cameraman was also a dead loss, I was informed, so of course he'd had to invent his own ingenious camera angles. I began to wonder who, if not von Sternberg, had selected his team for the film in the first place, though I lacked the courage to ask. I also wondered how two such perfectionists as Dietrich and von Sternberg managed to survive each other for as long as they did.

While browsing the shops off the Piazza San Marco with von Sternberg the following day, I kept my eye open for a gift to take Pat Cavendish, whose guest at La Fiorentina I was to be in a few days. Some small token, I thought, classy but not ostentatious. Ahah! Von Sternberg found the "perfect" gift, a singularly unremarkable scarf from a rather tacky tourist shop. Rather than offend him, without objection I bought the thing, thinking Pat at least might enjoy the idea that it had been handpicked by "the man who created Dietrich," Josef von Sternberg himself. Later, prudently, I sneaked off to pick up a bottle of Balmain's *Vent Vert* as a backup.

Back on my *Colliers* assignment, I made a quick swing down to Rome where I had a pleasant, if not totally enlightening lunch with Alberto Moravia at Rosati's, his usual hangout in the Piazza del Popolo. It was a delicious meal, but I barely gathered enough material for more than a few paragraphs, although I hoped it would suffice, especially as his latest novel, *Racconti romani* was rumored to have been bought by Joe Levine for Sophia Loren. At that time, my Italian was basic at best, and Moravia's English not much better. I don't know what kind of information I expected, but I certainly didn't get much.

Earlier, in New York, when Pat Cavendish had invited me, I'd had no idea what to expect when I arrived at La Fiorentina. I was understandably bowled over by the villa's breathtaking beauty and opulence. The Colgates' mansion paled in comparison to this Palladian palace. Saint Jean Cap Ferrat, on whose tip the villa was situated, is a tiny peninsula between Nice and Monaco and was, at that time, the quintessential Riviera haven for the international elite. Pat's mother, Lady Enid Kenmare, I later learned, also owned a vast "farm" in Kenya, and staffed her villa entirely with Kenyans, who were meticulous in every respect. I was greeted at the entrance by the major-domo and shown to my room, which was more than comfortable and exquisitely appointed. Pat appeared to welcome me, and I presented her with the cheap, gauzy scarf from Venice, explaining that it had been selected for her by the great Josef von Sternberg himself. Unimpressed by the object, she said she'd never heard of von Sternberg. I carefully explained that he was Dietrich's "Svengali," which also failed to impress. To my relief, she, at least, seemed to appreciate the perfume.

When I emerged from my room at seven for drinks before dinner, neither guests nor hosts had assembled as yet, so I decided to check out the library. Dominating the room from above the fireplace was a life-sized, full-length portrait of the legendary Lady Enid Kenmare herself, painted when she was in her most splendid youth. Enchanted by the portrait, I failed to hear someone enter and slip silently up behind me. A voice whispered in my ear, "They say she murdered all three of her husbands."

I turned around and found myself nose to nose with a snaggletoothed young man with overpoweringly bad breath. When he introduced himself as David Hicks, I recognized the name at once. I'd never met him, but, by coincidence, his reputation, like his breath, had preceded him. Friends in London had earlier warned me to avoid his antique shop in Knightsbridge unless I didn't mind being seriously groped.

I turned to the portrait, commenting how much I'd been admiring it. Still in annoyingly close proximity, my new acquaintance recounted with evident relish Enid Kenmare's rumored notorious history, describing how she'd purportedly amassed a fortune by murdering all three of her husbands. The sound of voices from the next room interrupted further revelations

The gathering that first night was hosted by Pat and her half-brother, Rory Cameron, editor of *L'Oeil,* France's prestigious interior-design magazine. Their other houseguests consisted of Hicks; biographer Peter Quennell and his wife at the time, Spider; American Woolworth heiress Barbara Hutton and her current protégé, Jimmy Douglas, a young Chicago piano virtuoso. There was also a charming Danish millionaire whose name I've long forgotten. I must say, considering my own socioeconomic status, I felt outnumbered, outclassed, and out of my depth, although almost everyone was treating me, well, not quite royally, but certainly with respect.

Hicks, it was revealed over cocktails, had flown down from London for the weekend to beg his friend, Pat, to intercede on his behalf with her dear friend, Pamela Mountbatten, daughter of the duke of Edinburgh's uncle, Earl Louis Mountbatten, to accept his proposal of marriage. In view of what lying rumor had led me to believe about Mr. Hicks, it will come as no surprise that I was duly dumbfounded by this news, but I had little time to ponder it when the subject swiftly veered toward James Dean. Mercifully, before I could be grilled, conversation stopped and all eyes swung to the grand staircase at one side of the room. Descending at measured pace was our legendary hostess, Enid Kenmare, now somewhat an aging shadow of her youthful portrait, although still boasting vestiges of her fabled beauty. Elegantly gowned for the evening, she bore on her shoulder, quite incongruously, a small "dassy," that is, a hyrax, a small mammal resembling a woodchuck that she'd brought from her farm in Kenya and was apparently her frequent companion. I later learned that it had tiny hooves and was actually related to the elephant.

After drinks, we all set out for dinner in La Tourbie, a village high above the Grand Corniche, stopping to take in a Germaine Richier sculpture exhibit at the tiny Grimaldi Museum in Antibes. It was nearly closing time when we arrived, and we were the only visitors in the place. After viewing the sculptures, I made the supreme mistake of heading upstairs by myself, to check out the museum's top floor, but unexpectedly found myself within breathing distance of my library companion again. Without uttering a word, he slammed me up against a display case and started to unzip my fly. The possibility that someone might come up and surprise us was bad enough, quite aside from the idea of contact with someone I found so repellent.

I grabbed his wrist, reminding him that others could walk in at any moment. Obviously confident that they wouldn't, he continued working at my zipper, determined to find out "what James Dean thought so hot," as he put it. Failing to see the humor of the situation, I shoved him away, wondering if he really figured this was worth risking his hopes of marrying Pamela Mountbatten. "Were you the fucker or fuckee?" he grinned, obviously unconcerned, as I extricated myself and fled downstairs to join the others.

We dined at a restaurant with a splendid view of the Riviera coast far below. All through dinner, presumably miffed by my behavior earlier and in a style reminiscent of Rogers Brackett, Hicks took every opportunity to make wisecracks at my expense. Obviously, in his book, I had demonstrated an unsporting attitude, and I, of course, never uttered a word to anyone about the museum incident. Maybe such behavior was par for the course around here. Or maybe I was just a very naïve twenty-six-year-old American, and Jimmy was giving me a much needed education in the ways of the world.

After lunch the following day, as usual we each went our own way, generally to our rooms for a nap. Lady Kenmare, however, having only just risen, retreated to the library for her customary afternoon bridge game. That day she was joined by the Quennells and her neighbor, aging literary giant W. Somerset Maugham—"Willie," familiarly—who had toddled over to join them from his Villa Mauresque next door. As for me, I collapsed on top of my bed, exhausted by an earlier bout of water-skiing, and fell into a deep sleep.

It must have been an hour or so later when I was only vaguely aware of a tap at my door and barely heard it open. At the sound of a pair of sandals scraping across the marbled floor, I opened my eyes to see an old man shuffling toward my bathroom. He had the face of a grumpy walrus, was wearing a short-sleeved Lacoste tennis shirt that revealed two tanned, withering arms, and a pair of tennis shorts that revealed a pair of tanned, withering legs. It was Willie Maugham, well into his eighties and quite frail by then. Noticing that he had wakened me, he apologized, never stopping his progress toward my bathroom while explaining that he needed to pee. They'd told him my toilet was the nearest.

While he was in there, I must have dozed off again because I was only vaguely aware of the toilet flushing and the bathroom door opening again. When I opened my eyes, he was standing at the foot of my bed, studying me. I didn't know what to say.

"You must have loved him very much," he said finally. I must've looked confused, because he explained, "It was there, between the lines." He'd read my book.

Shuffling closer to perch on the bed beside me, he reassured, "Still, it was something you'll always have." He placed his hand on my thigh and patted it gently. "Mustn't let them spoil it for you."

Touched, I replied, "I'm trying not to."

"Good," he nodded, then he got to his feet and shuffled out of the room.

As for Barbara Hutton, in whose company I spent considerable time over those two weeks, it struck me as odd that only she among all the others never once mentioned Dean, never asked me anything about him. It was only after someone mentioned her son, Lance Reventlow, that the reason for her evasion occurred to me. Reventlow, like Jimmy, was also into racing. I vaguely recalled that Jimmy had mentioned they'd met at the races in Palm Springs and hit it off rather well. In fact, I believe they saw each other that last day while Jimmy was en route for Salinas. In light of this, it occurred to me that perhaps Barbara didn't want to know about James Dean, didn't even want to think about him, especially about the way he died. Jimmy's untimely death at the wheel of a race car may have been too vivid a reminder of deep-seated fears she harbored for her own son. Sadly, however, Reventlow would ultimately die, not behind the wheel of a race car, but in an airplane crash some years later.

Recently, I came across a tale, in one of the many James Dean biographies, that Barbara picked up Jimmy at Googie's one night, lured him back to her suite at the Chateau Marmont on Sunset Strip, and after polishing off a bottle of Pouilly Fuissé, fucked him, and sent him off on his motorcycle. Barbara Hutton? Googie's? Pouilly Fuissé? Please.

28

Reliving the Past

BACK IN LONDON, I SPENT THE NEXT TWO YEARS WRITING FOR British television. I also wrote my first feature film, not the projected, updated take on *Jekyll and Hyde* that Jimmy and I had planned eleven years previously, but rather an unlikely combination of cowboys and dinosaurs, *The Valley of Gwangi*, which was brought to life by the technical wizardry of the king of "Dynamation," Ray Harryhausen. During that period, I settled into what would become a stable and enduring relationship with Paul Huson, a young designer from the BBC. We moved to Los Angeles in 1968 where for the next four years, my writing career progressed from writing episodic television to writing television movies. In 1974, Elizabeth Montgomery agreed to play the title role in my *Legend of Lizzie Borden*. As the picture was both a critical, and more important to the industry, major ratings success, it was perhaps inevitable that soon afterward, with the looming advent of the twentieth anniversary of Jimmy's death, I would be approached to do a television adaptation of my 1956 Dean biography.

Understandably, I was reluctant to open Pandora's box once more, but the two earnest young television producers, Jerry Isenberg and Gerry Abrams, under whose company banner the picture was to be produced, seemed honorable and were willing to let me produce as well as write the adaptation.

I didn't want to be a part of some inauthentic, mythologizing biopic of James Dean, so I insisted on a meeting with the NBC brass who had initiated the project. At the meeting, I expressed my reluctance to make the movie, mainly because of the problem of finding an actor to portray James Dean, a star whose physical features, mannerisms, voice, and unique style were still indelibly stamped on the memories of the moviegoing public. Frankly, I didn't think the movie should be made, period. The network executive was prepared for me, however. Sparing the subtleties, he informed me that the network was determined to do a movie about James Dean, with or without me or my book. The implication was that were I to refuse, I could abandon any hope of control over the project, including Jimmy's physical portrayal, his character, his private life, and possibly mine, as well.

It should be understood that, when it came to what went on air, the networks had the final say. That was my greatest fear: that they would have the last word about every scene, every line and, truth be damned, able to turn my life and Jimmy's into what it wasn't, turn Jimmy into the character they imagined their audience would want, avoiding even any hint of what might be considered "questionable" in their or their sponsors' terms.

Fortunately, I had a very smart lawyer, Skip Brittenham, who was fairly confident he could protect my interests with a tough contract. As the network stubbornly refused to give me control over the ultimate characterization of Jimmy in the film, Skip persuaded them to agree at least to the "reasonable" request that I be granted control over only those scenes in which my character appeared. To my astonishment, they agreed. Apparently, they hadn't read my book, but Skip had. He'd noticed that, as narrator and primary witness to Dean's life during his last five years, my character appeared in almost every scene. Realizing that, since the tale would be told and Jimmy perceived entirely from my perspective, he saw that I would have virtual control over almost every scene in the script. In the end, the folks at NBC were not entirely happy about this, but frankly, my dears, I didn't give a damn. However, they flexed their muscle by changing my title from *James Dean: Portrait of a Friend,* to the simpler and embarrassingly all-embracing *James Dean,* as if stating the claim to be the definitive biography of Jimmy, not simply my perspective, not at all my intention. Still, it was a small sacrifice in comparison to what I'd gained.

It was our good fortune that Isenberg and Abrams managed to persuade Robert Butler, one of television's top directors of movies at the time, to take the reins. If that name seems familiar, it's not only because Bob Butler is and was one of the best in the business, but also because, very early in this story, he had inadvertently played a minor, but significant role in shaping James Dean's destiny. As the reader may or may not recall, after I managed to get Jimmy a job as an usher at CBS Hollywood in 1951, Bob Butler was the head usher who fired him after only one week on the ushering staff. That action resulted in Jimmy taking the job in the CBS parking lot, which is where he met Rogers Brackett, and so on. Granted, Hollywood is a remarkably small world—or, perhaps Jimmy was pulling the strings from somewhere beyond. Jimmy the jester at work again. In any case, I'm not sure Bob was even aware of this little twist of fate, but when the time came to take command of our movie, he did so with the sensitivity and dedication of an artist and the focus of a zealot, albeit a gentle zealot.

Once my script was approved by the network, we started the search for our cast. I embarked upon this task realistically accepting the fact that none of the actors we would hire in the end, least of all the one to play James Dean, would conform to my memory of the actual people they represented. Even if some came close in looks, none would convey the actual sense and possess the exact mannerisms of the originals. Such are the inherent shortcomings of all biographical films, which had been one of the main reasons for my resistance to making this film in the first place. However, I had made my pact with the devil, and once under way, there was no going back. Approximations would have to do.

Nonetheless, casting the role of James Dean was still one of the most difficult tasks I have ever undertaken. We auditioned dozens of actors, and although there were a number who acquitted themselves extremely well, they simply didn't give one enough of a sense of either the Jimmy I knew or the James Dean the audience would remember. Some came close, but where they captured the persona, they didn't convey the image. Conversely, where others approached the image, they didn't convey the persona. In the end, I had to abandon any idea of replicating Jimmy and settle for a persuasive facsimile, a seasoned actor who had a grasp of the material, with enough of the look and a sense of James Dean, enough at least to suspend the audience's disbelief for two hours. No one would ever be perfect. At best we could only expect an imitation of life. But I think we came reasonably close with Stephen McHattie's skillful performance, though we had to sacrifice some of Jimmy's boyish looks and mannerisms.

As for Michael Brandon, who was cast as yours truly, though he proved himself a consummate actor, there was no physical similarity between him and myself. Like Stephen in the case of Jimmy, Michael also looked more mature than I at the time of the story, but did convey a naïve, boyish quality. Fortunately, as nobody out there in television land knew from Bill Bast, none of that mattered. It was about Jimmy, not me.

In casting the other roles, we had an easier time. Meg Foster, a fine actress with a lush mane of hair, was cast as Dizzy; Katherine Helmond played Isabel Draesemer, Jimmy's first agent; Dane Clark played James Whitmore, who was sadly too old by then to play his youthful self; Brooke Adams played Beverly; and Candy Clark, Chris White. Interestingly, although I hadn't seen the real Chris in twenty years, I managed to locate her living in West Hollywood. In another somewhat bizarre touch, she agreed to play the role of an anonymous Actors Studio secretary who summons the character "Christine White" (Candy Clark) and "James Dean" (Stephen McHattie) into the audition that gets them both admitted to the Studio. Chris verified for me Jimmy's panic before the audition and his attempt to run out on her. She also helped us recreate the actual scene she had written for the audition.

When the picture was finally aired, NBC was relieved to

find it garnered excellent ratings for them and gratifying reviews in the press. Among the latter, Kevin Thomas's piece in the *Los Angeles Times* made me especially happy. "William Bast's script," he wrote, "and [Stephen] McHattie's dazzling performance combine with Robert Butler's authoritative but unobtrusive direction to create one of the most compelling films within recent memory."

However, for all the kudos, there was a negative side. NBC's national publicity for the movie generated a new spate of personal publicity, once again focusing the attention of Dean fans on me. Over the years, my Dean fan mail had dwindled, although my association with Dean brought me into fairly regular contact with Dean biographers researching their own books. But after the airing of the television movie, Dean fan letters started pouring in again. However, now I had no publisher to act as a buffer, and some of the mail, specifically from one particular source, proved disturbing.

Like many in Hollywood, I tend to keep a low profile and try to keep my home phone and address private. Any fan mail for me was being sent either to NBC or the Writers Guild of America, both of which were readdressing the envelopes and forwarding them on. One day, I received a letter forwarded by the WGA in which the writer claimed to be Jimmy's reincarnation. Further, he asserted that only I could verify this and requested a meeting. Over the years, I have received letters making outrageous claims, though none from anyone making this particular one. This was a first, and in the hope that it would be the last, I decided not to reply. I was not, and never have been, into reincarnation.

Unfortunately, my silence did nothing to discourage my correspondent. Rather the opposite. His letters started coming at the rate of three or four a week, and their messages only confirmed my initial suspicion that this was a deeply disturbed person. My refusal to reply only seemed to fuel his determination. Over a period of weeks, his letters grew more insistent, then angry at my refusal to reply, and finally menacing. Now I was more convinced than ever that I shouldn't encourage him, far less reply. I worried that one of his letters, forwarded to me

by the WGA with its address crossed off and mine written in
its place, might be misdelivered and returned to him by the
post office, at which point he would know exactly where I
lived. I asked the WGA mail room to have all my future mail
forwarded to me in WGA envelopes, featuring only their return address.

Finally he sent me an audio tape. Listening to his sad, angry, incoherent ramblings as if he were in the room next to me
was all the confirmation my growing paranoia needed. He
confided that he could describe to me in detail private experiences and confidences that Jimmy and I had shared, things that
only I would know about. In quiet, mumbling tones, he also
informed me that my silence was disappointing to him, was
causing him to lose patience with me, and he now referred to
a gun collection that he intended to acquaint me with. I chose
not to report this to the police, at least for the time being, but
the incident was having a disturbing effect on me.

The scene was Orso's in West Hollywood, one of Hollywood's most favored and convivial restaurants. A party of
eight was gathered around a large round table to celebrate the
seventy-fifth birthday of Olga Lehmann, Paul's mother. In order to accommodate the party of eight, the management had
placed a larger, circular tabletop atop the smaller tabletop for
only six, which they often did for larger parties. I was seated
in a corner facing the room with Paul on one side of me, Olga
on the other. I spotted the kid first. He was approaching from
across the room, his eyes fixed on me. There was no mistaking him; not unlike the James Dean impersonator in London
many years before, he had dyed blond hair and was wearing
that same zippered red jacket and jeans. Noting my look of
apprehension as I stared at him, the others at my table turned
to see what I was reacting to.

He stepped up to the table, excused himself politely for
intruding, and asked if I was the William Bast who was James
Dean's friend. I asked how I might help him. Slipping one
hand inside his jacket pocket, he grinned and said he had
something to show me. I knew then what was about to happen. As he started to pull out the gun, I shoved Olga's elbows

off the table and, with one heave, upended the false tabletop, scattering our guests as it flipped over onto the intruder, knocking him to the floor. In the commotion that followed, several waiters rushed up and secured him, wresting the gun from his hand—and I awoke from the second-worst nightmare of my life. It remains an unexplained, but very welcome coincidence, that after that dream, the disturbing letters and tapes stopped arriving in the mail.

Fortunately, most of Jimmy's admirers have been kind, respectful, and life-affirming, among them, most notably, Seita Ohnishi. I first met this extraordinary Japanese businessman at noon in the parking lot of Paramount Pictures. His American lawyer-cum-translator had phoned me a week prior to explain that his client, an avid James Dean fan since his youth, had come from Japan in hopes of meeting me and possibly seeing my television movie, as it had not as yet been broadcast in Japan. I was informed that Mr. Ohnishi would also like to take me to lunch afterward to discuss a special project he had in mind to honor James Dean. I said I would be happy to set up the screening and delighted to have lunch with Mr. Ohnishi. As I'd seen the film many times, I explained that I would meet Mr. Ohnishi outside the Paramount screening room after the screening.

When I arrived in the Paramount parking lot, I was somewhat surprised to find a half-dozen identical Mercedes-Benz town cars parked all in a row, each with a dark-suited driver in attendance. Mr. Ohnishi, it seemed, had come with an entourage. After five minutes or so, the screening let out, and Mr. Ohnishi, his lawyer-translator, and a number of Japanese gentlemen in business suits joined me in the adjacent parking lot. Introductions were made by the translator, during which there was much bowing and handshaking, and the interpreter passed on Mr. Ohnishi's high praise for my film and his great pleasure in meeting me in person, for which I thanked him and assured him the pleasure was all mine. The interpreter added that Mr. Ohnishi had been deeply moved by my film and was most grateful for my having arranged the screening.

He then asked me if I would mind posing for a few photos with Mr. Ohnishi before leaving, presumably for lunch. I agreed, of course, bowing politely.

After posing together for eight or ten shots, Mr. Ohnishi gave some curt-sounding instructions to his interpreter in Japanese, which were passed on to the others in his party, also in Japanese. I figuring we were about to leave for lunch. Instead, after one final handshake, Ohnishi, his lawyer-interpreter, and all the others in his party piled into their waiting fleet of Mercedes and were driven off, leaving me standing there, alone in the parking lot. As no one had offered me a ride or told me where I was to meet them for lunch, I went back to my office and had a sandwich at my desk.

I'd all but put the incident out of my mind when, a month or so later, I got another phone call, this time from a gentle-spoken Japanese lady. Nellie Mitani explained that she was Mr. Ohnishi's new lawyer and interpreter. Ohnishi-san had returned from Japan and wanted to take me to lunch to discuss a rather important matter. I explained what had happened the last time Mr. Ohnishi had invited me to lunch and politely declined the invitation. Ten minutes later, Mrs. Mitani called back to apologize for Mr. Ohnishi. It seems no one had told him that I'd been invited to join him for lunch the last time, so he hadn't realized, until she explained, how rudely I had been treated. He begged me to forgive him and offered to take me to the restaurant of my choice for lunch to make up for it. Not one to hold a grudge over an innocent mishap, I agreed.

We met at the Polo Lounge of the Beverly Hills Hotel the following day. Over a pleasant lunch, through his interpreter, Mrs. Mitani, Mr. Ohnishi explained his proposal. He intended to raise a monument in honor of his boyhood hero, James Dean, and was seeking my advice and guidance for the elaborate undertaking. He had brought with him a yard-long, scrolled architectural drawing, which Mrs. Mitani explained was the plan for the monument. Having the waiter clear the table after lunch, he unscrolled the plan, as conversations stopped, heads turned, and necks craned all around us. This was, after all, Hollywood.

Mr. Ohnishi explained that he proposed to erect the monument near the intersection where Jimmy had been killed, at a place called Cholame, a desolate, windswept hamlet a hundred or so miles north of Los Angeles that was populated by half a dozen stoic souls and at the time consisted of a gas station, a country store, and a tiny post office. The memorial would be positioned directly in front of the post office, within view of the accident site nearby. The architectural rendering suggested a postmodern, polished steel version of a Shinto *Torii* gate. However, instead of a simple gatelike structure, it had been bent into a stylized, angular frame, designed to embrace the trunk of a large tree. Mr. Ohnishi had chosen the tree in front of the post office as the site because trees are held sacred in Japan and because he had learned from the locals of Cholame that this particular tree was a Tree of Heaven (*Ailanthus altissima*), which he found especially meaningful.

Considering the size and scope of the enterprise, I was impressed that he would undertake so great a task and asked him the reason. He would only explain that he was a great admirer of James Dean and was fulfilling a promise to himself that he'd made many years before. When I asked him what he intended to inscribe on his monument, he pointed to the upper front span of the structure as if he could already see it engraved there and proclaimed quite proudly, "James Dean—*East of Eden*." I wondered why he had chosen to include only that film, as Jimmy had starred in two others. He explained quite simply that *East of Eden* was his favorite. As tactfully as possible, I explained that posting just "James Dean—*East of Eden*" on the monument like that might cause people to think of it as a movie marquee advertising the picture showing in the building behind, which, though a post office, might be taken for a rural movie theater by strangers to the area. He gave it a moment's thought and agreed that that could be a problem, then asked what I would suggest instead. I offered the more appropriate: "JAMES DEAN—2/8/31–9/30/55," suggesting, also, that he might want to follow the dates defining Jimmy's life on earth with the symbol for infinity, more or less a figure eight on its side. After all, I reminded him, James

Dean would never really die in the minds and hearts of his fans. Mr. Ohnishi seemed to like that. I also suggested that Jimmy's favorite quote from Saint-Exupéry's *The Little Prince*, "What is essential is invisible to the eye," might also be inscribed somewhere on the monument.

So, after many months of careful planning with the help of a local architectural firm and a number of trips back and forth between Japan and Los Angeles, Mr. Ohnishi's dream finally became a reality, more or less as we had discussed it that day in the Beverly Hills Hotel Polo Lounge.

Beulah Roth, Paul, and I were invited to the monument's unveiling. Beulah, long widowed, was now sharing a house with her brother in Beverly Hills. Reunited with her after so long, I'd found myself surrounded by many of the familiar old mementos of her life with Sandy in Europe that had so fascinated Jimmy and me twenty-five years previously. Sandy was long gone, but his photographs of Jimmy were everywhere. Beulah still had the same tall chair Jimmy used to sit in, now roped off with a silken hawser like some coronation throne, to prevent anyone else from sitting in it. Over drinks with her one evening, Paul and I were joined by Beulah's brother, noted screenwriter Leonard Spigelgass, who, it transpired, had also been a friend of Rogers Brackett. Leonard didn't have a single good word to say about Jimmy, indeed, plenty of bad ones. Yet another side to Jimmy, I thought. Maybe the side he revealed to Rogers? But Beulah wouldn't have any of it. She still loved her Jimmy as deeply as she always had.

On the day of the monument's unveiling, Beulah, Paul, and I drove up to Cholame and joined Mr. Ohnishi and a group of his friends and associates for the ceremony, followed by a picnic lunch set up under the Tree of Heaven. I must admit that, when it was unveiled, I was duly impressed by the beautifully polished, mirrorlike stainless-steel structure. Then, as I studied the inscription, I was suddenly struck by the realization that, just to the right of the dates after Jimmy's name, and over the symbol for infinity, the mirrored surface reflected the actual site of the accident, perhaps a few hundred yards up the road behind me. When the frisson passed, I pointed this out to Mr.

Ohnishi and asked him if he had intentionally positioned the monument to capture that particular reflection. Apparently as shaken as I at the eerie coincidence, he assured me that he had not. Those hidden strings had been pulled again.

As I circled the tree, studying the inscriptions, I came upon something else that gave me pause, engraved into the base at one side. Etched forever there in steel was a footnote, a brief explanation of the quotation from *The Little Prince* inscribed above, a footnote written in my hand and signed by me. Unaware of its ultimate destiny at the time, and to my everlasting embarrassment, the note so everlastingly engraved was written, no, *scrawled* in haste on the stationery of a San Francisco hotel, as I was rushing to leave for a dinner date with friends waiting downstairs in the lobby. I had almost been out the door, when Mr. Ohnishi phoned from Japan and, through his translator, made an urgent request that I take a moment to write him a brief note explaining why that particular quote from Saint Exupéry was so important to Jimmy. I assumed he wanted to know for purposes of his own. Or perhaps he simply needed to be able to explain the reason himself, if asked. Had he said that he intended to immortalize my note by etching it into the monument itself, I would have given far greater consideration to my explanation and certainly greater care with my penmanship. As it was, I dashed off the hasty explanation in two minutes flat, shoved it into a hotel envelope, dropped it at the front desk for mailing to Japan, and rushed off to dinner. So there it stands, hardly legible, memorialized in steel for all time, among other things a permanent metaphor of ill-considered haste.

Yet despite my misgivings about its shallow content and illegible handwriting, I was suddenly quite moved to find myself so intimately, so permanently linked to Jimmy. Yes, twenty-five years back, I had written the book, which some might consider a lasting testament to our friendship, but this was different somehow. A book is paper, and paper yellows with time. It dries and crumbles into dust and is often committed to the trash heap. The copies of my first testament to my friendship with Jimmy, *James Dean: a biography*, that I keep on my office bookshelf are fast becoming evidence of this inevitability. But this magnificent object, this was steel! It would last forever. I recalled a devastating photograph that I'd come across once of Hiroshima after the atom blast. It showed a city totally flattened by the bomb with only the skeletons of what once were a few tall structures, steel girders left standing in the center of the devastation, obviously the frameworks of the city's several skyscrapers. The photo was captioned simply "Steel Stood."

Though I haven't been back to Cholame to see the condition of the monument for myself, those who have bear reports that have taken the luster off my romantic notion of everlastingness somewhat. Like Jimmy's grave marker, it has suffered the ravages of time, weather, and souvenir seekers.

Yet, it stands.

Epilogue

I suppose it was to be expected that my fixation on Jimmy would deter me from exploring other avenues for love while he was alive. As a result, it wasn't until well after his death that I ventured into the arena of romance, so powerful was his hold on me.

Of course I loved him. Not a day goes by when I don't wonder what it would have been like, had he lived, moving in with him again, this time as his lover. Could I have trusted him with my love, my devotion, my life? I doubted it then, and I doubt it still, but the bigger question persists: Would I really have risked it, for better or worse, at least to find out if it could have worked?

I had long been his witness. I knew who he was, what he was. Rather than bisexual or homosexual—one or the other by now a given where James Dean is concerned—let us also consider potentially bipolar. As a result, I lived with the daunting belief that I could foresee the inevitable outcome, that I knew who would be the loser in the end. I had convinced myself that I was dealing with Jekyll and Hyde and that Mr. Hyde would prevail, just as the picture I had started to write for Jimmy was intended to end.

As for love and devotion, I asked myself, on whose terms? His, of course, I felt sure, selfish at best, cruel at worst. What about my terms? Selfish, too, undoubtedly, but never cruel; well, rarely, anyway, and never viciously. But I had learned over our years together that there were no other terms for Jimmy, only his, and I had witnessed enough to know that his terms were not for me. I have been foolish at times in my life, monumentally on occasion, but seldom deliberately self-destructive, and, frankly, entrusting my heart to his care scared the hell out of me.

More than anything, his career had become paramount. If nothing else, I could foresee that it would dictate his life more than he would have liked to admit, and it would never tolerate any such relationship. Forget about everything else, we would have been living in a celluloid closet and only for as long as they let us. A week? A month? A year? And all the while, I'd have been playing invisible partner, not a role I would have taken to easily, I suspect.

Whenever the dilemma has plagued me, I've tormented myself with the same question again and again: Where would it all have ended? But end it did, abruptly and shockingly and far, far too soon, and all my doubts and questions were moot. The decision was not to be mine. No matter how often you rewind the tape, the ending never changes. Did the timing of his death spare me or cheat me? I will never know. And that, for me, is the hardest fact to live with: I will never know.

When Jimmy drove into oblivion, he didn't take my love with him. It lived on to torment the rest of my days with a simple question: What if? Why did destiny step in just as I finally made my decision to go for broke? Whatever the explanation, that choice, long avoided, having been snatched away before it could be realized, has cost me dearly. I have known loss, of course—not just Jimmy's, but many others since—some near and dear, others less so, but all painful to bear, like the host of friends and acquaintances who fell victim to AIDS, especially in the early years. The trouble is, despite having known loss, I have never learned to survive it well. I grieve too hard and too long. At such times, I would rather be stone. Unfortunately, I can't change my composition, and of all the losses I have had to bear, the effect of Jimmy's has endured the longest.

On the other hand, there has been compensation. He did leave me with this amazing lifelong odyssey. For such precious gifts, I shall always be beholden, exactly as he promised me. And, in a surreal way, he's still here, refusing to become just a memory. More often than not, he looks exactly like I remember him, sometimes even dressed in clothes I recognize, not merely costumes worn in his film roles, but the clothes he wore in real life. Weirdly, some of them are my clothes, clothes now familiar to the world at large through photographs of Jimmy, like the one of him strolling down the middle of New York's West Sixty-eighth Street, wearing my tan corduroy sports jacket. It was one of the few belongings I had left in his care when I abandoned New York for Hollywood, that and his annotated copy of *The Little Prince*. He had always coveted that jacket. I had briefly treasured the book.

How intimate those pictures now feel to me, how near he seems in those clothes. The sensation is extraordinary, almost metaphysical, like one time, while in preproduction for my television movie about Jimmy. We had to select the costume that Stephen McHattie was to wear for a certain scene, clothes meant to duplicate those Jimmy wore in *East of Eden*. As it happened, the TV movie was being shot on the Warner Brothers lot where some of *Eden* had been shot so many years before. Going through Warners' vast wardrobe stock, I selected a pair of pants we thought looked similar enough. At the fitting, however, when checking them one last time before alterations were made, we discovered something quite astounding. Sewn inside the waistband was a timeworn tag that read, "James Dean—East of Eden." They were the same pants he had worn for that scene in the film. In the few moments that I held them, staring at that tag, I could almost feel his presence and hear the echo of his laughter at my astonishment.

But that is the beauty and, ironically, the pain of memory. Usually when one dreams of the dead, they are rarely dead, but almost tangibly alive, as indeed Jimmy appeared in that devastating nightmare in which he begged me to save him. For me, because of his persistently ubiquitous image, Jimmy remains alive in my mind's eye, alive and forever young, as he was when we first met and when we last parted. Perhaps this should please me, yet, in fact, it saddens me. You see I never had the reward of watching him grow older, more mature, of watching him evolve into a long-loved friend and companion. On the other hand, I, in my mirror, grow alarmingly older year after year and now only vaguely familiar, while he, in ads, on book jackets, souvenir T-shirts, video covers, in ancient publicity photos, on never-ending television and cable reruns of his films, he remains alive and young and immediate. In this sense, it could be argued that he has fulfilled his fondest dream. He has become immortal, at least as immortal as any modern icon can hope to be. Eternally James Dean.

As for me, he left me behind, bound, it would appear, for my own rather dubious form of immortality, as a dim figure, hardly discernible in the giant shadow he has cast as a twentieth-century phenomenon. Jimmy long ago took center stage, and I was simply a spectator watching from the darkened wings where he left me. I suppose my greatest regret is the fact that I never got to let him know how much he really meant to me. However, I did find one consolation, a somewhat cynical one. After Jimmy died, but still early in my gay life, when I was young and in love again, but uncertain and ever cautious about committing myself to a potential partner, an old Southern queen of my acquaintance gave me some advice while in her cups.

"Honey," she drawled. "Never make a long-term commitment. All that love stuff don't last. You start out lovers, and you wind up sisters."

Looking back, there's one thing I can say for sure. I never imagined myself winding up as James Dean's sister.